THE SUSPENSION OF SERIOUSNESS

SUNY SERIES IN
LATIN AMERICAN AND IBERIAN THOUGHT AND CULTURE
Jorge J. E. Gracia and Rosemary Geisdorfer Feal, editors

THE SUSPENSION OF SERIOUSNESS

On the Phenomenology of Jorge Portilla

Carlos Alberto Sánchez

The appendix contains Jorge Portilla's *Fenomenología del relajo*
translated by Eleanor Marsh and Carlos Alberto Sánchez

Published by State University of New York Press, Albany

For information, contact State University of New York Press, Albany, NY
www.sunypress.edu

Production by Ryan Morris
Marketing by Kate McDonnell

Library of Congress Cataloging-in-Publication Data

Sánchez, Carlos Alberto.
  The suspension of seriousness : on the phenomenology of Jorge Portilla / Carlos Alberto Sánchez.
       p. cm. — (SUNY series in Latin American and Iberian thought and culture)
  "The appendix contains Jorge Portilla's Fenomenología del relajo, translated by Eleanor Marsh & Carlos Alberto Sánchez."
  Includes bibliographical references (p. 217–221) and index.
  ISBN 978-1-4384-4468-0 (paperback : alk. paper)
  ISBN 978-1-4384-4467-3 (hardcover : alk. paper)   1. Portilla, Jorge, 1918–1963.
2. Portilla, Jorge, 1918–1963. Fenomenología del relajo. 3 . Phenomenology.
4. Philosophy, Mexican—20th century. I. Portilla, Jorge, 1918–1963. Fenomenología del relajo. English. II. Title.
  B1019.P674S26 2012
  199'.72--dc23

                              2012003381

For my parents,
Guillermina and Patricio,
and my sons,
Julian and Ismael

Contents

Acknowledgments

This book could not have existed without the generosity of many. I thank professors Antonio Zirión Quijano, Guillermo Hurtado, Eduardo Mendieta, Iain Thomson, and Amy Oliver, for setting the mark and for their encouragement and mentorship during the formative stages of this project. I also thank my colleagues in the Department of Philosophy at San Jose State University, especially Rita Manning, Richard Tiezsen, and Peter Hadreas for their professional and moral support, students in my Latin American philosophy courses, Claudio Perez and Jesus Ramirez for reading and discussing an earlier draft of the manuscript without complaining, and Dean Karl Toepfer of the College of Humanities and Arts for his leadership and institutional support. I am especially indebted to Eleanor Marsh for her tireless work on the translation of Jorge Portilla's *Fenomenología del relajo*, which is contained in the appendix, and to the folks at the Fondo de Cultura Económica, for permission to publish it. Finally, I thank Dr. Beth Bouloukos and her staff at the State University of New York Press for their patience and dedication.

CHAPTER ONE

Matters of Life and Death

> And López Wilson, astigmatic revolutionist come to spy upon his enemy's terrain, to piss on that frivolous earth and be eyewitness to the dying of capitalism while at the same time enjoying its death-orgies.
> —Carlos Fuentes, *La región más transparente* (1958)

Introduction

Twentieth-century Mexican philosophy properly considered boasts of a number of great thinkers worthy of inclusion in any and all philosophical narratives. The better known of these, Leopoldo Zea, José Vasconcelos, Antonio Caso, Samuel Ramos, and, to a great extent, Octavio Paz, have received their fair share of attention in the United States over the last fifty years, partly due to a concerted effort by a few philosophy professors in the US academy who find it necessary to discombobulate the Eurocentric philosophical canon with *outsiders*. For reasons which I hope to make clear in what follows, Jorge Portilla is not one of these *outsiders* to which attention has been paid—even in his homeland, where he is more likely to be recognized, not as one of Mexico's most penetrating and attuned minds, but rather by his replicant, López Wilson, a caricature of intelligence and hedonism immortalized by Carlos Fuentes in his first novel. This oversight is unfortunate, since Portilla is by far more *outside* than the rest; in fact, the rest find approval precisely because they do not stray too far afield, keeping to themes and methodologies in tune with the Western cannon. One major reason for

1

Character in a Fuentes novel

the lack of attention paid to Portilla has to do with his output, restricted as it is to a handful of essays and the posthumously published text of his major work, *Fenomenología del relajo*.

Fenomenología del relajo, hereafter *Fenomenología*, should have firmly situated Portilla as a central figure in Mexico's rich philosophical history. His premature death (at forty-five) and the mythology that hovered about him while alive, a mythology that followed him to his grave, and beyond, to the posthumous publication of the *Fenomenología*, instead relegated Portilla to the realm of legend and his work to that of curiosity. So Portilla has yet to be given his proper place in the history of philosophy—Latin American or otherwise. Placing Portilla would require a return to the *Fenomenología* with the intent of drawing out the significant consequences of this work.

Portilla was introduced to the English-speaking philosophical community for the first time by the contemporary Mexican philosopher Antonio Zirión Quijano, who in 2000 published a paper on the history of phenomenology in Mexico, listing Portilla as a key figure (Zirión 2000). However, Zirión tells us there that Portilla is an "an almost forgotten figure who deserves to be remembered or even rescued" (Zirión 2000, 75) and calls upon the English-speaking philosophical community to "study, rescue, and translate" Portilla's valuable contributions, especially his work on "relajo" (Zirión 2000, 89). Zirión goes on to praise Portilla's *Fenomenología* as "the most brilliant and penetrating phenomenological essay written in Mexico to date" (Zirión 2000, 89). He repeats this again in 2004, calling it "the *only* original essay properly phenomenological which has been written by a Mexican philosopher" (Zirión 2004, 302). He laments that "there is very little written about Jorge Portilla, and about his most ambitious essay, *Fenomenología del relajo*, there is even less" (Zirión 2004, 301). In spite of Zirión Quijano's pleas, nothing has yet appeared to answer his call for work that "rescues" Portilla from eternal anonymity.

What follows is a rescue attempt by way of a recovery and introduction of Jorge Portilla *and* his *Fenomenología*. The chapters that follow will critically engage Portilla's text and in the process draw out Portilla's unique appropriation of the history of Western philosophy, especially existentialism and phenomenology, culminating in, what I take to be, a critique of modernity and subjectivity that I believe best represents the struggle and the triumph of post–World War II Mexican philosophy. Ultimately, the picture I hope to paint is one of a monumental figure whose encounters with that which was most familiar in his circumstance gave rise to a philosophical vision that allows us to understand not only certain predicaments of twentieth-century Mexican culture but also our post-911 world and its complex crises of value, commitment, and identity.

The present chapter is introductory in several senses: it introduces us to Jorge Portilla, his life, and his death; it gives us the theme of his *Fenomenología*, namely, *"relajo"*; it invites us to attend to the complexities of his *method*; and, finally, it readies us for the critique of modern subjectivity that, I claim, is the more significant contribution of Portilla's text. My treatment in this chapter relies primarily on four sources; while these are brief introductions, and while they are all in Spanish, they are the only instances in which Portilla's life and thought have become thematic. The first, by Rosa Krauze, appears as a eulogy in 1966 in *Revista de la Universidad de México*; the second, thirty-seven years after Krauze's, is an article from 2003 by Juan José Reyes in *La Cronica de Hoy*; the third is included in Antonio Zirión Quijano's impressive *Historia de la fenomenología en México*, which appeared in 2004; and the fourth, and most recent treatment, is by Guillermo Hurtado in his introduction to the anthology *Hiperión*, published in 2006. After a summary view of his life, thought, and method, I provide an outline for the chapters to follow.

Jorge Portilla: An Anonymous Life

Jorge Portilla was born in Mexico City in 1919 and died of a heart attack in 1963, at the age of forty-four. In between, he studied law and philosophy; became a father and a prominent member of the philosophical group el Hiperión (founded in 1947); was an existentialist, a Marxist, a phenomenologist, and, some say, a devout Catholic. He is said to be the model for several fictional eccentrics in a couple of Mexican novels, for instance, and most prominently, for López Wilson, the "eyewitness to the dying of capitalism" in *La región mas transparente* (1958). Despite Fuentes' close association with Portilla,[1] the picture that emerges there is one of a Marxist whose disillusionment hides whatever philosophical prowess he might have possessed. In this way, aside from certain facts, such as his membership in el Hiperión and his death, most of what we know about Jorge Portilla is pieced together from clues he leaves in his own writings, memories of friends, or just hearsay. After all is said, and the layers are properly peeled, a nonfictional picture emerges of a Mexican Socrates, one who frequented the intellectual hot spots and cafés of Mexico City during the 1940s and '50s with the aim of disturbing the bourgeois complacency of those in the know, as *gadflies* are prone to do, while carefully noting and dissecting the forms of life that would later come to preoccupy him, including those "death orgies" that Fuentes has him enjoying.

There is not much information on his youth or adolescence. We know that Portilla's father, Segundo, owned a bar on the outskirts of the Zócalo, the old historical center of the Mexican capital (Reyes 2003). Here, the younger Portilla would begin to gather the themes that would populate his *Fenomenología*—themes such as revelry, drunkenness, nihilism, irony, laughter, seriousness, and what he calls *"relajo."* In the 1940s, Portilla attends the University of Mascarones, at that time Mexico City's intellectual center. After Mascarones (it is not clear if he graduates) he dedicates himself to the life of the intellectual. The Mexican novelist Juan Jóse Reyes, son of Portilla's fellow *hiperión,* José Reyes Nevarez, provides a snippet of Portilla's intellectual bent: "He was open to conversation, life amongst friends, to happiness or to tremendous misery, among women or in solitude; he loved Mexican popular music as much as the realm of ideas which were no match for his exceptional intelligence" (Reyes 2003, 1). And he knew he was exceptionally intelligent, which led to a widespread conviction that Portilla was arrogant and mean. It is said that he sought others with whom he could engage and who could challenge him intellectually; some say that what motivated him was not the possibility of intelligent conversation, but the prospect of victory in argument (Reyes 2003, 1).[2] While this suggests arrogance, others saw it as a manifestation of his love of *being with others.* As Rosa Krauze puts it: "His life escaped him in conversation . . . Indubitably, Jorge Portilla would give everything away when he spoke, and would give it with the warmest generosity" (Krauze 1966, 9).

Accounts indicate, however, that this generosity disguised as arrogance was but a facet of a more complex personality—one that informs his philosophy through and through. Christopher Domínguez Michael summarizes the man in the following way: "Charming and paradoxical, star of barrooms and cenacles, Jorge Portilla was 'a drinker, a wanderer and a gambler' in the most tender and pathetic sense of that Mexican expression" (Michael 1996, 10).[3] Guillermo Hurtado, who in 2006 publishes the first anthology of *Hiperión* essays, introduces Portilla as "incapable of being measured within academic parameters: he was a man of superior intelligence, charismatic, and tormented" (Hurtado 2006, x). Indeed, most accounts agree that Portilla was tormented, that he was a drinker—and even more, *a drunk*. Krauze recounts a man who would "take sleeping pills while asking for whiskey" (Krauze 1966, 9). Domínguez Michael identifies Portilla with his philosophy, or, rather, with the themes which preoccupied him, and diagnoses him as a "bohemian" and a *relajiento*, terms that, as we will see, are synonymous with irresponsibility. In the end, Michael concludes, Portilla becomes a *"filósofo fracasado,"* a failed philosopher (Michael 1996, 10).[4]

The conclusion that Portilla was a *filósofo fracasado* is based, however, on a narrow understanding of the philosophical life in general, and of a superficial reading of Portilla's *Fenomenología* in particular. The narrow view of the philosophical life finds the "philosopher" institutionalized in the classroom or in the faculty—indeed "measured by academic parameters." But what would that make Socrates? Or Spinoza? Like them, Portilla never held a university position; however, "he gave lectures, and turned his kitchen table into a classroom [*aula*] where he explained Hegel's texts to a group of university students" on a regular basis (Krauze 1966, 9). As for his *Fenomenología*, it is a much more complex work than Domínguez Michael leads one to believe. Michael unsympathetically categorizes it as some version of Sartrean existentialism, one seeking ground in the later Sartre's Marxist-Leninism. The result is a failed Marxist text! Michael, like many before him, misunderstands the *Fenomenología*.

Portilla's death on August 18, 1963, was announced in several Mexico City news outlets. From these quick obituaries we get a sense that his death was both tragic and anticipated. It was tragic by virtue of it being *the death of someone*. The weekly *México en la Cultura* (September 1, 1963, 754) posts a small picture of Portilla with the caption, "Jorge Portilla has died. May he rest in peace. Of his intelligence no one could speak without enthusiasm." But his death was also anticipated, and anticipated in a double sense: in one sense, it was commonly believed that the life he led, one of heavy drinking, drugs, and *parranda* (as Krauze recounts) could only result in an early death; and, more interestingly, his death was anticipated because it signaled the arrival of his unpublished work. Indeed, in a late notice of his death, one published almost four months after the fact (December 1, 1963; *Cultura Nacional*, no. 857), we read: "Portilla died recently and we now hope to see some of those essays he promised and that will certainly be of the highest quality, like all of his work." As if Portilla's *life* was an obstacle to the revelation of his thought, as if his talent never belonged to him at all, but to us all: "He died just in time," writes Domínguez Michael, "before he subjected that damned talent of his to the hateful tyranny of [another philosophy in vogue]" (Michael 1996, 10).

The anticipated work would come three years later as *Fenomenología del relajo*. Collected by his friends and fellow philosophers, Luis Villoro, Alejandro Rossi, and Víctor Flores Olea, it required some editing on their part, although they claim not to have disturbed either the ideas or the style of its author "*en lo más mínimo*" (in the least).

A Crisis of *Relajo*

In the introduction to the *Fenomenología*, Villoro, Rossi, and Olea write that "philosophy for [Portilla] was not the exclusive preoccupation of schools or academics, but a form of life which demanded, to whomever would embrace it, the painful task of ceaselessly questioning the world in its everydayness [*el mundo cotidiano*]" (Portilla 1984, 3). This conception of philosophy explains Portilla's principal theme in the *Fenomenología*, namely, what he calls "relajo."

"Relajo" is a complex term indicating both an attitude and a manner of being for which there is no straightforward equivalent in English. It comes from the Latin *relaxare*, to loosen, which translates into English as "to relax." In colloquial Spanish it is used in the phrase "*echar relajo*," which is equivalent to the meaning of the phrase "letting loose." But "relax" or "letting loose" does not capture Portilla's phenomenological reading of the term, which he redefines to mean "a suspension of seriousness" [18, 25].[5] By "seriousness," Portilla has in mind the way in which we commit ourselves to values. Our commitment is such that we want to work toward their realization. Every situation is regulated by a value or values which make that situation what it is. For instance, a religious ceremony is governed by values which prescribe religious obedience, such as the value of silence, the value of prayer, the value of offering, and so on. While the ceremony is taking place, one is committed to those values—one is *serious* about them and their realization, since they are "what matters" in the situation. "Relajo" is the suspension of that seriousness and, thus, the impossibility of the realization of "what matters" in the moment.

Because of the lack of an English equivalent, I will "translate" "relajo" as *relajo*.[6]

There are few works in English that treat of *relajo* in one way or another. All of these cite Portilla as the most original in his conception. But none of them treats *relajo* extensively, and, none of them dedicates more than a paragraph to Portilla's treatment (Sobrevilla 1989; Lomnitz 1992; Levinson 2001; Castro 2000; Taylor 2003; Farr 2006; and Carpenter 2010). Most agree that *relajo* is an interruption or a disruption of mundane situations, while some conceive it literally, as an event of relaxation or jovial humor.

Portilla approaches the phenomenon of *relajo* in its everydayness, as it normally appears to people in their quixotic dealings with the world. His initial characterization is thus that it is "that form of repeated and sometimes loud collective joking that emerges sporadically in the daily life of our country [Mexico]." However, the everydayness of *relajo* is but a point of departure. Portilla will diagnose it as a "condition" which is at the root of that lack of community, solidarity, and responsibility that Portilla believes defines modern Mexico, and, more broadly, as I will argue, modernity in general. The recognition of this condition motivates Portilla's appeal to philosophy; the philosophical treatment of this condition is carried out from a sense of *personal responsibility* that Portilla feels for Mexico and Mexicans. The restriction of this feeling to the most familiar is necessary, as the familiar is what is closest to us. Beginning with what is closest, Portilla initiates his phenomenological analysis from the first-person perspective, situating himself in the time-space of contemporary Mexico, which is the historical moment of *relajo*:

> I belong to a generation whose best representatives lived for many years in an environment of the most unbearable and loud irresponsibility that could be imagined; in spite of this, I unfalteringly consider them the best representatives of that generation. Some of them were men of talent, others of a noble and generous character; all of them seemed absolutely incapable of

resisting any occasion for releasing a stream of coarse humor that, once flowing, became uncontrollable and continuously thwarted the emergence of their better qualities. It was as if they were afraid of their own excellence and as if they felt obligated to forbid its manifestation. They would only bring their excellence out when in conversation with a friend or when in a state of inebriation. I almost never witnessed them taking anything with real seriousness, even less so, their own capabilities and their own destiny. They were—I can see it clearly now—a Nietzschean generation *avant la lettre* that, in the midst of continual laughter, lived dangerously, devoted in actual fact to a slow process of self-destruction. [14–15]

This is Portilla hovering above those "death-orgies" Carlos Fuentes attributes to Lopéz Wilson. Portilla calls them manifestations of *relajo*, which is the real crisis. It is a crisis belonging to Mexico *and* Portilla. It is a *generational* crisis of history, spirit, and subjectivity that Portilla *assumes*—he takes it as his—it was his to "enjoy," and it is his to denounce. As Rosa Krauze recalls, for Portilla "the intellectual who lives on the margins of political and social circumstances does not have justification. . . . Portilla believed that the intellectual who was not shocked by what happened around him, was as guilty as everyone else" (Krauze 1966, 10). In this way, Portilla's philosophy begins from a sense of responsibility *for his generation*. And, as he confesses in the quote above, he digs it out of, what Juan Jóse Reyes calls, "autobiographical depths" (Reyes 2003, 1).

As to what *relajo* "is," Portilla finds its essence and provides guidelines for its overcoming. In general terms, *relajo* is the suspension of a determinate event through a repetitious interruption of the values which hold it together. The following minor example should suffice for now: during a visit to a local career training center, a congresswoman's speech promoting job creation was interrupted by an audience member who yelled out a question regarding the moral fortitude of a fellow congressman (who, he said, had been caught "with his pants down"). The question caught the congresswoman by surprise and, besides interrupting her speech, immediately diverted attention away from her point, namely, the promotion of programs that create jobs. Follow-up comments and questions on her colleague's questionable character took the discussion in a different direction: soon there was tension, laughter, and chaos. The value which held the meeting room together was a serious discussion about jobs and training. The interruption suspended the seriousness and the repetition of the interruption through follow-up comments, mocking remarks, and irreverent observations completely displaced the value that the speech aimed to highlight. The audience's focus was now on a different set of meanings and a different, and unorganized, context of significance which had no bearing on jobs or the economy. Simply put, the congresswoman's speech was overtaken by *relajo*.

This is a minor example. *Relajo* is a more encompassing phenomenon of daily life with possibly more serious consequences—even in *our* time and place. While today, and in that geopolitical space we call home, we might not call it "relajo," it is a recognizable happening that we often try to avoid by maintaining our focus on the matter at hand, or keeping our attention focused on the situation in which we might find ourselves, or at least, on that aspect of it that we consider important and for which we are willing to sacrifice our time and effort. The situation—for example, lecture, conversation, and charity work—will make its own demands upon us, requiring us to see it through to the end (via a fulfillment of its demands). This transcultural aspect of *relajo* must be kept in mind as we go on.

The Context of the Method

Portilla's philosophy is tied to his autobiography—to whom he is *as* a Mexican and an intellectual. That is, it begins in the existential dimension of his own life. It begins in Mexico and in the drama of his own generation. As the editors (Villoro, Rossi, and Olea) put it in their "introductory note," or "*advertencia*": "A man of crisis, Portilla lived the spiritual and social conflicts of our time, *in the flesh*" [10]. He was an *existentialist* in the most common sense of that term. But he was a phenomenologist in his philosophical approach. Hence, while the *Fenomenología*'s existential feel at times leaves it without method— it is at times fragmented and unsystematic—it is deeply rooted in a phenomenological tradition that includes Edmund Husserl, Martin Heidegger, Max Scheler, and, of course, Jean-Paul Sartre.

This is not surprising. Midtwentieth-century Mexico City is alive with existentialism and phenomenology, largely due to the efforts of Spanish intellectuals fleeing Franco's Spain after the breakout of the Spanish Civil War (July 1936 to April 1939). One of these exiles, José

Gaos, spearheads an existential-phenomenological "movement" rooted in Heidegger's *Being and Time* and French existentialism.[7] Another, Eduardo Nicol, tells his students that "philosophy [is] phenomenology or it isn't philosophy" (Camarena 2004, 153). Gaos' students convene el Grupo Hiperión and hold conferences and lectures where they study, analyze, and apply the lessons of Sartre and Heidegger to the search for a Mexican philosophical identity ("lo mexicano"). In Portilla's *Fenomenología*, the obvious influences are Sartre, Edmund Husserl, and a mutated version of Marxist criticism. But these influences are *appropriated*, which means that Portilla takes from them only those methodological or conceptual elements best capable of disclosing the "truth" of his theme. What we get is Portilla's own philosophical method. My working assumption here at the start is that it is possible to pry open the appropriation and recover the Sartrean, the Husserlian, and the "critical" influences.

Jean-Paul Sartre

Portilla, the man, can best be described as an existentialist, but not because of his philosophical method, rather because of his *attitude*. Krauze recounts: "Jorge Portilla despaired at his own impotence. He felt devoured by neurosis. He was afraid of *this and that* and he suffered a nervous anxiety that would take him to the arms of women or the analyst's chair" (Krauze 1966, 9). This existentialist attitude is clearly displayed in Portilla's "autobiographical" beginning to his *Fenomenología*, one that situates him in that "Nietzschian generation *avant la lettre* that, in the midst of continual laughter, lived dangerously devoted in actual fact to a slow process of self-destruction" (15). Thus, his beginning is a reactionary one; Portilla is assuming responsibility for his life and the lives of those around him. Portilla's philosophical assumption of responsibility personifies Sartre's insight, when the latter writes: "When we say that man chooses his own self, we mean that every one of us does likewise; but we also mean by that, that *in making this choice he also chooses all men*" (Sartre 1947, 20; my emphasis).[8]

While Portilla was a Catholic—or at least claimed to be (Krauze 1966)—he assumed Sartre's position regarding the lack of God-given, or objective, values. Values are to be found in the world in which one lives, and not in an a priori hierarchy on the top of which one finds "supreme" values (Max Scheler held this view, for instance [Scheler

1973]). Portilla's attraction to his theme, that is, *relajo*, can be understood as rooted in the belief that, when in a state of *relajo*, the modern Mexican subject is *choosing not to choose*. Sartre wrote that the human person "is condemned every moment to invent" herself (Sartre 1947, 48). What Portilla realizes is that those around him are choosing not to choose this condemnation. Hence, Mexicans, when fallen in *relajo*, have ceased inventing themselves and, as such, are stuck in a perpetually repeating now. They have lost the future.

As we will see, the situation of fallenness that Portilla describes in his *Fenomenología* is as severe as are the quietism, bad faith, and false consciousness that Sartre analyses, for instance, in *Being and Nothingness* and in *Existentialism*. Not surprisingly, Sartre's analysis of freedom plays a crucial role in Portilla's text. But while Portilla echoes much of what Sartre says about freedom and the ways of its realization, he stops short of appealing to a "Sartrean" method of investigation. And this, perhaps, is because Sartre's method is itself indebted to Edmund Husserl's phenomenology and Martin Heidegger's existential analytic. But neither does Portilla obediently subscribe to the orthodoxy of the phenomenological method. Given that Sartre's, Husserl's, and Heidegger's crises are their own, European, crises (whatever they might be), Portilla appropriates aspects of the Husserlian method in such a way that the appropriation responds and is adapted to his own, historical and subjective, crisis.

EDMUND HUSSERL

Husserl's phenomenology heavily informs Portilla's method of analysis. Portilla aims to find the invariant essence of *relajo*, and to do this, he appropriates Husserl's methods. But, as Zirión Quijano points out, we should not expect to find the "systematic scientific vision" that we find in Husserl (Zirión 2004, 303). The method Portilla appropriates is the phenomenological method as expounded in Husserl's 1913 *Ideas Pertaining to a Pure Phenomenology and to a Phenomenological Philosophy* (Husserl 1998). While Husserl's own ambitions for the "method" were grand—he wanted it to found "systematic scientific vision"—those who followed (philosophers and social scientists alike) have enjoyed and benefited from the method in less spectacular ways.

The goal of Husserl's phenomenological method is straightforward: to "seize upon essences" (Husserl 1998, 156), or to put it another way, to come to understand the "whatness" of a thing, to understand what makes it *what* it is. Theoretically, we can come to know or understand the essence of atoms, tables, practices, commitments, concepts, and even human existence, by subjecting these to the method of phenomenological reduction, which involves *perception, suspension, variation,* and *intuition* of the *essence* of those things or states of affairs.

Portilla's starting point, for instance, is his own life—his life as Mexican among Mexicans. He notices the pervasiveness of *relajo.* He considers *relajo* as it is given in experience; he is confronted with *relajo* as phenomenon of experience. The goal, however, is to arrive at the *essence* of "relajo" and the particular, individual manifestation of the *relajo* phenomenon is insufficient for this task. The next step is, therefore, to "suspend" whatever beliefs are attached to the phenomenon of *relajo,* for instance, that it is a harmless commotion or laughter. Husserl says that one must "put [those beliefs] out of action" (Husserl 1998, 59). Consequently, Portilla cannot continue to believe that *relajo* is *simply* the state of being relaxed or letting loose or laughing or causing a stir. But how to get the essence of *relajo*—how to *seize upon the essence*? Portilla must imagine every possible manifestation of *relajo* both in his own experience and in any possible experience. Husserl calls this exercise "free phantasy," or imaginative variation, and its purpose is to allow the phenomenological investigator to "attain clear intuitions from which [she] is exempted" by the particular experience (Husserl 1998, 158–59). Said differently: in imagination the phenomenological investigator is able to sort through the multitude of *relajo* instances, to run through every possible manifestation of the conduct. Interestingly enough, this imaginative exercise "is the source from which the cognition of 'eternal truths' is fed" as the phenomenologist runs through real and imagined encounters of the phenomenon, thereby opening up "access to the expanse of essential possibilities" (Husserl 1998, 160). This "expanse" allows Portilla to begin to *see* what remains invariant in the variation. This invariant is the essence, namely, that *relajo* is *essentially* "a suspension of seriousness."

CRITICISM/DECONSTRUCTION

There is no clear indication in the *Fenomenología* that Portilla subscribed to a Marxist-type of criticism that looks to unravel the immanent logic of Mexican culture. If there is an indication, it is not explicit. However, we do find a *critical method*, one similar to Karl Marx's but, surprisingly, more in line with Martin Heidegger's. This is surprising because Portilla never mentions Heidegger, either in the *Fenomenología* or in any of his other published writings (which are few and include newspaper columns written during the 1950s and up to 1962). But in reading the *Fenomenología* one does bump into the "specter of Marx," especially when Marx writes in his "Introduction: Towards a Critique of Hegel's Philosophy of Right," that "the essential task" of philosophy "is denunciation" (Marx 1977, 65). Portilla aims to denounce "an aspect of Mexican morality" [14] that he suspects is itself an aspect of "the human situation [*la situación del hombre*]" [13]. "So as to give them courage," wrote Marx, "we must teach the people to be shocked by themselves" (Marx 1977, 66). Indeed, a "phenomenology of *relajo*" is undertaken more in the spirit of denunciation and exposure than for the sake of pushing the boundaries of phenomenological practice.

Portilla's denunciations, making up his critical method, take the form of a "destruction" in the Heideggerian sense. By this we mean that Portilla destroys, or "deconstructs," the basic presuppositions that give rise to the cultural blindness which keeps people, and philosophers, ignorant of *relajo* and its negations. With this destructive approach, which Heidegger says when describing his own, is a "criticism . . . aimed at 'today'" (Heidegger 1962, 44), Portilla labors to denounce a crisis which he thinks blinds "today" to its promise and its potency—it is the "today" of *relajo*, which promises nothing but an impossible tomorrow. He says: "*Relajo* is a desperate attempt to prevent the moral life from manifesting itself as a spirited appeal to an ennobling and a spiritualization of human life" [84]. The critical destruction of "today" is not meant to bring about the "ennobling and spiritualization of human life," but through a deconstruction of those beliefs and behaviors that suffocate the moral life and keep it from showing itself, it is meant to expose the impotency of Mexicans on the grand stage of modernity, where this "spiritualization" is supposed to take place. In this complex manner, the "eidetic phenomenology" of Husserl is secretly married to a critical humanism resembling Marx's, and through phenomenological bloodlines, bolstered by the destructive/critical approach of Heidegger.

In the *Fenomenología*, critical humanism serves as a background for the moral considerations to which Portilla will have to attend; Sartre validates his effort, as *relajo* summons him to responsibility; and

Heidegger's destructive approach amends Husserl's method, which he takes as the most appropriate for his task. But perhaps "takes" is not the right word here. While Portilla certainly takes, the *taking* is not without consequence, since the taking manipulates what it takes, namely, the obligation, theme, or method, thereby transforming them. This is especially the case with Portilla's "taking" of Husserl's insight into the noetic-noematic correlation that emerges in intentional analysis. This taking, or appropriation, of the correlation serves to highlight the fact that "relajo" has a "sense" and not, as would be expected, to show "how" subjects experience *relajo* itself [22n3]. This appropriation shows that Portilla is dependent on Husserl's method to some extent, but, at the same time, it shows that he is willing to break with that method if and when the object demands it. Furthermore, Portilla's analysis of *relajo* will not involve a description of the structures of consciousness involved in the recognition or cognition of the phenomenon—as it would for Husserl.

Despite the methodological context which informs Portilla's *Fenomenología*, we do not find Portilla pledging allegiance to any one of these influences. Instead, we find him struggling with his theme in a genuine effort to unravel and possess it so as to expose its structure and its universal philosophical significance in the clearest possible way. This desire for clarity is a mark of Portilla's *philosophy* more generally: "Clarity is the very task of the philosopher, if one considers philosophy as a specific function of the culture of a community" [16]. In other words, if Portilla considers philosophy as a function of the culture of the community, which he does, then his own task is defined by the demands of "clarity." If the achievement of clarity requires a more aggressive manipulation of the tradition, then Portilla would be the one to aggressively manipulate it.

In Portilla, philosophy's role in culture is to make clarity possible by opening up the space of conversation by promoting reason. He puts it thus: "From this point of view, philosophy has the function of promoting reason in a specific society, of clearly putting before the collective consciousness the ultimate base of its thinking, of its feeling, and of its acting" [16]. But how else could this promotion take place if not through acts of destruction and denunciation? Portilla's appropriation of Husserlian phenomenology, Sartrean existentialism, Heideggerian destruction, and Marxist criticism are appropriations in the service of promoting reason via a denouncing of cultural configurations (i.e., *relajo*) which hinder the promotion of reason. In this way, Portilla's philosophy takes *philosophy as a tool to open up. reflexion. making available truth sets you free* [handwritten annotation]

shape as a philosophy of liberation, but not liberation in the political sense, rather liberation in the existential, personal, sense. Not a general liberation, but a particular, and specific, liberation. Portilla sums it up in the following way: "The truth sets me free, and perhaps the ultimate sense of all authentic philosophy is this liberating operation of 'logos' and not the creation of a framework of concepts as a mirror of reality" [16]. Ultimately, clarity, as made possible by philosophy, is liberation.

We can provisionally categorize Portilla's *method* in the *Fenomenología* as *a critical-phenomenological appropriation*: using autobiography as the sphere of givenness of the phenomenon (Sartre), Portilla *reconstructs* (through eidetic variation) the various manifestation of *relajo* to reveal its essential relations and its "noema" (Husserl), which, he says, is "value" [22n3]. Afterward, Portilla *deconstructs* (Heidegger) the *place*, and *time*, of the *relajo* event to uncover its subjective and intersubjective dimensions. This deconstruction reveals different forces at work in the time-space, that is, in the culture, of *relajo*. The revelation itself serves as a denunciation (criticism) which calls for a *prescriptive* account, what I will call "dialogical ethics." Portilla's normative account is set against a critique of modern subjectivity which, overtaken by *relajo*, is in need of salvation.

In the end, what we discover is that, unlike Husserl's "pure" phenomenology, or even Heidegger's existential hermeneutic, Portilla does not hold back in addressing those problems of existence usually reserved for philosophical anthropology, such as investigating the manners of existence belonging to the individual possessed by *relajo*. So long as the investigation is sanctioned by reason, then the investigation is worthy of being carried out, since, he says, "no subject is too insignificant for reason" [13]. Rationally treating the theme in question gives the investigation and whatever conclusions emerge, what Husserl called, "a mark of distinction" (Husserl 1998, 327).

On Subjectivity

A significant contribution to issues of contemporary concern is Portilla's critique of modern subjectivity by way of his critique of the individual who succumbs to or initiates *relajo*. This individual, the "relajiento," is emblematic of the more general crisis of modernity that I believe Portilla is addressing. In order to draw contrasts, three other modes of being a subject are presented in Portilla's text. In each case, the subject is conceived in accordance to the specific relationship that subject has to value(s) and/or its realization—to whether or not he or she is committed to, embodies, or creates value(s) in some way. Those "subjects," or that subjectivity, toward which Portilla directs his critical gaze, what we can refer to as the "nonsubjects" of modernity, will be characterized below by (a) "*relajiento*" and (b) "*apretado*," while (c), the "Socratic/Ironic" subject, is the contrast; (d), the "transcendental subject," is the "ideal" subject.

A. RELAJIENTO

[handwritten: laughs off responsibility — careless pretense? of lack of concern.]

The individual who embodies the crisis of *relajo*, Portilla calls a "*relajiento*." The *relajiento* has assumed the life of a perpetual suspension. Values that demand realization are suspended, and with that, the processes of subjectivity. Portilla describes *relajientos* in the following way: "A 'relajiento' is, literally, an individual without a future . . . He or she refuses to take anything seriously, to commit to anything; that is to say, a 'relajiento' refuses to guarantee any of his or her own behavior in the future. The 'relajiento' assumes no responsibility for anything; he or she does not risk doing anything; he or she is simply a good-humored witness of the banality of life" [39–40]. The *relajiento* individual is thus someone who has suspended the event of subjectivity altogether. The *relajiento* is, literally, "one who is full of relajo," overflowing with suspensions and without a future. In Portilla's account, then, the *relajiento* is a *subject in suspense*; he or she is not fully a subject, or even subject-in-progress, but a *nonsubject*. While Portilla finds in this nonsubject the root of nihilism and irresponsibility in modern Mexico, below I will explore the positive aspects of this idea of suspending seriousness, and consequently, subjectivity—an idea now in vogue in certain postcolonial and postmodern accounts. I will also suggest that the *relajiento* is a concept of critique applicable to the subject of modernity more generally understood.

[handwritten: not an authentic life nor does the apretado]

B. APRETADO

The *apretado*, of which "snob" is a translation, *embodies* value.

ref: Sartre's text on the
inauthenticity RIGID
= BAD FAITH

The spirit of seriousness is that attitude of consciousness which refuses to take notice of the distance between "being" and "value," in any manner in which this could occur. In this sense, it can be an incidental determination of any individual. But in the individual that is called an "apretado" in Mexico, this attitude is a habit. The "apretado" individual considers him or herself valuable, without any considerations or reservations of any type. The external expression of this attitude, its most peripheral manifestation, is this individual's outward appearance. "Apretado" individuals worry about their physical appearance, which is the expression of their internal being. They dress impeccably; they are elegant people, or at least they try to be at all costs. Their exterior shows the massiveness with no fissures according to which they interpret their own interiority. "Apretado" individuals are a little bit too impeccable; their self-esteem shines forth in their meticulous care for all the details of their external figure. Our colonialist naïveté says that these individuals are "very British," and they themselves have [a]—often self-proclaimed—weakness for what they call "good English taste." [87–88]

Sartre

not living his authentic self —
denying yourself freedom,

The *apretado* is the dialectical other of the *relajiento*—he represents the *relajiento's* extreme opposite in the spectrum of *being human* in terms of mannerism, world-views, and commitments. The subjectivity of the *apretado* is defined through his identification with values imposed from the outside, values definitive of behavior, style, taste, and so on. The *apretado* allows the external world to constitute his or her identity. He embodies values and thus lacks the freedom to deviate from them. That he *lacks freedom* makes authentic subjectivity impossible. The *apretado*, like the *relajiento*, is a "nonsubject," or what Portilla calls a "negated subject."

C. SOCRATIC/IRONIC

The Mexican comedic actor Mario Moreno, a.k.a. "Cantinflas," serves as a model for a subjectivity *beyond relajo*. Like Socrates, Cantinflas' deployment of irony before the demands of seriousness is meant not to suspend value but to "unravel" it. Portilla says, "There is no situation, no matter how serious, that is not completely defused by the demolishing expressiveness of this great mime" [27]. Of course, the unraveling of seriousness is also constitutive of *relajo*, so Portilla adds to this the importance of Socratic irony. Irony proves to be the antidote to *relajo*. The Socratic irony-subject is a subject who searches for truth by unraveling that which is proposed as truth. The irony-subject is, in existentialist terms, always in the process of becoming. Portilla writes: "Irony is, then, immanent to a consciousness that judges and that notices the distance between the possible realization of a value and its supposed realization by someone with a pretense of fulfilling it. It is, so to speak, the adequate response to the 'pretentious person'" [65]. Further, "Irony is something which can penetrate logic and reality" [68]. And, "In Socrates, irony is an act of liberation; it is distancing oneself from mere appearances in order to adequately orient the pursuit of truth. In irony, one transcends an obstacle toward truth" [69]. In other words, the irony- or Socratic subject is a *transcending* subject. Most important, however, the irony-subject is, opposed to the *relajiento,* a committed subject, and opposed to the *apretado*, always in the process of becoming due to her unrelenting pursuit of truth.

commitment to truth

D. THE TRANSCENDENTAL SUBJECT

*active liberation.
self-deception
need to transcend
own subjectivity to
be your true self*

Portilla idealized the subject. According to this idealization, subjectivity is an inwardness which projects out to the world in acts of engagement and world making. Throughout his *Fenomenología*, Portilla's concern is the arrival of a subject who will take responsibility for the future of Mexico, one who transcends the appeal of nonsubjectivity, of suspense (or suspension), and undertakes the drama of world building. This is a responsible, liberated subject and a maker of worlds. He hints at this authentic subjectivity in several places (I go into more detail in chapter 5). For instance: "The free variations of my subjectivity, the changes of attitude in pure interiority—some of which can be characterized as liberations and that produce a concomitant change in the appearance of the world—in operating this change of appearance open up several different possibilities for my behavior: This is what interests us here" [63].
    Perhaps the Socratic/Ironic subject is the condition for the possibility for the "ideal" subject, one who is free of its determinations and

transcending irony + humor?

willing to create. A subjectivity unencumbered by history and circumstance is an authentic subjectivity. It is, he says, "pure interiority," and an "*interior* event" [63] that "produces" change in the world, which is, in other words, world-constituting. This is a subjectivity beyond the determination that oppresses the *relajiento* and the *apretado*, but also beyond Socrates, since it is free of the need for irony and humor as tools for liberation.   *unencumbered by lived history*

A Critic of Modernity

The promises of modernity cannot be realized unless they are taken *seriously*. The modernizing project, whose internal logic aims to make Mexico more economically productive and competitive, demands seriousness. At its core, it requires a sober attitude toward what might be perceived as a nostalgic relationship Mexicans have toward their own history (the conquest, colonization, independence, revolution). Simultaneously, it requires a recalibration of cultural attitudes and commitments toward capital, efficiency, management, and labor. The modernizing project seeks the future of Mexico in the emerging opportunities presenting themselves ever more rapidly in the global marketplace. But its fulfillment also demands that the *relajiento*, and the social and cultural conditions that make *relajo* possible, be subsumed. *Relajo* must be overcome. But neither will a dogmatic defense of values, some of which are obviously oppressive and impediments to social progress, bring about the completion of a modernizing project begun five hundred years prior. The *apretado* must also be transcended. Socratic seriousness provides the *model* for the type of commitment needed to welcome the future.

But what is sought is a free and transcendent subjectivity. The person who embodies this ideal will freely choose what is right, valuable, and good in agreement with a free and liberated intersubjectivity, that is, community. The Socratic irony-subject is not yet the realization of this ideal, but it makes it possible. No longer oppressed by the determinations of history and circumstance, authentic intersubjectivity expresses itself in communal acts of dialogue, generosity, and creative world making.

We can dare to generalize and say that Portilla's idealized subjectivity is the hope of those on the margins of world history. That this idealized subjectivity is left unrealized even in the modern centers of power tells us that, perhaps, we are all marginal in some way—that modernity is the state of *being* marginal. That Portilla structured his critique of *relajo* as a critique of an essential way of displacing this ideal suggests that his critique is more ambitious than it first appears. Portilla's is a critique of our inability to be who we can be—Mexicans or not, then or now.

Predictions

Portilla suggested that what must be overcome in order to achieve a meaningful life is the seduction of *relajo,* the seduction of its irresponsibility and its call for detachment from those values constitutive of meaningful experience. What must be transcended, in other words, are the suspensions of *relajo*. Mexican history, as well as the history of Hispanic America, is one of violence, encroachment, and erasure; thus, it is tempting to hold off on taking a stand, on declaring one's subjectivity before the ills of that history. The "suspensions of *relajo*" are harmful to the historically colonized and marginalized: in their displacements and suspensions they seem to further colonize and marginalize. From this acknowledgment we get Portilla's efforts to expose the phenomenon from *autobiographical depths*. Portilla's life grounds a phenomenological investigation that seeks to uncover the path to authentic or genuine subjectivity. His appropriations and deconstructions provide the method for such a task.

What follows is the attempt at recovery first urged by Zirión Quijano. Chapters 2 and 3 offer a reading of the *Fenomenlogía*. There, I unravel Portilla's main themes, such as *relajo*, seriousness, and those acts usually mistaken for *relajo*. I provide *relajo's* definition and its essential characteristics. Chapter 4 attempts to isolate Portilla's *method*. My claim is that Portilla's method is an "appropriation" of different strands of phenomenology, such as Husserl's eidetic method and Heidegger's deconstructive approach; Portilla's method also involves an ethical dimension, which I refer to as a "dialogical ethics." In chapter 5, I flush out Portilla's metaphysics of the subject. The claim will be that Portilla recognized the "ideal" of subjectivity as necessary for the overcoming of the crisis of modernity to which he was responding. Finally, chapter 6 provides a critical appreciation of Portilla's *Fenomenlogía*, paying particular attention to his methodological commitments and presuppositions. In this chapter I also argue that Portilla's critique of that form of life which he finds troubling is, more dramatically, a critique of the failed project of modernity. Portilla, I claim, is a critic of modernity, and not just of the trace of it he finds in Mexico. His is a universal concern.

CHAPTER TWO

Reading *Fenomenología del relajo*, Part 1

> This cannot be philosophy! This cannot be philosophy! . . . What
> kind of human beings are we that we are unable to create a sys-
> tem, that we are incapable of bringing about a philosopher who
> resembles [*asemeje*] one of the many who are and have been key
> players in the history of philosophy? . . . In this question will be
> the heart of the problem; the *why* of our demand for a supposed
> right to a special question.
> —Leopoldo Zea (1989, 11)

I mentioned at the outset that I was lured to Portilla's *Fenomenología del relajo* by Antonio Zirión Quijano's pronouncement that this work represented "the most brilliant and penetrating phenomenological essay written in Mexico to date" (Zirión 2000). What follows explores the manner of this essay's penetration and the intensity of its brilliance.

It is important before we begin that we situate Portilla's philosophical efforts in a definite historical context. In Portilla's case, the context is defined by his involvement in el Grupo Hiperión, or the Hyperion group, whose *philosophical* quest for "lo mexicano," for *Mexicanness* in the late 1940s, defined postwar Mexican philosophy.[1] Next, we provide a general overview of the *Fenomenología* as a whole—its aims and scope. This will be followed by a closer look at the main thematic concepts: *relajo*, value, seriousness, mockery, sarcasm, *choteo*, irony, laughter, and humor. Finally, we'll take a look at the two different kinds of personalities associated with *relajo*, and its antithesis, seriousness: *relajientos* and *apretados*.

Situating Ourselves: El Grupo Hiperión

The Spanish Civil War forced many in the Spanish liberal intelligentsia into exile. The exiles dispersed throughout Europe, but a great majority found sanctuary in the Americas. In Mexico, exiled philosophers, also known as *trasterrados*, or the "trans-planted,"[2] quickly anchored roots to the Mexican soil and took up the urgent task of defining a *Mexican philosophy*. Some of them sought the "reparation of the injustice committed by the History of Philosophy upon Mexican philosophy" (Gaos 1954, 355). This was an injustice observed in the lack of an authentic philosophical tradition in Mexico.

The task was urgent; the history of philosophy in Mexico showed a lack of originality and sensitivity to the Mexican circumstance in its most significant philosophical movements—for instance, Scholasticism in the colonial period and positivism in the nineteenth century. Philosophy in Mexico had been an affirmation of orthodoxy rather than an original, genuine attempt to *do* philosophy with a Mexican perspective. Thus, positivism, Scholasticism, and Marxism had been adopted by Mexican philosophers at face value and each time the same problem arose: the orthodox adoption of a foreign ideology *did not work* for, or did not "fit," the Mexican circumstance. This motivated a genuine attempt toward ideological self-reliance—one suggested by the Spanish exiles as a possibility. The *trasterrados* found an eager audience: young Mexican intellectuals ready to undertake a critical hermeneutic of contemporary Mexican history, culture, and spirit. Their aim was to consider, philosophically, the Mexican circumstance and to think *about* Mexico *for the sake of* Mexicans. A practical attitude was encouraged by the *transterrados* and quickly adopted by their pupils. This attitude required a fearless critique of self and circumstance as the central *philosophical* task.

The arrival of the Spanish exiles was a major event in the history of Mexican philosophy, if not for initiating a new philosophical trajectory for Mexican thinkers, then at least for making possible the emergence of el Grupo Hiperión, or the Hyperion group.[3] Hyperion was formed in the fall of 1948, when a group of young intellectuals, under the influence and tutelage of the *transterrado* José Gaos, set to work on a Mexican philosophy of the present. In a gesture of solidarity and youthful exuberance the group baptized itself as "Hiperión," after the mythical titan sun god Hyperion, the Greek god of illumination. Faithful to the name, members of Hyperion considered themselves rightful heirs to the project of *illuminating*, the implicit yet ordinary existential particularities of the Mexican ethos.[4] They charged themselves with exposing the phenomena (both positive and negative) constituting what it means *to be* Mexican ("lo mexicano")[5] and ultimately, of *proposing* the tasks appropriate for the creation of authentic and responsible Mexican subjects.[6]

Members of el Grupo Hiperión included Leopoldo Zea, Emilio Uranga, Jorge Portilla, Ricardo Guerra, Joaquín Sánchez Macgrégor, Salvador Reyes Nevarez, Fausto Vega, and Luis Villoro. But while the group took a name in common, suggesting the adoption of a similar methodology, each of its members pursued different approaches to the problem of the Mexican present, of "lo mexicano." Zea dealt with the problem through a phenomenology of history (see Sáenz 1999), Uranga through ontological analysis (see Sánchez 2008), Portilla with a phenomenology of values (see Sánchez 2006, 2010), Macgregor with existential moods, Reyes Nevarez via aesthetics, Vega through an examination of social dynamics, and Villoro (in those days) through an analysis of cultural identity (see Guerra 1984; Hurtado 2006).

Zea is the most (perhaps only) recognizable figure in Anglo-American philosophical circles. This is due both to his longevity—he lived from 1912 to 2004—and his copious philosophical output.[7] The other relevant members of Hyperion neither lived as long as Zea nor produced as much. They are not, however, any less significant. Emilio Uranga, for instance, is at the time of Hyperion acknowledged as the most gifted philosopher of the group, referred to by his peers as *primus inter pares,* "first among equals" (Hurtado 2006, x). Uranga, convinced that post-Revolutionary Mexican philosophy has lost itself in an obscurantist metaphysics and lacking roots on the Mexican present, approaches Mexican reality with Martin Heidegger's existential analytic and a Marxist existentialism inspired by Maurice Merleau-Ponty. Portilla, the more elusive member of Hyperion, is likewise committed to a revaluation of values grounded on phenomenology and existential humanism. Despite their apparent differences, Portilla's aim is coincident with Zea's and Uranga's in that at stake in their projects is the overcoming of the alienating self-conceptions and alienating ideologies which Mexicans have, historically, adopted and which estrange Mexicans from their cultural, historical, and existential possibilities. Uranga explains: "The generational theme of Hyperion is precisely the ontological characterization of the being of the Mexican; a moment, to our understanding the most radical moment, in the autognosis of the Mexican . . . We don't just want to live, but *know* and understand what we are living, if it is possible simultaneously . . . Reflection is not meant to even out the field for action (*enmendarle la plana a la acción*), but rather it is the effort to throw oneself into action fully conscious of our limitations (*finalidades*)" (Uranga 1952, 64–65). To "throw oneself fully into action" involves, they believe, a critical project of awakening (what I will call below, "destruction"), one that calls on their fellows to own up to the reality of their reality, to the presence of the present, so that they may realize, better late than never, the promises of modernity. Hence, as Guillermo Hurtado rightly observes, "The philosophy of *lo Mexicano* of *Hiperión* was more than a metaphysical philosophy, it was a philosophy oriented toward action, particularly toward liberating action" (Hurtado 2006, xix). And nowhere is this clearer than with Portilla, whose "phenomenology" gives way to an "ethics" meant to reestablish the space of rational discourse, fulfill the possibility of modernity, and, consequently, bring about the realization of (authentic) freedom.

Approaching the *Fenomenología del relajo*

Portilla died in 1963. His friends and fellow philosophers, Víctor Flores Olea, Alejandro Rossi, and Luis Villoro, publish the *Fenomenología* in 1966. It is a work, they tell us in the editors' introduction, many years in development; its genesis is traceable to the Hiperión years (1948–1952) and, as is obvious from its theme, a result of reflections undertaken as a result of his involvement with the group. Aside from some general remarks about Portilla's final years, when he "attempted a more direct communication with the public through newspaper columns" [11], the editors do not say anything about the content or approach of what they simply refer to as "the essay" (*el ensayo*).

The *Fenomenología* endeavors to show that to which Mexican philosophy can aspire: a historically determinate philosophizing with universal ambitions and a moral vision. Portilla, whose political affinities were always Marxist, wants philosophy to do more than *interpret*; he wants it to be a means of change. A friend, Rosa Krauze, recalls: "[For Portilla] the intellectual who lives on the margins of political or social events has no excuse. [He] maintained that that intellectual who is not shocked by what happens around her is as guilty as the professional politicians in regard to the harmful consequences of the cold war . . . [She] has to take philosophy out to the streets and ease the spiritual tension which drowns contemporary humanity" (Krauze 1966, 10). Hence, the *Fenomenología* will do more than what its title indicates: it will be more than a *descriptive* project meant to get to the essence of *relajo* (a concept better left untranslated, explained in chapter 1). While the phenomenology of *relajo* will take up part 1 of Portilla's text, its moral significance will take up part 2.

Especially for those familiar with the history of phenomenology, what stands out when one first encounters "the essay" is the title. For those of us trained in the "standard" history of phenomenology, it seems out of place, weird, or somehow unauthorized by that history. There are phenomenologies of perception, time, consciousness, the body, the life-world, Spirit, culture, reading, hearing, talking, language, and death—but a phenomenology of "relajo"? The title itself suggests an eccentric undertaking. It tells us that what is contained therein is a phenomenology of some culturally determinate phenomenon that could be skipped if we are either unfamiliar with the culture or uninterested in capricious and self-serving philosophical exercises. The title forces us to choose. We either take a chance and read, hoping for more than allowed by our preconception, or we skip the book in favor of something more familiar. If we take a chance, we must wait for a proper orientation, which takes a few pages to arrive. "Relajo" is not explained either by the editors or by the first few pages of the text itself. We thus have to suspend judgment on the meaning of the term, especially if one has some working knowledge of the Spanish language, since it would be easy to assume to know what this phenomenology is a phenomenology of. Although easy to "look up," or to ask an experienced Spanish speaker, we must refrain from doing so—the aim is an ideal "presuppositionless" phenomenological beginning. We must practice phenomenology in order to begin to read the *Fenomenología*.

Before getting on with the descriptive project (with the *phenomenology*) of *relajo* in part 1, Portilla situates himself in the specific crisis that has brought him to put pen to paper. Addressing the reader, he writes: "allow me to situate autobiographically the origin of this research . . . whose] purpose is simply to gain—for myself and for those who may find it useful—the greatest possible clarity regarding the subject" [14]. He goes on to define the crisis as one of values, in which those he knows and has known (thus, his "autobiographical" beginning) are incapable of taking a stand, of committing themselves in any significant way to what matters, to what demands their commitment. This lack of commitment is, or has, been felt by Portilla himself as the will-to-death of those he has, or had, come to respect. He laments that "many of the members of this generation died tragically, or disappeared, swallowed up by the most extravagant varieties of vice" [15]. Portilla is perhaps here thinking of himself, and his own will to self-destruction. As Krauze recalls: "[Portilla] swayed to and fro from euphoria to dejection, which exhausted him; he drank whiskey with sleeping pills" (Krauz 1966, 9). We could easily attribute this bi-polarity to Portilla's unique psychology, but then we would have to attribute the same to an entire generation, since the "swaying" is all around him. "I belong to a generation," he says, and to "an environment of the most unbearable and loud irresponsibility" [14–15]. This sense of belonging is perhaps what best defines his philosophical personality; because he belongs to the generation, he is responsible for it, and thus he feels the responsibility to *respond*. The *Fenomenología* is thus a response in the form of a confession and a plea from the heart of the crisis.

Portilla assures us that he aims to go beyond a mere relative interpretation of a local mannerism. He aims to speak to humanity; his aim is to aspire, philosophically, to universality. This desire notwithstanding, his phenomenological approach allows him to begin from his immediate, most familiar, situation. Thus, he finds himself in the generational crisis of values. But this crisis is also a national crisis and a human crisis. Portilla is confident that *reason* can prevail in this crisis—that reason can, that *philosophy* can, in Mexico as everywhere else, *liberate*: "In Mexico nothing seems more necessary than the liberating action of *logos*" [16].

The Descriptive Project

What Is *Relajo*?

Once Portilla situates his project autobiographically, or from the first-person experience of *relajo*, the phenomenological work begins. In chapter 1, I mentioned the difficulty in translating "relajo" into English. The difficulty is even greater when the goal is to translate *Portilla's* use of the concept of "relajo," which in many respects is radically different than the common understanding of the term. So I leave it untranslated and hope that we can make sense of it by appealing to its *sense*. I have encountered scholarly translations of "relajo" ranging from "privileged insult, banter" (Lauria 1964), "lackadaisical attitude" (Sobrevilla 1989), "chaotic disorganization," and "vicarious chaotic pleasure" (Lomniz 1992), "fun and relaxation but also carnival like inversion" (Farr 2006), to "joking behavior" (Castro 2000). Some of these, such as "chaotic pleasure," are closer to Portilla's notion, while several of these, for instance, "privileged insult" and "joking behavior," are misleading for they suggest that Portilla thinks *relajo* is somehow a harmless and inconsequential manifestation of social playfulness. Portilla does not think this to be the case, as we will see below.

In everyday, pretheoretical life the word is usually used in conjunction with the verb "*echar*," roughly, "to throw." In everyday life, individuals will occasionally "*echar relajo*." There are a myriad of examples one could use to illustrate "*echar relajo*, but Portilla's examples are personal. Lamenting the lost generation to which he belongs, he says of his closest friends that they would not miss an opportunity to "[release] a current of coarse humor that, once flowing, became uncontrollable and continuously frustrated the showing of their better qualities" [15]. These individuals, who could rather be exploring their "better qualities," perhaps through civil conversation about poetry or politics, instead curse and laugh at and with each other, preventing that exploration of their excellences to even get underway. This is that to which "*echar relajo*" usually refers. But Portilla sees in this behavior, and in all of its manifestations of the *event* of *relajo*, the root of a crisis. It is not that individuals are capable of initiating *relajo* ("*echar relajo*") that Portilla finds conducive to the crisis of value gripping his fellows, but, rather, it is that *relajo* is left unidentified as the root of that crisis. *Relajo* must be denounced.

But if *relajo* is not that harmless, playful, and relaxing activity, then what is it? It certainly involves, although not always, bouts of cursing, yelling, drinking, chaos, disorganization, joking, and laughing, but *relajo* itself is something distinct, an event to which these simpler acts tend, more intricate and more encompassing.

Portilla begins by differentiating "relajo" as a mere behavior (as it is normally understood, e.g., by Castro above) from "relajo" as a "*unitary sense* of a complex behavior" [17; my empahsis]. This differentiation highlights Portilla's idea that *relajo* is more than what it is thought to be. It is more than the banter of drunks or joking around of youth; relajo is a conduct saturated with meaning and with *purpose* (although this purpose is for the most part irrational or prerational).

Portilla "defines" *relajo* as follows: "The sense or meaning of *relajo* is the suspension of seriousness. [*La significación o sentido del relajo es suspender la seriedad*]; That is to say, suspending or annihilating a subject's adherence to a value proposed to his or her freedom" [18]. The meaning of *relajo* is the suspension of seriousness—and, when achieved, it manifests itself as an act of rejection of the value and its imposition. The value might be forcibly imposed, so its suspension or destruction (the word Portilla uses is "annihilation" [*aniquilar*]) is an act of freedom. This means that the phenomenological manifestation of this complex conduct gives itself as a "no" to value. In this negation, *relajo* suspends seriousness and destroys one's attachment to values. And it does so in a "unitary act" made up of three "moments" given simultaneously: (a) a displacement of attention, (b) an invitation for an end to solidarity [*desolidarización*], and (c) the expression of the act [19].

Ultimately, this behavior, uncritically understood in terms of a *harmless* joking around or putting off, is in fact, and critically considered, a violent event which, when (c) announced, usually repeatedly and loudly, (a) displaces, or takes-out-of-place, the attentive act committed to the seriousness of a particular value, and (b) encourages others to *break* from their own commitments to that value. It has intersubjective implications.

When, with a provocative word or gesture, one interrupts a lecture, the attentive investment of those in attendance is *taken-out* of play, or cancelled, and with it the value or significance that held the lecture together. Sure, it is easy to call the meeting back to order; but the reverberation of the interruption will be felt for the rest of the lecture. In the event of *relajo*, calling the meeting back to order is prohibited as the interruption is prolonged through the *repetition* of the original act of displacement by either the original instigator or by those who fall victim to the provocation, and who, as victims, *repeat* the behavior. Repetition is essential to the *relajo*-event:

> *Relajo* is a reiterated action. A single joke that, for example, interrupts a speech being delivered by a speaker is not enough to transform the interruption into *relajo*. The suspensive interruption of seriousness must be repeated indefinitely whether or not the agent [of *relajo*] achieves his or her purpose. It is necessary

for the interrupting gesture or word to repeat continuously until the dizzying thrill of complicity in negation takes over the group which is the most paradoxical of all communities: the community of non-communicators, as a negative backdrop that makes the activity of the value's agent impossible or useless. [24]

It is the repetition of the act which brings about the "dizzying thrill of complicity in negation" from others. In situations like this, one (teacher or student) feels the urge to just give up, since the repetition of the interrupting act or gesture offends the seriousness of the situation and displaces the commitment required to get the point across. In this way, *relajo* is a prolonged digression or interruption that encourages displacement and discourages commitment. This is why some interpreters have suggested that *relajo* is "festive" (Farr 2006; Castro 2001), since a *fiesta* is thought to be a kind of prolonged displacement of commitment. Portilla's phenomenological reading of *relajo*, however, has it that the *fiesta* is antithetical to *relajo*—fiestas uphold their own values, such as the value of "joy." *Relajo* suspends seriousness and commitment to values and, what is most important, displaces attention:

> *Relajo*, in reality, always implies the characteristic of "digression": it is always a certain "deviation from something." It is not an original and direct act but rather one that is derived and reflexive. It requires an occasion, which is to say, the appearance of a value that offers itself to the subject's freedom and from which a dissent can begin. In this way, the displacement of attention is like the axis around which the entire moral meaning of *relajo* revolves: it is the basis of all the meanings that constitute this behavior. [20]

Relajo as "digression," "deviation," interruption, or dissention can surely take over an occasion, a situation, a community, and, as Portilla testifies, an entire generation; it can take over the entire modern epoch when we understand this epoch as lacking seriousness or commitment. As such, Portilla finds in it a moral significance, an examination which he undertakes in the second part of the *Fenomenología*.

Relajo is a temporal event. Time, like freedom, is its condition of possibility. *Relajo* is not a flash in the pan; it is not a spontaneous act; it is complex, and it is spread out in time. The temporal horizon of *relajo* is, ideally, infinite. *Relajo* can last as long as the interruption is repeated, as long as attention continues to be displaced. Of course, an infinite interruption is hard to imagine (unless life itself is such an inconvenient repetitive displacement of attention). In actual experience, the time of *relajo* is usually determined by our attentional investments.

Because it is temporal, because the interruption, the displacement, and the negation are reiterated in time, *relajo* is able to spill into the social realm, into the temporally structured world of intersubjective acknowledgment. Once infiltrated, the space of intersubjectivity must reckon with *relajo*'s suspensions. It can reckon in two ways, either by struggling for order and the recuperation of the value which held them (the community or group) together, or by surrendering to it, taking up its deviations and its suspensions of value. In either case, reckoning with *relajo* will change the dynamic of the group and, ultimately, the state of affairs in which the group/community resides—regardless of what this reckoning must involve. Portilla refers to this effect of *relajo* as a "provoking of the 'state of things' among people" [27]. Provoking the intersubjective sphere in this way cannot be without consequence. This means that as the *relajo*-event comes to an end, its provocations will necessitate a reorganization of the community or group or a reconsideration of "what really matters" to its members. At the very least, members of the community/group will have to be more vigilant, and *this* is something of a forced change.

Submission to the disorganization, dissention, chaos, and noise of *relajo* is not inevitable. A complex of values to which commitment is strong also points to the strength of values. *Relajo* breaks out with difficulty in certain cases. In some cases, the approach of *relajo* is thwarted by stronger values. Portilla offers the following illustration:

> During a screening of a film version of Shakespeare's *Julius Caesar*, in the scene in which Cassius falls pierced by his own sword, the expectant silence in the movie theater was broken by a long groan that invincibly provoked laughter among the audience. It is true that the performance did not collapse into a case of *relajo*, but had such joking expressions from the viewers continued, between the mocking attitude of some and the indignation of others, disorder and confusion could have proliferated, putting an end to the aesthetic situation.

The prolonged groan was not, evidently, produced in its author by the suggestive power of the events unfolding on the screen. It was, no doubt, an intentional act directed toward the dissolution of the aesthetic complex "drama performed before an audience." [28]

That the aesthetic situation did not come to an end shows that perhaps the value of "Shakespearean drama" is strong enough to overcome the provocations of *relajo*, that a value such as "bourgeois pleasure" is strong enough to hold the audience in this example together. Whatever the case may be, a value stronger than the provocations of *relajo* keeps attention in place. There are other examples. The now-famous shoe-throwing incident involving former US president George W. Bush could have degenerated into *relajo* had those present "continued to mock the situation" bringing about "disorder and confusion." That is, if the *gesture*, and not necessarily the throwing of a shoe at the president, would have been repeated by those in attendance through either insults, screams, laughter, or mocking. Assuming that the president's words were not explicitly inviting the *gesture* (as far as we know, he did not say, "Now, let the shoes fly!"), then the shoe throwing was an intentional act (a "provocation") "directed toward the dissolution" of the *value* of the political event and, as such, the gesture meant to suspend the seriousness of the situation.

From what has been said, several *essential* characteristics for the sense of *relajo* are revealed. *Relajo* is essentially:

- the suspension of seriousness,
- a displacement of attention,
- an invocation to others (to members of a group),
- a disruption,
- an interruption,
- repetitive,
- a negation of the past,
- a suspension of the future,
- a resistance,
- a provocation.

All of these characteristics share an essence: *they are critical moments of events in time.* We can say that these critical moments are moments of crisis within events. A provocation, for instance, will fracture the determination of an event, thus forcing a crisis within the event itself. In this way, *relajo* is a crisis. This is not to say that in every historical event that possesses one of these moments we will find a crisis of *relajo*. What we can say is that it is possible that all events can be disrupted or interrupted,by *relajo*, even when, as in the case of a different language, the concept to capture its appearance might be lacking. In this way, Portilla's phenomenological description of *relajo* aims at universality; it is a universal phenomenon of human existence.

FOUR EXAMPLES OF "*RELAJO*"

To the examples already given, we can add a few more that should illustrate the way in which the *relajo*-event, what I am also calling the *relajo*-phenomenon, manifests itself. The following descriptive characteristic must be kept in mind:

> constitutive of the essence of *relajo* is the ability to manifest itself in actions of the most varied nature. These can range form the most imperceptible facial expression to the *formulation of perfectly coherent and rational positions* [regarding the value]. In the middle of this range there are bodily attitudes, words, shouts, noises, etc., that imply a call to others to adopt the negation of the proposed value. This characteristic constitutes an action *per se*, an external act that leaves a mark on the surrounding world, in contrast with the "intimate" nature of the two previous ones. [21; emphasis added]

The examples that follow are obviously not exhaustive, and they are not meant to exemplify the manifestation of "perfectly coherent and rational positions," but are meant simply to illustrate the possible diversity of occasions in which *relajo* might emerge.

Fiestas

The "fiesta" brings together a neighborhood or a community for the purposes of celebrating any one of a number of accomplishments, days, persons, saints, events, and so on. A Friday night "party" signaling the end of the work week would count as a fiesta; so would a Sunday afternoon gathering in celebration of a birthday or a victory. There is music, laughter, food, joviality, dancing, hugging, gossip, drinking, and courtship in the fiesta. According to Portilla, the value that regulates the fiesta is "joy" [*alegría*], so the drinking, the gossip, the courtship, the laughter, and the dancing are all moments in the realization of *alegría*. Growing up in a migrant-farmworker community, fiestas were a routine and a necessity. Folks would gather on weekends and celebrate themselves, their triumph, and their suffering. They sought *alegría* with each other through the fiesta. Frequently, the drinking would turn otherwise happy and friendly people into loud and/or violent personalities. A man we knew as "el Lobo," or the wolf (because of his overwheleming facial hair), would be the first to fall victim to his vices. And we expected it. He would stumble onto the dance floor, interrupting and forcing the dancers to stop dancing; he would hug strangers, whose discomfort was noticeable; he would interrupt courtships, to the anger of the possible lovers. Others would get involved: they would try to calm him down, hold him up, fight him off, slap him around, push him aside, yell and scream at him, until the joy was sucked out of the fiesta. The music would stop, the food would fall to the floor, people would yell at each other, and children (like myself), would cower by adults, watching the scene that a few moments earlier seemed like a celebration of life degenerate into chaos. The seriousness with which members of the fiesta pursued "joy" was suspended; their dislocated attention was now focused on the *relajiento*, the Wolf, who had instigated the suspension. *Relajo* had descended upon the fiesta; or rather, the fiesta had become the site of *relajo*. No one knew what was next but *alegría* was impossible; many other events where possible, like violence, gunfire, or drunkenness. Afterward, as the crowd dispersed, we would forget why we gathered in the first place, what the point of it was. *Relajo* had proved too strong against the value that motivated the community forward toward *alegría*. *Relajo* has destroyed the fiesta.

"Hanging out"

Teenagers "hang out" with friends in living rooms, back yards, garages, malls, parks, or anywhere where there is space and the illusion of absolute freedom. There appears to be little purpose to hanging out, except, perhaps, to get away from one's parents or be with one's friends. But we continue "hanging out" as adults. We meet in bars, restaurants, parking lots, parks, for the same reasons (although most of us are at an age when we are not trying to get away from our parents). In either case, Portilla would say that even a situation like "hanging out," which seems to have no real purpose, has its guiding value. One hangs out with one's friends for the camaraderie, or the sense of belonging. *Relajo* could manifest itself if the value of camaraderie was displaced through a repetitive, and burdensome, introduction of another guiding value which would make camaraderie impossible. Often, when hanging out with my adult friends, the critical moment is when "Smith" shows up. Smith's political and religious views are contrary to the views of some of the members of the group. Our pursuit of the value of camaraderie usually involves keeping the conversation away from politics and religion, especially when Smith is present. But Smith always finds a reason to insert his political or religious views into the conversations. Soon, the rather friendly atmosphere turns tense and unfriendly. The conversation splinters into several different monologues, as each member of the group stakes a claim to a viewpoint and yells it to the next person. There is no listening, only speaking; the value "camaraderie" has been displaced via Smith's interruption of the seriousness in which we pursued it. Smith introduced a provocation that turned our friendly gathering into *relajo*.

The Political Scene

Our political involvement is guided by the value of social responsibility. Meetings of politically involved, socially responsible people are very serious, as the tasks at hand are never easy. The value is pursued with every gesture and every word. There are rules and orders that must be followed if the agenda items are to be completed. There are rules of decency and decorum that must be obeyed. Because of the seriousness of the political scene and the solidity of the values pursued, *relajo* is an always present danger. A joke which interrupts the person who "has the floor" is enough to provoke laughter among those present; the repetition of the joke, or similar jokes, is enough to bring about *relajo*. In early 2010, Swiss Finance Minister Hans-Rudolf Merz made news for his sudden outbreak of the giggles during a speech to Parliament. Although he was talking about a serious matter, the minister's giggling spread, and those present desperately tried to contain themselves, to hold fast to the value which brought them together. The television networks replayed the scene for several days, and one could not help but wonder how the scene did not degrade into chaos. This situation was on the cusp of the *relajo*-event—the scene itself invited others to participate, but those present kept their composure, and so the scene held together, and Parliament was able to go about its business, to continue pursuing its guiding value, that is, the social good. This highlights a key characteristic of *relajo*, namely, that what initiates it must be repeated.

Terrorism

From the point of view of the bystander, the citizen, or the victim, an act of terrorism is an act of *relajo* in a monumental scale. The terrorist act is not constituted by laughter, playful banter, or joking around. And while the act itself should be taken seriously, our seriousness is replaced by fear, terror, and anxiety. The events of September 11, 2001, suspended all seriousness and annihilated our essential link to our most cherished values. How was this done? As a people, most Americans take seriously the direction of the country and we live our lives according to values that we believe define us as American, for example, freedom, economic security, peace of mind, confidence. The planes that struck the Twin Towers interrupted our pursuit of those values. Our attention was immediately displaced; we were no longer attending to our freedom, but to terror; the value of economic security was replaced by the fear of our neighbor; peace of mind gave way to the thought of war; and the value of American confidence was undermined—we valued suspicion. The constant repetition of the "act" in the mass media kept the act "alive." The "act's" invocation was clear, and voiced by our own leaders, and by the victims: "you are either with us, or against us!" Under these circumstances we perpetuated the terror through fear and suspicion and lost sight of those values which guided us before 9/11.

The terrorist act is an act of resistance against values, and as such, it is a manifestation of *relajo*—its negations are severe: it negates the past, inverts the now, and, because it destroys values, makes the future impossible. As we'll see later (chapter 6), in this temporally-significant sense the terrorist act is an act of *relajo and* death.

Seriousness

Seriousness and value are inseparable in Portilla's analysis. The displacement of value is contiguous with the suspension of seriousness; suspending seriousness signals the displacement of value, and displacing value signals the suspension of seriousness. At this point in our reading of the *Fenomenología* we ask ourselves if suspending seriousness or displacing value is worrisome enough to merit phenomenological scrutiny. Given Mexico's historical circumstance as marginal to Western history, we might wonder whether *relajo* is an act of resistance against the forces of history and violence which have imposed value onto and demanded seriousness from the colonized and oppressed (perhaps this is what the "shoe thrower" had in mind). But Portilla does not seem willing to yield to this suggestion. Seriousness is good; value is good; so whatever disrupts these is not good. Seriousness and value are thus the two main operative concepts that need to be clarified in order to fully comprehend what I call the "event" or "phenomenon" of *relajo*.

Portilla defines *relajo* as a suspension of seriousness. But why "seriousness"? Because seriousness is a virtue. The "serious" types are those who think before they act. They are the last to be suspected of a crime, as they are sure to have carefully considered the consequences and opted for a more "rational" course of action. Seriousness is oftentimes used interchangeably with sobriety and devotion and intelligence. Thus, we like to think that Martin Luther was serious, that Jesus Christ was serious, that Mohammad was serious; we ascribe seriousness to Plato, Kant, and Hegel. But some of the most astute philosophers have questioned the very standard of seriousness. Søren Kierkegaard, for instance, tells us via his pseudonym "Anti-Climacus" that "what edifies is seriousness," but not when the edification is a result of "disinterested knowledge," in which case seriousness is "frivolity and pretense" (Kierkegaard 1989, 36). Nietzsche is clearer about his skepticism regarding the standard of seriousness, or the *motives* of seriousness. In *The Gay Science*, Nietzsche writes: "For most people, the intellect is an awkward, gloomy, creaking machine that is hard to start: when they want to work with this machine and think well, they call it 'taking the matter *seriously*'—oh, how taking good thinking must be for them! The lovely human beast seems to lose its good mood when it thinks well; it becomes 'serious'! And 'where laughter and gaiety are found, thinking is good for nothing'—that is the prejudice of this serious beast against all 'gay science.' Well then, let us prove it as a prejudice" (Nietzsche 2003, 182–83). We will see how Portilla is wrapped up in this "prejudice" (chapter 6). His notion of "seriousness" falls in line with that of "the serious beast." According to Portilla, seriousness is a *state of being* in relation to the world which requires "loyalty and commitment" [19]. This sort of state is one noticeable by the individual's ability to "think well" under any circumstance, a state which, Nietzsche says, may make you lose your "good spirits," as serious matters should not be taken lightly. Loyalty and commitment, after all, require certain sacrifices, and one of them is to forgo one's good spirits to maintain them. Seriousness is this type of commitment and respect to that which has value or is valuable. The *point* of seriousness or "thinking well" in a particular situation is to keep the situation from falling apart. Seriousness exudes control. When a speaker "keeps her composure" despite an interruption, we usually praise her for preventing the occasion from falling into chaos. We might say that she is known to be a serious person, so chaos was never a possibility. According to Portilla, this kind of composure would be a reflection on that commitment she has to "maintain the value [of the occasion] in existence" [19]. On Nietzsche's account, however, Portilla is simply, or dogmatically, adopting a standard about how one ought to behave oneself, a standard passed down via certain master narratives.

Clearly, Portilla does not share Nietzsche's reservations, which means that as far as Portilla's worry goes, to suspend seriousness is to suspend composure, thinking well, and commitment. In this way, *relajo* is an offense to the "lovely beast" who "becomes serious." This act is defiant against the purported *edification* of social rules and customs, inherited rules for progress, order, and civility. Seriousness edifies, as Kierkegaard believes—it makes one think well—but *relajo* defies these virtues as impositions "placed on one's liberty" by the "machines" of institutional government, colonialism, modernity, globalization, the US, Europe, and so on.

However, there are two kinds of seriousness: on the one hand, "the spirit of seriousness," which gives rise to a certain type of subject which Portilla will call a "snob" [*apretado*], and on the other, "authentic seriousness," which constitutes a free, liberated subject. Portilla describes the difference: "The spirit of seriousness is pure gesticulation, an exaggerated exteriorization that tends more toward showing one's own excellence and toward underscoring one's own importance than toward the realization of the value. The spirit of seriousness is reflexive; seriousness is pure spontaneity; the former projects outward, while the latter is "intimate"; the former is a behavior toward others; in [the case of] genuine seriousness, I am alone with myself before the value" [19]. This distinction is not new, as Portilla could have readily found it in Sartre's *Being and Nothingness* (1953, 544ff). Hence, Portilla describes the "spirit of seriousness," with Sartre, as a pretention, where the individual pretends to embody the value and *be* the value. Opposed to this, "authentic seriousness" is a manner of committing to values where the commitment depends on the strength of the value and its relation to truth. The commitment of the person possessing the "spirit of serious-ness" is absolute; the commitment of the person who is "authentically serious" is contingent on truth. But *relajo* suspends both kinds of seri-ousness. On the one hand, the pretension is itself structured around values which are being realized for the sake of seriousness itself; who-ever takes up the "spirit of seriousness" is committed to *being serious*. So *relajo* suspends this commitment. On the other hand, *relajo* disrupts the presencing of value itself, making authentic seriousness impossible.

A THEORY OF VALUE

Portilla's *Fenomenología* has been described as a work in "the phenom-enology of value" (Zirión 2004, 304), and for good reason. Central to Portilla's understanding of *relajo* is the phenomenological givenness of values—the "how" of their apprehension and the nature of their "demands." By "values," Portilla has in mind both moral and nonmoral values. Thus, for instance, standards of good, evil, and right and wrong are values—moral values (nonmoral values include standards of beauty, intelligence, community, civility, and utility, to name a few). Values, for Portilla, are "how" we encounter our world. Portilla explains:

> Let us say, for the moment, that all human life is steeped in value. Wherever we turn our gaze, value gives sense and depth to reality. Lived values are not those essences that are presented in philosophy manuals, like pearls of meaning organized hier-archically beyond being. Value underscores and organizes the things in the world. The coolness of the water I drink on a hot day is a value. The gracefulness of the woman that one crosses paths with in the street is a value. The softness and the good design of the armchair in which I sit down to rest is a value. The intelligence of this friend or the good humor of that one is a value. [32]

Thus, according to Portilla, values mediate our relation to objects, states of affairs, and others. Humans, as "steeped in value," cannot escape this determinate way of perceiving their world. But this is not to say that this mediation takes the same form for everyone, at all times, and in all places. That is, some will prefer "beauty" to "gracefulness" and thus interact with their world on that basis. This suggests that the aspect of subjective, and intersubjective, preferring is always at play in our value-saturated lives, as some values are preferred over others—that is, some values *demand* to be preferred over others. But, the point is that *everything* is valuable.

If everything in the human world is valuable, then everything in the human world calls for our attention. That is, values are not given emptily *as* values, but with content, which Portilla calls "demands" [18]. When we apprehend an object, person, or state of affairs, we are thus immediately confronted with a value's demands.

> All value, when grasped, appears surrounded by an aura of demands, endowed with a certain weight and with a certain gravity that brings it from its pure ideality toward the world of reality. The value solicits its realization. The mere grasping of the value carries with it the fulfillment of that demand, of that call to its own realization in the world; and in order for this demand—which appears in the objective realm of the lived experiences of the value—to be realized, the subject, in turn, performs an act, a movement of loyalty [to the value] that is a kind of "yes," like an affirmative response. This is the first outline of what, when grasped reflexively, we call "duty." [18]

Here Portilla tells us that value "solicits its realization"; it calls us and calls on us *to do* something, namely, what it is important, according to it, for us to do. The immediate apprehension of value is simultaneously the apprehension of its demand, of its "aura of demands" *as* possibilities. For example, in greeting someone, the value apprehended demands the performance of a certain ritual, like shaking the person's hand or, especially in certain Latin American countries, hugging or kissing the other person on the cheek. To refrain from proceeding with the ritual is to undermine the value; simply, it is taken as a sign of disrespect (both for the value of the ritual and the person). We can see that the reiterated refusal to perform the ritual, and turning the greeting into a spectacle that lasts a period of time and involves everyone present, signals the approach of the *relajo* event.

That value *solicits* its realization should mean that value is somehow *lacking* in itself. But values do not *lack*; *we* lack. Here, Portilla's Platonism rears its head. By way of summary, toward the end of the text, he tells us that "value always transcends its contingent actualizations. An act of punctuality does not make me be punctual. Value and being do not seem to ever be able to unite in a definitive manner, or, at least, there doesn't seem to be any experience or object in the area of our human experience in which this coincidence occurs fully. The sweet flavor of a fruit or the coolness of water is not "sweetness" or "coolness" as such, made fully real. Values in themselves always are beyond their possible manifestations; they are not exhausted in any of their realizations" [71–72]. Differently put: values are ideas. As ideas, our conscious relation to them is contingent, because we, and our commitments, are contingent. The contingency of our commitments makes them susceptible to interruption and dislocation. Our fragile encounter with our values, with what matters to us, reveals that a certain kind of sobriety, or seriousness, must be the ground or foundation of our commitment. Thus, *relajo* exposes our contingency and our fragile commitments, and in this sense it also exposes the fragility of values, since they cannot realize themselves.

Portilla's views on value suggest a certain metaphysical commitment on his part regarding the objectivity of value, the view that values stand *outside* the subjective realm and possess an independent existence. After all, he says that a value's demand or exigency is part of the "objective aspect of the experience of value," while our affirmation of the demand, or, in the case of *relajo*, our dissention, is the subjective part. Values, it seems, are objective. This is the theory of value that we find in figures like Plato, for whom values such as Truth stand outside the contingent world of mortals. Opposed to this, a theory of value may hold that values are direct expressions of subjective preferences or aversions, and thus *not* objective.[8] But Portilla, rejects the Platonic idea and the subjectivist position, preferring instead to remain neutral regarding these metaphysical or epistemological positions. "What interests us," he says, "is to clarify the manner in which value gives itself in everyday life before any speculation about its essence, its hierarchy, or its polarity" [31–32].

From a purely philosophical point of view, his avoidance of the metaphysical status of value is not satisfactory. Clearly, he maintains the view that value is objective—or, at least, that its demands are objective. To this, Portilla responds that what he means is not that value *is* objective, but rather that value *appears objective*. This classic phenomenological move allows Portilla to situate value in the human world as constituted in that world without affirming or denying its ideality or its reality. Hence, he calls value "lived" [32], and a "norm of my self-constitution" [33] that is, nonetheless, a "quality of the world" [32]. In effect, Portilla is going between the horns of the traditional dichotomy by not committing himself to either an objective or a purely subjective theory of values. After all, the commitment that value demands is too fragile to be objective, and, at the same time, the value itself is too demanding to be subjective. This fragility can be seen in the fact that *relajientos* can always refuse the demands of value (Portilla says, "One can refuse to follow the fragile indications of pure value. One can perpetually pass by the unconditional demands of morality" [82]), and value objectivity gives itself in the persistence of value in all of human life. In this way, Portilla maintains a metaphysical neutrality regarding the being of values.

Despite this refusal to commit to a value metaphysics, Portilla makes the relation of value and *relajo* clear. *Relajo* is resistance to the demands of value. This, of course, is tied to the "sense" of *relajo*, which is a "suspension of seriousness," which, again, is that sanctified space wherein "I am alone with myself before value" [19].

RELAJO IS NOT MOCKERY, "BURLA," SARCASM, OR TEASING "CHOTEO"

What is called "relajo" is not a specific Mexican phenomenon. In fact, this phenomenon appears in every other culture on earth. Most of us have experienced this phenomenon at one time or another. The signifier changes, but the signified stays the same. In some languages, like English, there is no name for the activity Portilla describes. The vulgar phrase "fucking around" comes closer than any other. But "fucking around" lacks the sense of disruption of *relajo* as well as its "displacement of attention." It is synonymous with "harmless goofing off," which is not a synonym of *relajo*, despite what some translators have suggested (see Castro 2001). While "fucking around" can be chaotic, it is usually easy to control. Those who "fuck around" can be placed under the guardianship of stronger values, like "law" or "propriety." This is not to say that the activity that *relajo* describes does not exist; it is simply, as far as I know, known by many names or none at all. There is no commonly acknowledged metaphor that captures it in English.[9] This explains my hesitation in translating "relajo." We find the same difficulty with "*burla*" and "*choteo*." Nevertheless, the occasions, situations, circumstances, events, or moments these words denote should be familiar to those of us who have occasionally fallen victim (willingly or unwillingly) to the suspension of seriousness or the seemingly perpetual deferment of a commitment to some value or other.

Relajo is often associated with mockery, "*burla*"—defined as scornful derision or ridicule. As a boy growing up in central California, I was once sprayed by a skunk. The next day my mother forced me to go to school. Once the other kids got wind of me, they teased and ridiculed me all day long. I came home and told my mother what the other kids had done. She told my father: "Le hicieron burla," "They made fun of him." Of course, "*burla*" is harsher than a simple making-fun-of. It is to be mocked, which is never simple and often emotionally scarring. *Burla*, what I am translating as "mockery," will usually involve one or more individuals who are *making fun of* others. But this is not *relajo*. There is no value that is being suppressed, no commitment that is annihilated, and, more telling still, mockery could very well be serious and guided by a value.

According to Portilla, mockery [*burla*] plays "an instrumental relation" with *relajo*. The mocking jabs or harsh teasing *can* be used in the service of the *relajo* event, which, as we have seen, aims to *suspend seriousness*. One derides someone's appearance, but in order for that derision to be *relajo*, it must be taken over by an intentionality which aims to suspend seriousness and destroy a relation to values: the derision must be repeated indefinitely, and everyone present must, willfully or not, participate in it, at which point whatever values held the gathering, the group, the community, together are suspended along with the commitment to realize them. In this way, one is no longer experiencing mockery but *relajo*. The power of *relajo* which allows it to subvert other forms of social disruption under it allows Portilla to say that "*relajo* is the transcendental unity of sense toward which [these] acts are directed" [28]. So not only is *relajo* a suspension, a provocation, a detour, a disruption but it is also a *transcendental condition*. *Relajo* is thus much more complex than simply *making fun of* or mocking.

Neither is *relajo* sarcasm. Portilla identifies sarcasm as a *kind of mockery*. But, he says, sarcasm "cannot be considered instrumental" in relation to *relajo*, as it is "offensive" and "bitter" [29]. The purpose of sarcasm is not to *make fun of* or to suspend, but to offend. "*Relajo* creates a void regarding value; sarcasm eats away at a person" [29]. The sarcastic word or gesture is directed at an individual with the purpose of offending or emotionally scarring that person. Portilla says that "sarcasm can provoke an atmosphere of uncomfortable expectation that is full of threats of violence, like an insult or like a slap in the face" [29], whereas *relajo* discourages all expectation. But the more important difference between sarcasm and *relajo* is that the former's temporal horizon is closed off as soon as the sarcastic remark or utterance is accomplished; sarcasm might linger in the mind of the victim or the perpetrator, but it does not linger long enough to suspend value or prohibit commitment. As Portilla puts it: "Sarcasm paralyzes; *relajo* is an invitation to chaotic movement," and "sarcasm is an individual act . . . whereas *relajo* does not exist without the repetition of those acts which constitute it" [29].

Finally, *relajo* is not teasing, or *choteo*.[10] The Cuban intellectual Jorge Mañach first offers a philosophical analysis of this concept in 1928, which he defines in the following way: "Choteo consists in 'not taking anything seriously' . . . Choteo consists in 'letting all fall away into relajo' . . . [It is] a repugnance of all authority" (Mañach 2009, 15). Mañach's analysis is first rate and deserves its proper study. In fact, Portilla's analysis resembles Mañach's in many respects, but particularly, in their choice of theme. Portilla, however, has chosen the phenomenon into which *choteo* ultimately tends, *relajo*, its transcendental condition.

Nevertheless, these two terms are used interchangeably in the everyday life of some Spanish speakers. When discussing this subject with a Spanish speaker, the speaker identified *relajo* with *choteo*, explaining that "nothing happens" in either case—by which she meant that "nothing gets done." This alludes to Portilla's idea that some value is not being realized; hence, nothing is accomplished. *Relajo*, like *choteo*, is also anti-authoritarian. It is a resistance to authority and its representations, that is, to values and seriousness. Their difference lies in their *intentionality*. Portilla puts the matter in the following way:

> Teasing [*choteo*] is not distinguished from *relajo* in that, as the latter, it is repeated action, but the intentionalities of teasing and *relajo* are radically different. Teasing demands the stability and the preservation of the relationship between the subject and his or her interlocutor, since only in this way can the presumed superiority of one over the other manifest itself, such that *relajo* always ends up totally neutralizing the people or situations that are its object and it ends up directed exclusively to itself, to the maintaining of an atmosphere of disorder and detachment. In

teasing, the agent is interested in holding the attention of a possible spectator on its object; teasing lacks the intentionality of
deviation that we have signaled as an essential moment of *relajo*.
On the other hand, the individual who teases presents him or
herself as, and turns into, a focus of attention, as the one who
can, as one who surpasses the other in wit, one who totally transcends the other. Thus the teaser draws a bipolar and linear field
of communication in contrast to the three-dimensional nature of
the quasi-space inherent to *relajo*. [29–30]

So while *relajo* is intentionally directed to the displacement of attention,
to bringing about and maintaining "chaos and detachment," *choteo* is
intentionally directed to *preserving attention*, namely, upon the perpetrator of *choteo*. The self-reference of *choteo* is lacking in *relajo*; in
choteo, it seems, there is the expectation that others will notice my superiority over my interlocutor. In *relajo*, the self-reference is missing. Once
fallen in *relajo,* the self seems to disappear in the chaos and the noise,
or it fragments into the "tridimensional nature" and the "quasispace"
of chaos and deviation.

LAUGHTER AND *RELAJO*

One of the essential characteristics of *relajo* is its infectiousness. That is,
the spread of *relajo* is quickened both by the ease in which it is assumed
by those present when it "breaks out" and by its essential spatiality—its
three-dimensional nature. Signs that *relajo* has broken out are not hard
to miss. Suddenly, an utterance or gesture initiates a giggle or a smirk
which ripples through the audience, who repeat the utterance or gesture,
now in an exaggerated tone, until there is a crescendo of laughs, and
even those who are unaware of what is going on begin to laugh until
laughter has taken over the audience, who by now have lost sight (at
least for the moment) of the task at hand and who "make themselves
at home" in the chaos. Making oneself at home in the chaos is easier
when laughter is present. Portilla tells us, "*Relajo* manifests itself, in
the general majority of cases, accompanied by hilarity" [42]. This does
not mean, however, that of necessity whenever there is hilarity there is
relajo, or vice versa.

Portilla's analysis of laughter is more substantial than his analysis of mockery or *choteo*. The reason for this attention is two-fold: on the one hand, laughter's contiguity with *relajo*, or the fact that we expect laughter where there is *relajo,* and, on the other, Portilla's belief that laughter as an intentional act has not been properly treated. Portilla does not "properly" treat laughter either, but he offers a sketch for a theory of laughter that guides us into the next part of the work, namely, the discussion of the moral significance of *relajo*.

In keeping with the phenomenological approach to his study (I will discuss this approach in chapter 4), Portilla begins by highlighting the presuppositions upon which theories of laughter have been based. One such presupposition has it that laughter is *caused* by something funny, what he calls "the comic." His objection is Humean in nature and rather straightforward: "To say that laughter is an effect of the comic is just as absurd as saying that study is an effect of science or that rage is an effect of evil or of some other *cause*" [43]. In other words, just because there is evil, that does not mean that there will be cholera, just as it is not necessary that in the presence of tragedy there will be sadness or laughter in the presence of "the comic." This is to say that laughter can have many other causes or that it may not have a cause at all; one just spontaneously laughs. Because Portilla believes that laughter has its own directionality (i.e., its own intentionality) and is usually directed to the comic (thereby avoiding the idea that it is *caused* by it), he concludes that "it would seem that laughter is a way of *designating* the comic" [43]. Thus, Portilla's phenomenological definition of laughter: "Laughter is a peculiar act in which consciousness is *directed* to the comic" [44; emphasis added].

So it is not that laughter is *caused* by the comic, but, rather that laughter *seeks* or is *called* by the comic. But what is "the comic"? The comic is understood as a humorous or amusing situation comprised of jokes and types of discourse usually accompanied by laughter. But this way of conceiving the comic leaves out its essential aspect, namely, that it is a "degradation of values." Portilla cites Alfred Stern's *The Philosophy of Laughter and Tears*: "The comic is any incident and any action that displaces our attention from a value to a non-value or from an intrinsic value to an instrumental value. The two cases are equivalent to a degradation of values that *provokes* the instinctive negative value judgment that is laughter" [46]. Portilla disagrees with Stern on the judgmental quality of laughter, as well as on the notion that laughter is essentially provoked by the comic. What he retains from Stern is the idea that the comic is "a displacement of attention from value to a non-value"—a "degradation" or displacement carried out by *relajo* in Portilla's analysis. The comic situation displaces attention in the same way as *relajo*, although in the comic attention goes away from the misery of human existence and to the ridiculous or the humorous, while in *relajo* attention goes away from the values which constitute the overcoming of that misery and to something completely unrelated, to nonvalues that do not invoke my participation. Laughter might be present in both cases. In the comic, like in *relajo*, the presence of laughter will invite others to "fall" into it. This presence, however, is not "caused" by the comic or by the *relajo*-situation; rather, it is merely concomitant with it.

Because the comic is, like *relajo*, a degradation of values, a displacement of attention, and so on, and laughter is concomitant with the comic, then the presence of laughter signals the possibility of a degradation of values. Portilla warns that any degradation of value is dangerous (a warning that must, of course, extend to *relajo*). The degradation of values, he says, "is something threatening. The *fact* of the degradation of a value opens up the horizon of a possible universal degradation of values and even of the absolute extinction of the value" [47].

One has to wonder: if comedy has been around since the dawn of human civilization, then why has not this "absolute extinction of value" come about? The value degradation must be held in check by some internal or external mechanism of the comic situation itself. Portilla believes that laughter is this mechanism and that it is intentionally directed, not to the comic generally, but specifically to the value degradation which the comic brings about. By laughing at the degradation, one "affirms" the degradation itself, an affirmation that situates the degradation in the "totality of the world of value" and makes one feel "that joyful sentiment of being safe" with the recognition that the degraded value does not destabilize the totality. He says, "Laughter would then be a form of consciousness that, faced with the degradation of value and precisely *because* of this degradation, would try to secure for itself its [own] freedom with respect to such a degradation and, at the same time, to ensure the invulnerable character of the world of value in general" [47]. While Portilla does not think that laughter is merely an "emotion" or a "sentiment," since it is a "form of consciousness," he agrees with Stern that laugher is liberating or, at least, tends toward freedom.

Liberation is thus "essential to laughter" [49]. This insight is common both to the existentialist and the Marxist traditions that inform Portilla's thought. The critical Marxist Mikhail Bakhtin tells us, "Laughter purifies the consciousness of men from false seriousness, from dogmatism, from all confusing emotions" (Bakhtin 1984, 141). Sartre spends some time treating laughter in his book on Gustave Flaubert, and portrays laughter as a defense against the extinction of values (Sartre 1989). In both cases, laughter liberates one from the dread and anxiety that situations, both comic and not, can bring about when these force us into corners. It liberates us from circumstances that might otherwise imprison us, from fate and determination. To laugh is to affirm our condition and recognize that it is *not as bad as it could be*.

An example from the Golden Age of Mexican cinema seems appropriate. Consider *Ahí está el detalle*, or *There's the Rub*, a classic 1940 film starring the comedic genius Mario Moreno, "Cantinflas."[11] In the climactic scene, Cantinflas is in court before a judge, accused of murder and facing "the wall" if found guilty. He is accused of killing "Bobi," whom the prosecutor believes is a man, but who (as the audience knows) is really a dog. "Did you kill Bobi?" asks the prosecutor. "You mean that dog?" answers Cantinflas, which allows the prosecutor to highlight for the jury the callousness of the accused. The defense, unaware that Bobi is a dog, tries to help Cantinflas by suggesting that he killed Bobi in self-defense, to which Cantinflas answers: "No, I wanted to kill him!" and "I had him in my sights for a while" (or something to that effect). This scene is always accompanied by laughter. The degraded value here is justice itself. We are certain that justice is not being served due to the original misunderstanding. And if Cantinflas is found guilty, justice will never be served. We laugh at the exchange *in order to* hold off the anxiety that would otherwise grip us. According to Portilla, we laugh at the exchange to perpetuate the misunderstanding and to remind ourselves that the value "justice" is *not that easy* to degrade. We liberate ourselves from the anxiety and the threat that, in this case, the value of justice might be extinguished.

Relajo is not necessarily constituted by bouts of laughter; laughter is not essential to *relajo*. This insight troubles Portilla, since this means that the crucial mechanism that keeps the degradation of value from degrading further in the comic is missing in *relajo*, which, in Mexico, "creates an atmosphere of anxiety that, more than provoking laughter, impedes it" [50]. What has been said corrects a misunderstanding in the scant literature on *relajo*. Adding to a brief and somewhat lacking characterization of *relajo*, Diana Taylor writes that "*relajo* proves non-threatening, because it is humorous and subversive in ways that allow for critical distancing rather than revolutionary challenge" (Taylor 2003, 129). This is clearly wrong. *Relajo* threatens values, and, since laughter is not essential to it, it is not always humorous.

The discussions of laughter, mockery, sarcasm, and *choteo* are undertaken for similar reasons: to unravel the presuppositions through which *relajo* is commonly understood. *Relajo* is all of these things and none of these things; it is more complex than any single act of *choteo* and less direct than every act of sarcasm. It may involve laughter, but laughter is not essential to it.

CHAPTER THREE

Reading *Fenomenología del relajo*, Part 2

Every philosophy is practical, even the one which at first appears to be the most contemplative. Its method is a social and political weapon.

—Jean Paul Sartre (1968, 5)

*R*elajo names a "suspension of seriousness" and a "displacement of attention" relative to value, to "what matters," to the call of duty. It is a suspension and a displacement which transcend Mexico and Mexican society. That other countries outside Latin America are unfamiliar with *relajo* does not mean that the situation that *relajo* names does not exist there as well. So Portilla's "description" aims to be of universal significance.

The moral reach of *relajo* is thus not restricted to its local origins. While Portilla's autobiographical beginning suggests a genuine worry over his own people [*el pueblo*], the denouncement is meant to transcend Mexican borders, to be genuinely universal since, he says, "the *fact* of the degradation of a value opens up the horizon of a possible universal degradation of values and even of the absolute extinction of the value" [47]. Phenomenology allows Portilla to peel away the layers of the *relajo*-phenomenon and get at its core, at its essence, which itself speaks universally about *relajo*. But this peeling away is not enough to address his motivating worry: description is not enough. The second part of the *Fenomenología* considers the moral import of the *relajo*-phenomenon not only on those with whom he is familiar, namely, his

51

Mexican contemporaries, but also on his human contemporaries, on those who recognize *relajo* and those who do not know its name, those who are its victims or those who are its perpetrators.

Portilla situates the moral significance of *relajo* within a traditional moral framework centered on *freedom*. He considers the effect of the *relajo*-event on freedom and the relationship of *relajo* to acts which promote freedom or liberation, including *ironic* and *humorous* acts. Portilla crafts part 1 as a descriptive project, while part 2 is a normative one. He writes, at the start of part 2, "We abandon the territory of certainty to enter into that of possibility . . . [We will] shift from the key of 'is' to the key of 'perhaps' [*tal vez*] to continue our reflections" [51]. We will take this "perhaps" as Portilla's entry into the realm of the moral "ought." Here he asks about how one *ought* to behave as opposed to how one does behave. He concludes the normative discussions of part 2, and the work itself, with the personality types which embody both *relajo* and its opposite, seriousness. These two types, he claims, endanger the emergence of the kind of subjectivity (see chapter 4) that might be able to transcend the perils of *relajo*; these individual types, he suggests, stifle freedom's authentic realization in history and, I argue, the unfolding of modernity's destiny in the Americas.

On Freedom

Edmund Husserl's phenomenological method structures Portilla's approach to part 1 of the *Fenomenología del relajo*. Jean-Paul Sartre's existentialism informs the core of part 2, namely, Portilla's discussion of freedom. In *Being and Nothingness*, Sartre writes: "Thus my freedom is perpetually in question in my being; it is not a quality added on or a *property* of my nature. It is very exactly the stuff of my being; and as in my being, my being is in question, I must necessarily possess a certain comprehension of freedom" (Sartre 1956, 566). Likewise, Portilla believes, the comprehension of freedom is necessary for an understanding of *relajo*, "to understand, from the roots upward, this complex bundle of behaviors seemingly regulated by the idea of non-regulation, of disorder" [51]. Indeed, *relajo*, as has been described, seems like a perfect exercise of freedom. One *freely* disrupts an event; one *freely* repeats an offense; one *freely* suspends seriousness. "Freedom," Portilla observes, "appears on the horizon of *relajo* as a condition of its possibility" [51], which is another way to say that "*relajo* is a possibility of freedom" [52].

But what is freedom? Taking a page from Sartre, Portilla believes that our understanding of freedom should not be prejudiced by the historical debate between determinism and free will (Sartre 1956, 563). Freedom, according to Portilla, is not "absolute"; absolute freedom is an "aesthetic doctrine" [54] dreamt up by the human imagination. This means that freedom is not an abstraction or an "empty concept," since "an act without a motive or without an end is an unthinkable and unrealizable act" [55]. But neither is one completely determined. Echoing Sartre, who believes freedom is the nature of consciousness and, thus, a "spontaneous choosing" to act (Sartre 1956, 594), Portilla calls it a "source of acts," "*fuente de actos*" [56]. However, just because this conception of freedom avoids the entanglements of the determinism-free will debate, Portilla, diverging somewhat from Sartre, argues that we must not discount the determinations of our embodiment or our history.[1] As a spontaneous choosing or as the source of acts, freedom is expressed both in creative or destructive acts that transcend those determinations and in those acts that are simply changes taking place inside our own skin. Portilla puts this in more philosophical terms:

> Indeed, freedom in general can be actualized in two clearly discernible ways. It can consist of an external liberation that implies the removal, destruction, or overcoming of an obstacle that is really present in the world, as occurs in the case of an individual that comes out of prison or in the case of a political change or a revolution. Freedom is here an end and a result of an action actually performed on things or situations. But it can also consist of a pure movement of interiority. It can consist simply of a change of attitude. There are possibilities of freedom that have no need of actual transcendence of consciousness, possibilities, that do not require a new real ordering of the world but that are free variations of attitude within pure interiority. [62]

In other words, freedom is actualized in acts that transform the world or our inner lives. There are then two different kinds of changes that can take place: external and internal. Neither kind of change, however, need not be positive; the acts need not bring about transformations considered good or beneficial to oneself or the greater good. I can change my attitude to reflect a new prejudice or a new animosity. I can change the world to exclude my fellows or harm their self-esteem. I can spontaneously choose to interrupt a funeral with quotations from my favorite television show, thereby changing the situation in which *we* find ourselves, that is, mourning. I can reiterate my interruption and bring about *relajo*.

However, I can change the world by obeying the demands of duty and value. This is because, as Isaiah Berlin pointed out a few years before Portilla (1958), we can distinguish, and thus act on, two ideas of freedom: *positive freedom* and *negative freedom*. Positive freedom is the freedom that we exercise when we obey law and moral duty, for example, as in Kantian moral theory. It is, Berlin says, "the freedom to" (Berlin 2000, 203). Negative freedom is the freedom to be free of interference or coercion, such as in Libertarian theories of justice. Berlin calls it a "freedom *from*" (Berlin 2000, 199). In Berlin's characterization, negative freedom is freedom to be left alone to do as I want and will to do, while positive freedom is the freedom to act on that which I care, or should care, most deeply about. It "derives from the wish on the part of the subject to be his own master," to say, "I wish to be somebody, not nobody; a doer" (Berlin 2000, 203). From this perspective, *relajo* is an expression of negative freedom. But negative freedom, Portilla is quick to point out, is *not* "authentic freedom." Authentic freedom or liberation requires, Portilla explains echoing Berlin, realizing the positive conception of freedom: "Freedom as pure negation, on the other hand, is not more than a mirage and a deception, since the 'freedom from,' the negative freedom, is but the negative side of a 'freedom to,' or the given of responsibility. In the first case, negative freedom is but an aspect of positive freedom that is indeed a genuine liberation, an opening up of the path for effective action in the realization of values. In the second, it is but the negative form of responsibility: I am responsible for my actions, then I am *not* absolutely subject to circumstances" [83]. Positive freedom, the "freedom for" or "freedom to," is the capacity to realize and choose values, to be a *doer*, and, thus, to be one's own master. The possibility to exercise freedom in this positive way is then what is sacrificed by, and in, *relajo*. In other words, this is the kind of freedom that must be assumed in order to overcome *relajo*—to transcend it along with the oppressive circumstance which its happenings create.

This last point brings us to the "moral" significance of *relajo*. *Relajo* is an exercise of negative freedom that, through the illusion of absolute liberation, oppresses others by "coercing" them into its disruptions and holding them captive while the value or values to be realized are displaced in acts that drown out the call of duty. These are moral implications, as those who are held captive are certainly not exercising their freedom; they are being deprived of both spontaneous choice and the possibility to act on what they care most deeply about. For Portilla, this means that *relajo* is something that itself must be transcended. The transcendence of *relajo* will make possible the authentic realization of freedom. Speaking of "resentment," which "forbids access to a whole sector of reality or of values" [61], and is thereby closely related to *relajo* (Sánchez 2011), Portilla writes that "overcoming of such attitudes [or *relajo* and resentment] is, evidently, a liberation" [62].

Hence, while *relajo* itself might *appear* as liberation from the seriousness of a moment or the values imposed by history or circumstance, Portilla believes that true liberation will be achieved only after *relajo* is overcome. *Relajo* is an act of resistance, but it is not yet, nor can it be, the realization of authentic human freedom. Portilla concludes that "*relajo* is an attitude that illegitimately identifies rebelliousness with freedom" [83]. The "illegitimacy" of this identification is still to be explained (chapter 6). Now we ask: how can *relajo* be overcome?

On Irony

It is telling that the concept of irony does not preoccupy Portilla until part 2 of the *Fenomenología*. *Relajo* is not the transcendental condition of irony, as it is for mockery, sarcasm, or *choteo*. In fact, irony will prove to be a means of transcending *relajo* or, at least, signal the way to its overcoming. The ironic personality will have a relation to value and seriousness that prescribes the framework for authentic human subjectivity. What differentiates irony from *relajo* is, ultimately, their respective relations to freedom—one to negative and the other to positive freedom. *Relajo* is an expression of negative freedom; irony, of positive freedom.

Irony, like *relajo*, is understood as a "relationship between consciousness and value" [64]. And, like *relajo*, it is an exercise of freedom. Irony is a manifestation of the second kind of freedom, namely, positive freedom or the kind exercised in the response to duty; irony is rooted in the will or subjective inwardness: "Irony . . . is a possible variation of the subjective attitude" [64]. This does not mean that irony does not have an external liberating effect: irony liberates *us*, the spectators of the ironic situation, the readers of the ironic drama, and the victims of those "claims to value" which oppress us and which irony displaces. Hence, irony is an act of consciousness that transcends its own limits.

Portilla takes us through certain "vague notions" of irony. One of these is that something ironic is contradictory. This identification is vague, and ultimately false, because not everything contradictory is necessarily ironic. According to Portilla, something else besides the presence of contradiction is required. There must be a "claim" which is contradicted. "In order for there to be irony, there is a need for something more than contradiction pure and simple. Our examples manifest a contradiction between a 'pretense' and a reality. A person has the pretense of being wise but acts ignorant. A historical period has the pretense of being in possession of the key to human happiness, but in furthering its inventions, it produces an instrument of destruction that sows anxiety among humankind" [65]. Modifying standard definitions which define irony merely as a "contradiction or incongruity between appearance or expectation and reality" (Murfin et. al., 1997, 176), Portilla stresses the positional structure of irony, that is, that for something to count as irony, there must be some sort of claim, a "pretension." In other words, either a personal voice or an entire cultural world-view must make a claim about reality which is then "contrasted" to what that person or that culture actually does.

The "pretension" makes a claim on value. More precisely, it is a claim to possess a value which is then contrasted with the reality of its realization. Someone claims to be mindful of the law but then acts like a criminal. Someone rails against the legality of immigration but employs an immigrant laborer. The contrast between the claim (to justice or about immigration) and what that person actually does, when highlighted, is irony. That it must be highlighted or made explicit is important, since without it being highlighted, or pointed out, or recognized, then it is not recognized *as* irony (the contrast certainly cannot recognize itself as irony). This recognition is made by the ironic consciousness. According to Portilla, the contrast is "not [a] real attribute of things," which means that it is somehow mind-dependent. He writes: "Irony is, then, immanent to a consciousness that judges and that notices the distance between the possible realization of a value and its supposed realization by someone with a pretense of fulfilling it" [65].

Irony ultimately proves to be that form of consciousness that serves as the cure for the generational crisis for which Portilla's *Fenomenología* serves as record. Since at the heart of this crisis lurks the irresponsible and invalidating suspensions of *relajo*, then it is irony that recovers responsibility and makes visible that which suspension has taken out of play. The paradigm case, or the ironic consciousness that must be appropriated for this recovery and return, is Socrates' irony, as illustrated in Plato's *Euthyphro*. Portilla summarizes the dialogue for us, concluding, "By means of irony, Socrates shows; he does not limit himself only to saying it, but rather he makes it visible: he *shows* that this Euthyphro knows not one word about piety. Socrates makes us catch him red-handed in his not-knowing about piety. He undresses Euthyphro of his pretenses in such a way that we almost feel a little pity for dear Euthyphro, who is there, before our eyes, trying to cover up his nakedness with some rag of thought. Irony has suddenly transformed Euthyphro the wise into Euthyphro the ignorant" [66]. Socratic irony represents here the *unmasking* of ignorance, the exposure of "claims" to value which are unjustified; irony is aletheic. It represents, Portilla says, "a will to truth" [68]. We see right away the absence of this *will to truth* in *relajo*. There is no desired end for those overtaken by *relajo*: there is neither a desired chaos (as in "fucking around" or, in Spanish, "*desmadre*") nor the revelatory moment of irony.

Irony manifests itself in Socrates as a two-dimensional destructive process. The two dimensions are irony-consciousness [*conciencia-ironía*] and irony-endeavor [*empresa-ironía*]. Irony-consciousness is the attitude which "sees" the "vanities in existence," and irony-endeavor is what names them and "in naming them, destroys them" [68]. Both dimensions in this destructive process are underscored by the will to truth, which in Socrates is itself driven by the recognition of his own ignorance. But this "destruction" is not so much a tearing down, as it is an unbuilding process, one which *frees*. Portilla thus calls irony "liberating": "We can say, then, that Socrates frees us totally, opens up the path toward the truth for us, through an act with which he frees himself—by means of irony—from Euthyphro's illegitimate authority—which at the same time seems illegitimate only after Socrates' irony" [69]. The liberating event brought about by irony, accomplished through a destruction of illegitimate claims to value, thus *happens* not only to Socrates, but to us, the readers of the Platonic text. This means that liberation through irony is a communal event—liberating a transtemporal, trans-spatial, and transcultural community. Not only is the experience of freedom brought about by irony in a communal event, but it also *founds* community. We come together to pursue the thread of the ironic, and once vanity and ignorance are exposed, we stay together in the pursuit of truth. "In transforming the world," Portilla argues, Socratic irony is "a foundational act of community: that of disciples, the community of those who seek the truth" [69].

But what does irony have to do with *relajo*? The atmosphere of *relajo* is reduced to clamor, interruptions, and the fragmentation of community and might contain something of the ironic. The irony of the comic Cantinflas, who says one thing and means another or means nothing at all, is often described as exemplifying *relajo* (Pilcher 2001). But the irony of the comedian exposes the ignorance of those he addresses and seeks something other than the chaotic disconfigurations and the tiring suspensions of *relajo*. He seeks truth, and we seek it with him. Cantinflas is *not* a *relajiento*. Speaking of Socrates, Portilla says, "His irony is founded on a supreme seriousness, since seriousness is nothing other than vocation for and unconditional devotion to a value" [69]. This means that while *relajo* suspends this ground and uproots community from it, irony fastens to it and maintains itself in and by it. Socrates' "liberating act is realized, then, from the depths of seriousness and responsibility" [71]. The association of seriousness with responsibility points to another major difference, namely, that irony is a responsible kind of being (a "freedom for"), while *relajo* is not. But this also means that seriousness is required for liberation—that freedom demands seriousness. In contrast, *relajo*, by suspending seriousness, is neither liberating nor a genuine expression of freedom. The ultimate difference between the two—that is, *relajo* and irony—boils down to a subjective appreciation of seriousness and a willingness to place limits on one's freedom.

Portilla ends the section on irony with the following words (which I here emphasize): "*Irony is a liberation that founds a freedom for the value. Relajo is a negation that founds a pseudo-freedom that is purely negative and thus infertile [infecunda]*" [71]. This conclusion is inevitable. Irony authentically liberates; relajo is a false liberation.

If a "moral" significance is what Portilla is after, then he discovers it here. *Relajo* is an intrusion into community, a suspension of the search for truth, and a negation of authentic freedom. This phenomenon, which has a name and a history in Mexico, *ought* to be overcome for the sake of Mexico, Mexicans, and the whole of humanity. The way of its overcoming does not lie in the repetitive discussion of its presence and its essence; the way of its overcoming is irony, a will to truth that can, and ought to, be pursued if freedom (and all that is attached to this) is, at the very least, an existential ideal.

On Humor

Relajo is a happening, an event, and a phenomenon that destroys, annuls, displaces, and interrupts a subject's commitment to values or to what should be regarded as signifincant in any given situation. In the process of its *happening*, it fractures the system of meaning which gives guidance to one's life and one's projects. In this state, values appear as if fragile and forcibly, or externally, "placed on our liberty." Existence becomes burdened by these values. In breaking our commitments and suspending the seriousness which allows us to faithfully realize the call of value, we find a certain kind of freedom, a liberation from our duty to *respond* and, thus, from responsibility. While still an expression of freedom, *relajo* is a manifestation of negative (absolute) freedom, one that invariably opens the door to irresponsibility. In *relajo* our existence becomes irresponsible.

Irony is an expression of a will to truth. As such, irony allows us to reconnect ourselves to a supreme value. Portilla thus says that "irony is transcendence toward value" [72]. But it is necessary that in recovering one's commitment to value, one also recover one's freedom. That is, not only is *relajo* to be overcome, but also the negative freedom which authorizes it, since "*relajo* drives us into a dead-end street, into the illusion of negative freedom" [83]. The opposite is the case with humor: "Humor can be defined . . . as a transcendence toward freedom" [72].

Characteristically, Portilla is short on illustrations. Perhaps he assumes that the reader knows what humor *is*. This assumption is not unfounded. After all, all of us have a "sense of humor," or at least we have been known to have one. That we have a "sense" of humor already points to an aspect of humor's essence: it is related to subjective mental states. Unlike the comic, which confronts *us* as an objective state of affairs or situation, humor emanates from the subject: it is our own way of dealing with that which confronts us. Here we find an important aspect of humor's essence: its referent is *freedom*. According to Portilla the fundamental aspect of humor's essence is its transcendence toward freedom, which means that it is a transcendence *away* from our own oppressive situatedness, or our "facticity." Portilla says that "humor liberates us . . . from adversity" [74]. And adversity, he says, is our unavoidable "human misery" [74].

Humor is liberating. In momentary bursts it liberates us from our misery, from our *circumstances*, and from the push and pull of immediate demands. Adversity, or *the* misery, is the full negativity of life, which can press down upon us at any moment. Recovering addicts or alcoholics who have managed to stay clean and sober for long periods of time are asked, by other addicts or alcoholics, to never forget that "life shows up." This simple phrase is a reminder that the misery and adversity which drove them to substance abuse will, of necessity, return. When life shows up, they must be ready to *deal* with it without the drugs or the alcohol. So they prepare. The preparation involves recognizing the inevitability of adversity and the universality of the misery. They are asked to develop their perspective so as to see life for what it is when it shows up. Developing a "sense of humor" is often the first lesson in that preparation. Portilla points to this capacity when he writes that "humor is the capacity to distance oneself" from one's own life [76]. In this way, humor and laughter serve the same liberating function, their difference resting on their intentionality: humor is transcendence *from* misery and toward freedom, while laughter is transcendence *from* misery and to an aspect of existence which it means to affirm (the comic).

Thus, humor joins irony as a means of overcoming the oppressiveness of the *relajo*-event and the interruption of the *relajo*-individual (what he calls "*relajiento*"). Portilla packages the difference between the three in the following way: "Irony wants truth, humor wants freedom, *relajo* wants irresponsibility" [84].

On Personality Types

Relajo would not pose any moral difficulties were it not for the fact that it intrudes on the specific development of the human spirit. In other words, *relajo* makes its way into the social sphere by *taking over* the personality of moral agents who take up *relajo* as their defining *manner of being*. These individuals will instigate *relajo* whenever they get the chance and will always find a way to maintain its suspensions and inter-ruptions. *Relajo* is the "how" of their being. But this is far from being conducive to the development of a subjectivity which is world-constitut-ing and authentically free. (I treat these personality types below.)

On the other end of the personality spectrum, Portilla identifies those individuals who have been taken over by *relajo's* opposite, namely, "the spirit of seriousness." We must remember that Socrates pursued truth from the depths of seriousness. But, while serious, Socrates was not pos-sessed by the "spirit of seriousness." He tells us the difference earlier on: "The spirit of seriousness is pure gesticulation, an exaggerated exte-riorization that tends more toward showing one's own excellence and toward underscoring one's own importance than toward the realization of the value. The spirit of seriousness is reflexive; seriousness is pure spontaneity; the former projects outward, while the latter is "intimate"; the former is a behavior toward others; in [the case of] genuine serious-ness, I am alone with myself before the value" [19].

Portilla dubs the person *possessed* by the spirit of seriousness an *apretado*, which literally translates to "the tight one," or, colloquially, "a tight wad," but which, given Portilla's description, is best to translate as "snob" (for the most part, I leave the term untranslated below).

The *apretado/a* is a person who we, observers, think takes things way too seriously. But this is not because things are serious or demand to be taken seriously; rather, it is because these are the kinds of things that the *apretado/a believes* should be taken seriously. This is a belief justi-fied through observation of others whom the *apretado/a* holds in high esteem or whom she wants to emulate. The snob commits to her values based on a false belief about the status of those values in the social hier-archy. The *apretado/a,* commits to what she finds valuable to the extent that she embodies them and regards in a negative light anyone who does not value what she values or commits in the way in which she com-mits. In the *apretado/a,* being and value are welded together and become a personality. Portilla says that the *apretado/a* is a "compact mass of value; they live themselves on the inside like a dense volume of value-filled 'being'" [88]. There is no distance between this serious type and the values she prefers; she *is* those values. This makes for an obvious dis-tinction: the *apretado/a* "appears as the absolute opposite of the man of *relajo*" [89]. In embodying her values, the *apretado* desires "order"; in suspending them, the *relajo*-individual, or *relajiento*-individual, "detests order and destroys it every time s/he can" [93].

Opposed to Socratic seriousness, the seriousness of the *apretado* is illusory and self-defeating. According to Portilla, this has to do with the fact that this kind of seriousness is, like the possibility of *relajo*, grounded in a conception of "negative freedom." Both personality types are consequently self-destructive and, as such, impediments to the creation of community and dialogue. Portilla concludes: "In both attitudes there is a negation of community. One and the other dissolve community" [94]. The *relajiento/a* dissolves community by prohibiting the realization of values, and the *apretado/a*, by internalizing values in such a way that they become oppressive and impediments to self-creation and solidarity.

Portilla's discussion of these two types is meant to illustrate the significance of the moral implications of either "the spirit of seriousness" or *relajo*. Virtue, of course, will be found in between these extremes. Authentic subjectivity will be achieved in the negotiation and overcoming of these two types, in the overcoming of the false belief that because the snob is the antithesis of the *relajo*-individual, then subjectivity (associated with positive freedom) rests with the snob. Portilla puts it thus:

> One could say that the figure of the former is antinomial to that of the latter in all respects. For now, the "apretado" individual seems similar to a fullness of affirmation against the pure negation of the "relajiento" individual. The "apretado" seems to be the positive pole of a unitary correlation, at the other extreme of which would be the negativity of *relajo*. If, as we have shown, relajo implies a non-freedom, a false, negative freedom, the "apretado" individual could seem to be a bringer of freedom. This individual would be genuinely free.
>
> But this is false: such a manner of reasoning is not more than an abstraction. Within reality, the spirit of seriousness ends up being just as negative and just as lacking in freedom as *relajo*. [89]

The *relajiento* exists in the unlawful space of negative freedom, which is a "nonfreedom," while the *apretado*, or snob, lives to portray himself *as* law itself, which is oppressive or "lacking in freedom." Authentic subjectivity lies in the mean between the extremes of *relajo* and "the spirit of seriousness," the model of which, for Portilla, is the Socratic subject who, through a rational (i.e., "serious") manipulation of irony and humor, can come to be "authentically free."

The *Fenomenología* as a Mirror of Society

In a recent study on "Chicano folklore," the author, citing Portilla, describes *relajo* as a "joking relationship, a bantering back and forth, which through the laughter relieves the tension and disintegrates the cause of the tension of the moment . . . [It] can be lighthearted joking around" (Castro 2000, 201). This definition is common, both in the literature and in everyday, prephilosophical understanding. But, as has been shown, *relajo* is more than this; it is an expression of negative freedom and a radical expression at that; it serves as the transcendental condition of this kind of "joking" or "bantering" or "mockery." In other words, *relajo* is that toward which they *are*. As Portilla puts it in regard to mockery: "Mocking, as such, is an action that tends to subtract or to deny the value of a person or situation, but which, when considered in isolation, *does not yet* constitute *relajo*" [28; emphasis added]. *Relajo*, being a suspension of seriousness, is a rather serious problem, even if it is not considered so serious in our own time.[2] The crisis Portilla describes reflects a kind of social, historical, and cultural distraction which grips our human community, rendering it incapable of fashioning its future in accordance with its better excellences.

————<o>————

Portilla's *Fenomeonlogía del relajo* reveals a world that we could easily miss. Perhaps Portilla intended his text to open us up in this way. I think of walking through a busy marketplace in Mexico City—or, in *any* marketplace where different voices compete for an audience. Looking in one direction or another, we might encounter a group engrossed in *relajo*, in the rebellion of devaluing their own values and those of the circumstance in which they find themselves, ultimately doing a lot and accomplishing *nothing*; they are *relajientos*. Elsewhere in the marketplace, we find mockery in a scene where someone's bad fortune becomes a theme for ridicule; or we are victimized by a sarcastic remark coming from the fruit vendor, one meant to hurt us in some way; or we witness *choteo*, whereby someone aims to reveal her superiority by pointing out her comrade's intellectual shortcomings, for the entertainment of the group. On our way out, we overhear the ironic observation that a marketplace is a great place to exchange ideas; or one of us has the humorous realization that the smog makes umbrellas unnecessary. Behind us, a husband chastises his wife for her dress, reminding her that it is improper for a lady to show too much flesh and that he has a reputation to maintain—he is an *apretado*. In this way, the *Fenomenología* is truly a reflection of our noisy, stifling, value-ladened human condition.

CHAPTER FOUR

Phenomenology and *Fenomenología*

Mexican philosophy, if it is to be genuinely so, must take as its
point of departure a reflection about its own reality, or it must
originate in it. This reality is, for the most part and in many ways,
the same as that of other human beings.
                                    —Guillermo Hurtado (2010)

Mexican Philosophy in Profile

In Jorge Portilla, Mexican philosophy affirms itself. It affirms itself by
unhesitatingly asking its own kind of questions. In its affirmation,
it reveals itself. But it does so only in a limited way. That is, Portilla's
Fenomenología reveals Mexican philosophy in profile, since its questions are those demanded by the specific generational and cultural crisis
of value to which his philosophy is responding. Portilla's questions are
specific, for example: *What is the everyday manifestation of our cultural
crisis?* Understanding that *relajo* is this everyday manifestation, he then
asks: *How can relajo be overcome?* In asking these questions, Mexican
philosophy might appear provincial and relativistic, but according to
Portilla, these questions aim to reveal "essential characteristics belonging to the human condition" [13]. Of course, whether this particular-
universal structure is found in "Mexican philosophy" as a whole is a
matter for further study; we can say for certain, however, that it is found
in the profile we see of it in Portilla.[1] "Mexican philosophy," like "Latin
American philosophy" or "Analytic philosophy," cannot be seen in one

blow, but in aspects, in instances when it asks special questions which *resemble* what history might recognize as "philosophy."[2]

By saying that Mexican philosophy gives itself in profiles, I am not negating the possibility that there might be a common methodology or a common concern that gives Mexican philosophy its identifying flavor. What I am saying is that (and the case is the same with Latin American philosophy) the "philosophy" that we encounter when we read the works of José Vasconcelos, Leopoldo Zea, Antonio Caso, Samuel Ramos, or Jorge Portilla are but aspects of a more coherent commonality that might always elude us. Thus, Ramos' deconstruction of the Mexican character in *El Perfil del hombre y la cultura en México* (1934), or José Vasconcelos's fantastic speculations about the fate of *mestizos* in *La raza cósmica* (1925), are profiles of this eluding whole. Each profile is an instant of a Mexican philosophy, and each is an example of that which drives Mexican philosophy forward. I am inclined to believe that given a large enough sample of work done by Mexican philosophers or of work that treats themes related to philosophical thought in Mexico, that common drive, or *worry*, might emerge that we may call "the worry" belonging to "Mexican philosophy"—which might still not tell us what "Mexican" philosophy *is*.

The profile of Mexican philosophy that we find in our reading of Portilla (what we can call "Portilla's philosophy") is one where philosophy is *liberating* (although not a "philosophy of liberation," as we find in, for instance, Enrique Dussel). As such, Portilla's philosophy, as all authentic philosophy, is meant to liberate one from false beliefs and false idols. In the manner in which Portilla appropriates the tradition, we can say that he *responsively* appropriates it for the sake of liberation. Now, by "responsively," I mean that it responds to certain demands made upon it by the situation itself—by the crisis and the idols to be addressed; by "appropriation," I mean more than an assimilation of the history of philosophy, but a consumption, a confiscation, a synthesis, a sublation, and an enrichment of *method*. This appropriated (consumed, confiscated, synthesized, and sublated) method emerges in Portilla as a unique profile of Mexican philosophy, namely, the *fenomenología* of his *Fenomenología*. That is to say, Jorge Portilla's philosophy is an appropriation of phenomenology, particularly of the foundational *methods* of phenomenology, while simultaneously a rejection of that tradition as an inviolable mythology of the West—a rejection made apparent by the use and abuse it undergoes in Portilla's hands.

Chapter 1 already touched on certain key influences noticeable in Portilla's philosophy—Jean-Paul Sartre, Max Scheler, Martin Heidegger, and Edmund Husserl. From Sartre, Portilla takes his calling; from Scheler, the possibility of his theme, namely, values; and from Heidegger and Husserl, his method. And, indeed, the Husserlian method of phenomenology is the endoskeleton of Portilla's appropriated phenomenology.[3] To this endoskeleton is attached a method of "destruction" similar to one we find in Martin Heidegger's earlier writings (what we find in part 1 of the *Fenomenología*), as well as a moral perspective I describe as a "dialogical ethics," which informs the moral considerations of part 2 of Portilla's text.

Portilla's philosophy, characterized by its responsive appropriations or confiscations, is thus a unique *aspect* or *profile* of Mexican philosophy. But by portraying it as a mesh of confiscations, one could be led to read Portilla as an eclectic, perhaps *careless*, phenomenologist, one who simply got the method wrong and took overzealous liberties to compensate—or who did not know its limits, thereby mixing and matching as he saw fit. Zirión has argued, for instance, that the Mexican appropriations of Husserlian phenomenology have been "inappropriate and out of place" (Zirión 2004, 19). I do not think that Portilla was inappropriate at all; but I do think that he mixed and matched *as he saw fit* without being "out of place." This way of putting the matter, that he "saw fit" to appropriate the tradition in the way in which he did, hits upon something crucial about both the *Fenomenología* in particular and philosophy in general. Portilla's philosophy responds to a certain "lack of fit" between phenomenology proper (or "pure," uncontaminated phenomenology) and the object of the investigation, namely, *relajo* as itself an aspect of Mexican culture.

The lack of fit here is between "pure" phenomenology and *relajo*. As early as 1915, Martin Heidegger, then a novice to philosophy, surmised that a "method of research . . . is determined by the object . . . and the points of view under which it is examined" (Heidegger 2002, 50). With this insight, Heidegger himself argues that the object of the science of history, that is, human culture, demands a different methodological approach than the object of physics or the objects of biology, mathematics, etc. What Heidegger is suggesting is that objects to be studied demand their own particular method. When a scientific or philosophical method is imposed on an object, a method that that object has not itself demanded, then, he repeats in a 1920 article, "it might turn out that these objects become lost for good by being forced to conform to a particular type of apprehension alien to them" (Heidegger 2002, 78). My claim is that Portilla's philosophy is sensitive to the demands of the object under consideration, that he is aware that his object will "become lost" if he does not treat it appropriately, which means approaching it with a method suitable to its complexity and historical uniqueness.

In Portilla's philosophy, *relajo* is the complex and historically unique object—one which provokes and demands. This object is unlike other objects treated by phenomenologists, for instance, the physical world, time, consciousness, life, or triangles. It is unlike these objects in its specificity—it is not abstract like life or triangles, nor is it universally *felt* like time, nor is it universally acknowledged like consciousness or the contingency of the physical world. It is also different by being situated in a Mexican context. Again, this does not mean that it is not possibly a universal human crisis, but the fact that it is named and thematized in Mexico and Latin America suggests that it is given clearly there as an everyday and familiar experience. Because of this difference, which includes the complex and provocative manner of its givenness, *relajo* must be treated in a way that is accepting of its demands as a complex, historically unique phenomenon. Consequently, Portilla's philosophy, one that is open to the data of everyday culture and that "presupposes" the significance of the crisis of *relajo*, is justified in its response and its appropriations. At the same time, it is, in addition to a genuine example of "Mexican philosophy" in the sense indicated by Hurtado in the epigraph, responsible and *serious* philosophy.[4]

The Descriptive Method

Naturally, Portilla's fragmented appropriation of the phenomenological tradition will be looked upon with disfavor by those for whom the tradition's significance rests in its integrity and cohesion, and where the proper tasks of those who came after Husserl and Heidegger are to *interpret* rather than appropriate in the manner described. Appropriation can either be authentic or inauthentic; it can be true to the original, or it can be a careless misunderstanding. Zirión Quijano writes that "the history of phenomenology in Mexico . . . [is a history of the] diversifying and mixing of phenomenologies and notions of phenomenology . . . [of] disorientations and misunderstandings" (Zirión 2004, 20). While this is certainly the case with Portilla, I do not agree with what it suggests, namely, that the "mixing," or "diversifying," is careless in its understandings or blind in its orientations. On the contrary, in Portilla's case, the appropriation of the phenomenological tradition is grounded on a historically informed understanding of its origins and its limits, one that also suggests that it is clear in its orientation—it is clear about where it comes from and where it wants to go.

The first clue that this analysis will be phenomenological is, of course, in the title. The *Fenomenología del relajo* is meant to be just that, a "phenomenology" of *relajo*. This, in turn, suggests a descriptive, but specifically, an "eidetic" approach to *relajo*—that is, that we will be given different instances of the appearance of *relajo* out of which an essence will be extracted or "intuited." Each instance of *relajo*, after all, is a contingent manifestation. Husserl would say that it is a "matter of fact" which could be "otherwise," but to which belongs an "essence and therefore an *Eidos* which can be apprehended purely" (Husserl 1998, 7). This apprehension of "Eidos" or essence is "eidetic seeing"—the effort to see in this way constitutes the "eidetic" approach.[5]

Portilla *suggests* an eidetic approach to *relajo* with the title. But what we get in the *Fenomenología* falls short of such an approach. It is not a purely "eidetic phenomenology" for two reasons: one, the object under investigation does not lend itself to such a method, as this would presuppose a previous understanding of what Portilla is trying to get at, namely, the "what" of *relajo*; and, two, Portilla has greater intentions. "The purpose of this work," he writes, "is not analogous to that of a physician who offers a diagnosis, but rather to that of a person who begins a dialogue" [14]. Portilla's purpose is not merely to describe, or to find an essence (an *Eidos*), but to leave the essence indeterminate enough so as to "initiate" a conversation, which is less about defining an essence and more about *initiating* action.

Despite Portilla's applications of eidetic analysis, his method is still grounded on certain central Husserlian themes, primarily, on the *return* to consciousness. The repository of data for a proper study of the theme in question is, Portilla says, "the consciousness of these events" [15]. Because *relajo* is lived as a "spontenous attitude" of displacement, disattention, rebellion, and so on, its origin can be traced back to the lived experience of an active consciousness. Its analysis, therefore, must take the form of an analysis of consciousness, which, for Husserl, delimits the entire realm of human experience; it is the site of all experience.

Whether as spectator of *relajo*, its victim, or its perpetrator, the evidence of its happening gathers in consciousness as experience. Experience is itself the primary data. Portilla calls this return to consciousness a "general principle": "As *a general principle of this investigation*, at least in this first descriptive part, it must be established that all the descriptions presented refer to the spontaneous attitude of active consciousness, to the world of lived experience in general, without allowing for the incorporation of any reference to a theory of values as such" [31; emphasis added].

However, this return to consciousness, or what Husserl calls "reduction," is not carried far enough to meet Husserl's standards of rigor. Husserl himself carries his reduction to the level of transcendental experience, to that of "transcendental pure subjectivity," which gives "transcendentally pure data" via a "bracketing" whereby "this 'mundanization' of consciousness in the natural attitude is inhibited once and for all" (Husserl 1971, 86). In other words, Husserl's method demands a separation of pure consciousness from the historically situated consciousness belonging to individual persons. This allows a transcendental subjectivity to emerge which serves both as the possibility for meaning-creation and also as the possibility for intersubjective understanding. As we will see in the next chapter, for his own reasons Portilla appears enamored with the idea of a transcendental subjectivity, but he does not follow Husserl into the realms of "pure phenomenology," remaining instead *grounded* in the fallibility of his "personal experience" [16]. Thus, instead of worrying about the essential structures of pure consciousness, structures cleansed of their particularity and historical specificity, Portilla's concern is with "promoting reason in actual society," which involves taking "philosophy out onto the streets (its natural place)" [15]. Abstract philosophizing might initiate dialogues, but its liberating power gains its traction in the world, in the streets, where reason meets life.

But, even if he avoids tracking Husserl to the realms of purity and abstractness, Portilla retains another major Husserlian theme, namely, "intentional analysis." In a telling footnote, he says: "In the language of E. Husserl, the 'noema' of *relajo* is a value, even if the value is merely a noematic nucleus; the full noema is the theme: 'negated value,' 'value put in parenthesis,' 'neutralized value,' 'value to be degraded in the name of another value,' etc. The noematic nucleus (the value pure and simple) remains always invariable with its essential constituent of appealing to

my freedom" [22n2]. Another way to say this is this: when consciousness is presented with *relajo*, what it sees is a value, but not a value
which is demanding its actualization; what consciousness sees (when
subjected to intentional analysis) is a negated, parenthesized, degraded
value. This is *relajo*'s essence; its sense, or noema, fully intuitied, is the
negated or dislocated value. What intentional analysis reveals is just that
to *relajo* belongs a noema, or a sense, through which we experience *it*
and understand *it—we* understand *relajo* as a negation.

　　This means that *relajo* is not an intentional act like, for instance,
wishing, desiring, and willing. *Relajo* is not a specifically mental, or
reflective, act that seeks its fulfillment in experience. In other words,
while desire, for instance, is intentionally directed at whatever would
fulfill it and turn it into a desire fulfilled, *relajo* does not seek fulfillment
through the intuition of "negated values." We find *relajo* in the world,
not in our minds. But even if it were in our minds, as a happening that
we longed to bring about, it would be a longing, and not *relajo*, that we
would find. Besides, looking for such desires, longings, and *relajo* in our
minds is a self-defeating endeavor: "When reflecting on this phenomenon [of *relajo*] we [do not] discover in another subject an interiority that
is concealed to us and evident to him or her and that we will intuit that
lack of attention and disassociation from commitment as individual acts
that are 'lodged' in that subject's psyche" [21–22]. By limiting himself
in this way, Portilla avoids Husserl's notorious slip into the "problem
of other minds" and aligns himself with other notable phenomenologists who did the same, for instance, Martin Heidegger and Maurice
Merleau-Ponty.

　　The "event" of *relajo*, however, does have its own intentionality. Its
intentional object is negated value, that, because it is negated, is hardly
an object at all, and hardly a value. So its intentionality is *unlike* the
intentionality of mental acts. *Relajo*'s intentionality is manifested during the *relajo*-event itself: on the one hand, it is a "reference to others"
and an "invocation to others" to participate in the spectacle; and on the
other, it directs itself to the displacement of attention and the negation
of values. The first, Portilla calls "lateral intentionally toward others"
the second "negative intentionality toward value" [23]. While Portilla
does not say much about this analysis, it is easy to appreciate his insight.
Relajo, as we saw in the previous chapter, cannot come about without
the participation of others, who maintain the interruptions or perpetuate
the displacements. This is a "lateral" move; it spreads outwardly from

its center, from the origin of the suspension. *Relajo* is also an attempt to "dislocate" intentionality by displacing the attentive focus of spectators. In this way it exhibits a "negative intentionality"—or, we could also say, a negating intentionality.

Ultimately, Husserl's phenomenology powers Portilla's *Fenomenología* through its descriptive phase: the return to consciousness is a "general principle." But the phenomenological method that we find here is fragmented. Portilla's appropriations of the Husserlian method of analysis are meant to respond to the exigencies of his task. Thus, we find only remnants of the eidetic reduction (the search for "essence"); the reduction to consciousness stops with personal experience (it does not go into the "pure" transcendental realm); and intentional analysis is rebooted, taken out of consciousness, in order to meet the demands of the social nature of the *relajo*-phenomenon. This fragmentation of method has led some notable commentators, such as Zirión Quijano in his *Historia de la fenomenología en México*, to argue that in the *Fenomenología* "we cannot find a sufficient definition of method, just a few almost accidental outlines," and, worse yet, "missing is also a systematic scientific vision" (Zirión 2004, 303). Zirión Quijano is right that Portilla does not give us much in terms of deciphering his methodological approach, but I believe that what he gives us is enough to decipher *a* method. The outlines are *not* accidental. The method is fragmented for a reason; the appropriation is made with purpose. As I suggested above, the object of investigation does not demand the *assimilation* of method or a "systematic scientific vision." It demands, Portilla says, an "aspiration for clarity," *aspiración a la lucidez* [15], which systematic scientific visions might, in fact, impede.

The Destructive Method

"Clarity," writes Portilla, "is the obligation of the philosopher and the non-philosopher" [15]. In the search for clarity, he calls on the Husserlian phenomenological method—at least in part. But as we have seen, the Husserlian method only touches on a few key themes, leaving the rest to what might at first seem like a hodgepodge of methodologies or philosophical approaches, and threatening the very ideal of clarity. Closer inspection of part 1, however, reveals a methodological strategy that while in line with the phenomenological tradition seems to be unrecognized by Portilla himself. This approach is the method of "destruction" first introduced into the phenomenological bloodstream by Martin Heidegger some years before his famous formulation of *Destruktion* in *Being and Time*. It is, first and foremost, a method of "deconstruction," but, what is more important, a means to clarity.

Portilla's is not an ambitious "destruction" (*Destruktion*) of the history of Western metaphysics, as it is for Heidegger in *Being and Time*. Portilla's destruction, or deconstruction, like Heidegger's earlier *destructions*, aims to liberate the present from the obfuscating obscurity of false idols. Portilla says: "Philosophy, to the extent that it is a 'logos' on humankind, performs an educating and a liberating function. With it, what is concealed and implicit becomes present and explicit, and something can be transformed by its enlightening action" [16]. This highlights Portilla's unwavering faith in the liberating power of philosophy. The question turns on what he means by "philosophy." This is answered in the preceeding line: philosophy is the means of making "present and explicit," which is a less flowery way of saying that philosophy unearths, unconceals, reveals, and makes *known*.

With these words, Portilla is expressing the traditional faith in philosophy, one which goes back to the pre-Socratics. This was certainly Husserl's view, expressed by his famous formulation of the "phenomenological epoche"—the means to recovering the hidden and unconcealing the implicit via a rigorous "suspension" of presuppositions followed by eidetic analysis. Husserl formulates this method early, in 1907: "Everything transcendent that is involved must be bracketed, or be assigned the index of indifference, of epistemological nullity, an index which indicates: the existence of all these transcendencies, whether I believe in them or not, is not here my concern; this is not the place to make judgments about them; they are entirely irrelevant" (Husserl 1964, 4). Presuppositions of all kinds are "transcendent." But this is another instance where Portilla deviates from Husserl, since it is also clear that Portilla is not indifferent to those presuppositions which form his philosophical starting point. Not everything transcendent is epistemologically null. For instance, the validity of one's past or future self is not suspended or questioned. While Husserl suspends the certainty of that which is not immediately before me, Portilla hints at the persistence of one's past and future identity when he writes: "A person is not exactly equivalent to him or herself before and after having been understood. The person cannot be [the same], because the power of the word has transformed him or her. I cannot be the same person before and after knowing that, in a sense, the designation "petit bourgeois" applies to me. The word situates me, it creates me like a 'fiat' pronounced by others that makes me emerge before myself with a new appearance that I barely recognize but that I cannot reject outright either" [16] Several presuppositions otherwise bracketed by Husserl remain: for one, personality is not bracketed or nullified, and neither is the world, which "situates me"; there is a person who philosophizes and a person who is changed by that philosophizing (these are numerically identical persons), and there is the effect others have on me. That "others" are not "bracketed" is another instance of deviation from the Husserlian line. Ultimately, this passage illustrates a recurring theme in Portilla, namely, that he is not willing to follow Husserl to the realms of "pure" method. Presuppositions can be analyzed, deconstructed, replaced, and so on, but they cannot be suspended in toto as Husserl thought, or "assigned an index of indifference, or epistemological nullity." This view was shared by Heidegger, even during his years as Husserl's assistant.

Heidegger called his version of the *epoche* "destruction." In the process of interrogating Karl Jaspers' *Psychology of Worldviews*, Heidegger wonders about those "epistemological ideals" at work in Jaspers and asks whether "these ideals satisfy the fundamental sense of philosophizing, or whether they do not rather lead a shadowy life that has hardened into a long, degenerate, and spurious tradition" (Heidegger 2002, 73). The same concern over the "shadowy life" of epistemological ideals is carried over into his questioning of the theme of Jaspers' work, which is that of "psychological life." Indirectly criticizing Husserl by proclaiming the fruitlessness of approaching those hardened and degenerate *presuppositions* (those handed down by the tradition) by "creating" a "new philosophical program," that is, the phenomenological reduction, Heidegger suggests that the approach should not be to suspend presuppositions, but, rather, to "free [them] up" (Heidegger 2002, 72), to allow them to speak. Jaspers' dogmatic appeal to the traditional concept of "life" is one such presupposition that must be *set free* through a "critical approach":

This "how" of a critical approach always remains subject to a type of appropriation that must constantly renew itself in the form of a *destruction*. Our review [of Jaspers' work] is phenomenological in the genuine sense, but it is not "without presuppositions" in the bad sense. Here one turns what is imme-diately "on hand" in one's objective historical, intellectual situ-ation into the in-itself of the "things themselves. One fails to see what is characteristic of all intuition, namely, that it actualizes itself in the context of a definite orientation and an anticipatory foreconception of the respective region of experience. (Heidegger 2002, 74; emphasis added)

Heidegger's method of "destruction" is both a return to Husserl's *epoche* and its overcoming. It retains presuppositions because presuppositions are part of the way in which one understands the world; they structure its intelligibility. They are *always* there, "on hand," as other things. This is the reason why "one fails to see" the temporal nature of intuition itself when one begins from a "presuppositionless," since one fails to see how sense is constituted in time and by temporal creatures. Hence, the *method of destruction* will reveal the presuppositions or foreconceptions; next, it will "delve into the motivation, the sense, and the scope of the direction of inquiry that led to such foreconceptions, and become aware of what is *demanded* by the very sense of these foreconceptions," even if these "demands" were never understood "in an explicit manner" (Heidegger 2002, 77). We will come to see, finally, how presuppositions themselves "call for their own clarification" (Heidegger 2002, 77).

Whether Portilla conceived his approach as *destructive* in this, Heideggerian, sense is difficult to know for certain. But it I would like to propose that he is, at the very least, engaged in a project of destruction similar to Heidegger's (and, in this way, similar to Marx's project of "denunciation"). We find echoes of the method of *destruction* in the following lines:

It is indispensible that whoever takes on the descriptive task adopts a subjective point of view . . . In the descriptions just undertaken [that of *relajo*] we have placed ourselves within this "interior" position in the act of studying the phenomenon, adopting an attitude exclusively descriptive, that is, completely neutral with respect to every attempt at explanation (of "exterior" comprehension) which could have possibly crossed our minds [. . .] trying all the while not to be effected by philosophical theories, even if the most clear and profound which have been dedicated to it. [50–52]

In Portilla's approach, we first take the "subjective point of view" and "place ourselves within this 'interior' position in the act of studying the phenomena" (Heidegger says we "delve into the motivation, the sense, and scope"), then we try "not to be effected by philosophical theories" (*Destruktion* urges a becoming "aware of what is *demanded*" by the presuppositions). From here, the analysis proceeds *without* the theoretical requirements of Husserl's phenomenological reduction.

The method of destruction comes into play in consideration of two primary presuppositions through which *relajo* is normally understood. It is necessary for Portilla to confront these presuppositions and, in effect, "destroy" them. The first, and persistent, presupposition making up *relajo*'s cultural intelligibility is that it is "the behavior of dissidents" [35]. This means that *relajo* is an act of rebellion carried out in the spirit of freedom. *Relajo*, in other words, is liberating. It liberates one from commitments, the pull of community, social cohesiveness, and the oppressiveness of imposed values. In its everyday manifestation, *relajientos* are those individuals who *throw care to the wind*. People busied with work, family, and other social responsibilities will look upon these individuals as lazy, lackadaisical, and good-for-nothings, but, simultaneously, as "free" and unburdened by the social sanctions which *force* others into roles. This presupposition holds that the suspension of seriousness is the affirmation of defiance.

To properly destroy, or deconstruct, this presupposition, Portilla situates himself concretely in the most familiar, that is, his own (Mexican), generation. From there, he considers the motivation of the belief that *relajo* is liberating. He wonders whether the motivation for this belief is, rather, fear: "They were afraid of their own excellence" [15], he says of those he's known and who have been swept up by the irresponsibility of *relajo*. As he peels off the layers, Portilla argues that the sense of this idea stems from a perverted conception of freedom, which preferences *negative* freedom over and against *positive* freedom. Ultimately, the idea of *relajo* as liberating is found to be lacking in justification and reality. Its destruction does not mean, however, that it is destroyed in the sense of being obliterated and purged from its place in the web of significance surrounding the crisis of Mexican culture; its destruction means that the internal motivations and the scope of the preconceptions have been revealed and put into question. The presupposition will remain as a means of understanding *relajo*, but now fully exposed *as* presuppositions.

The second presupposition which faces deconstruction reveals itself as a *confusion* regarding other socially disruptive behaviors. It is presupposed that *relajo* is, as the name implies, a manner of "relaxing"; as such, it "involves fun and relaxation" (Farr 2006, 223). Fun and relaxation, in turn, involve laughter, humor, joking around, mockery, bouts of teasing, sarcasm, and ironic exchanges. Portilla takes this presupposition head on, arguing that what others see as part and parcel of *relajo* are also phenomena in their own right. Although they make up different features of *relajo*, some of these, like mockery and *choteo*, are possible only because *relajo* is itself their transcendental condition. Others, like laughter and irony, are antithetical to *relajo* and appear in the *relajo*-phenomena only accidentally (they are not *essential* to it).

We can see right away that Portilla's treatment of these different social phenomena is not meant as an *eidetic* variation, whereby varying the different ways in which *relajo* appears one can get at its "essence." Instead, their treatment is meant as a confrontation of "foreconceptions," or presuppositions through which *relajo* has been traditionally, or commonly, understood: it is a destruction.

Normative Considerations

This brings us to the ethical dimensions of the *Fenomenología*. In part 2, "El sentido moral del relajo," Portilla draws out the moral significance of this phenomenon and gives his project an ethical and a political feel, infused as it is with a "call for responsibility and empowerment" (Lomnitz 1992, 10). "Let us shift from the key of 'is'," of part 1, says Portilla, "to the key of 'ought'" [51]. The "method" remains destructive, and the target of destruction, or deconstruction, is now an entrenched, and confused, notion of freedom: "The concept from which we will take the necessary support for clarifying the moral sense of *relajo* is that of freedom" [51]. Portilla's analysis of freedom follows Sartre's in *Being and Nothingness*. Portilla characterizes freedom, like Sartre, as "a passage or transfer, [*tránsito o trasiego*], a passing from interiority to exteriority" [56]. Freedom is the possibility to move from the choice (interiority) to the act (exteriority). For Portilla, this means that authentic, or positive, freedom is actualized in confronting the values which give themselves to us in experience and committing to their realization—to do what the value demands. Moral behavior is behavior which makes this realization, or this "transit," possible; moral behavior realizes the possibility of positive freedom.

However, Portilla's analysis of freedom does not tells us much about the moral significance of *relajo*, other than the obvious, namely, that negative (or absolute) freedom is not conducive to proper moral behavior. Freedom is better expressed in commitments and the ability to respond to duty.

My impression is that the real moral significance of *relajo*, or the more tangible moral consequence that Portilla draws out, is his view that *relajo* destroys the possibility of dialogue. Earlier he writes: "If *relajo* is an attitude toward a value, it is also, at the same time, an attitude that indirectly alludes to 'others'" [22]. The invitation to others to participate in the disruption of value is at the same time an invitation to forgo meaningful communication. In other words, *relajo* is harmful to human sociality. Portilla does not fail to see this implication, but he does not make it an explicit theme of the moral evaluation that he is suggesting, instead focusing on the fact of *relajo*'s illusory freedom.

Thus, my suggestion is that what we get in part 2 of the *Fenomenología* is a *dialogical ethics* or, what is the same, an analysis of *relajo*'s impact on human community from the point of view of a communicative ethics. *Relajo* represents, at the very least, a suspension of the conditions for dialogical exchange. So apart from the phenomenological analyses of Husserl and Heidegger, we find a concern with the normative aspects of human communication, with its possibility and impossibility. Perhaps the best example of a dialogical ethics we can point to is Paulo Freire's, whose *Pedagogy of the Oppressed* (1970) was published four years after the *Fenomenología*.

In that work, Freire emphasizes the significance of dialogue: "Dialogue is the encounter between men, mediated by the world, in order to name the world. Hence, dialogue cannot occur between those who want to name the world and those who do not wish this naming—between those who deny others the right to speak their word and those whose right to speak had been denied them. Those who have been denied their primordial right to speak their word must first reclaim this right and prevent the continuation of this dehumanizing aggression" (Freire 2000, 88). Dialogical ethics requires the ability and opportunity for all to speak and participate in the naming of the world. An act is morally blameworthy, on this account, when it denies that ability or opportunity to speak and name. However, morally praiseworthy are acts which "reclaim this right" to speak and name.

Portilla suggests that *relajo* denies dialogue. It is of the essence of *relajo* that it appears in social or communal settings (*"Relajo* in solitude is unthinkable, or I should say, unimaginable" [23]). Because it is a suspension and an interruption through a gesture, a dislocation of attention away from a dominant value and an annihilation of commitments to value, *relajo* is, by necessity, a disruption of a community engaged in conversation. This disruption is manifested as a sudden interruption of a conversation *about* . . ., of a dialogue *regarding* . . ., or the communication *of* . . .acts taking place between and among members of a group. In *relajo* the conversation is hijacked by the attempt to suspend seriousness and bring about the negation of values to which the members of the group were, before the initial *event*, attempting to make manifest. Dialogue, discourse, conversation, is here suspended, perhaps indefinitely. Those who were *serious* about realizing a value, who aimed to identify their world through an effort of conversation and discussion, are marginalized and remain in the margins for the duration of the *relajo*-event. This marginalization is due to the fact that, as Freire writes above, "dialogue cannot occur between those who want to name the world and those who do not wish this naming": *relajientos* "do not wish this naming." As Portilla puts the matter: "The invocation to others is not, we insist, something accidental, but rather an essential constituent of *relajo* that is concomitant with all the other characteristics . . . The active subject [of *relajo*] creates a certain void around the person or situation imbued with the value and thus, he or she prevents the value from fully acquiring substance in reality. That being said, the void is not created only in the pure subjectivity of whoever promotes it; it is not a localized void, but rather it extends throughout an environment: the intersubjectivity of those present" [23]. The "invocation to others" brings with it the impossibility for dialogue and communication. Words will be spoken, perhaps shouted and pronounced, but meaningful discourse cannot take place. The "void" that is created by *relajo* is felt as an absence of commitment, an absence of freedom, a lack of authority, and a silencing of the call of duty, and, as such, morally problematic. Oppression and marginalization are, then, consequences of the negating presence of the *relajo*-event.

Portilla characterizes *relajo*'s displacement of attention and its "invocation to others" in terms of its "double intentionality": "It is constituted both by my lack of solidarity [with a value] as well as by my intent to involve others in this lack of solidarity, which creates a common environment of detachment before the value" [23]. Put differently, this doubling of *relajo's* intentional rays manifests itself as an intentionality aimed at disassociation (or the brining about of a lack of solidarity) and as the intentionality of invoking others. In Freire's analysis, a condition for liberation is the possibility of communication between persons that does not take the form of an imposition, or a "deposit" of information, by one person over others. But what is more important for Freire, "Dialogue cannot exist in the absence of profound love for the world and for people" (Freire 2006, 89). This means that *relajo's* "intention to commit others" is already an imposition, grounded on the suppositions that others are there to be committed; it is, then, antithetical to love and more akin to hate or evil. What makes dialogue impossible in the three-dimensional space of *relajo's* displacements is the effect of its double intentionality which brings about "a common atmosphere of indifference" through an interruption of a subject's commitment to truth inherent in purposeful dialogue.

As an interruption of a subject's commitment to the truth of an event (to its value), the creation of indifference through the act of *relajo* is an interruption of a subject's Socratic search for truth. Alain Badiou calls this sort of interruption "evil," where evil is understood simply as an interference of the pursuit of *a* good, which is *truth*. Truth, according to Badiou, is "the real process of a fidelity to an event" (Badiou 2001, 42). If one sacrifices this commitment, then one gives up the truth, and whatever intervenes in this commitment is evil. To remain committed, to maintain fidelity to the event of truth, brings about our subjectivity; it drags us out of our anonymity and makes us visible. In Badiou's terms: "The process of truth *induces* a subject" (Badiou 2001, 43). In simple terms, commitment makes us who and what we are. Badiou calls truth an "immanent break" (Badioiu 2001, 42). It is a break from routine, from the determined way of the world, from invisibility and inconsequence. "A truth punches a 'hole' in knowledges" (Badiou 2001, 71). Consequently, Badiou claims that "it is only because there are truths and only to the extent that there are subjects of these truths, that there is Evil" (Badiou 2001, 61). Evil is thus the interruption of a truth process. In other words, evil is to interrupt someone's fidelity, commitment, in his pursuit of truth; it is to get in the way of someone's commitment, or fidelity, to what gives meaning to his life. Thus, Badiou urges: "'Do all that you can to persevere in that which exceeds your perseverance. Persevere in the interruption. Seize in your being that which has seized and broken you'" (Badiou 2001, 47). Overcoming evil requires that you do what you can to persevere in that which is greater than yourself, namely, the value of your pursuits; persevere despite the interruptions (evil) that may befall you. In Badiou's schema, *relajo* would be evil, and overcoming it would require the perseverance of those in the act of conversation to keep speaking in spite of it. If overcoming evil is a moral act, then Portilla would say that overcoming *relajo* is likewise morally necessary.

What I am calling Portilla's dialogical ethics emerges from a consideration of *relajo* as morally problematic in both Badiou's dramatic and Freire's practical senses. Portilla is directly addressing that interruption of fidelity to commitment which is essential to *relajo*, what Badiou calls "evil." His is a critique of *relajo* as a condition for the impossibility of dialogue and, ultimately, of authentic human sociality and the basic human desire to safeguard that which makes life worthwhile—a project in line with, what Portilla calls, "human dignity" [55]. After all, dialogue is the means of access to those truths that matter to us and that give our lives direction; but it is also the way in which we find that common ground that gives meaning to our coexistence. It is what gives us the path to authenticity, fidelity, being, and, what is most important, respect. Portilla's dialogical ethics rooted in a critique of *relajo* echoes a sentiment recently expressed by Charles Taylor: "what is to respect people's integrity includes that of protecting their expressive freedom to express and develop their own opinions, to define their own conceptions, to draw up their own life-plans" (Taylor 1989, 25). The suspension of seriousness, the interruptions which displace attention and the devaluations essential to *relajo* disrespect that integrity necessary for developing opinions, defining conceptions, and drawing up plans. It is a disrespect which makes solidarity and self-fashioning impossible.

As a way of conclusion to the text, Portilla writes: "Indeed the foundation of a community, [of] coexistence, can be thought of as the continuous self-constitution of a group in reference to a value" [95]. *What matters* will be discussed, seriously considered, amongst friends, brothers, and lovers; this discussion and consideration of "what matters" solidifies one's role and one's identity in the group, community, or social context. The work of realizing the value is continuous and creative. One's identity emerges from this work. The "evil" of *relajo* impedes this emergence. As a suspension of seriousness with respect to value, *relajo* is also an undermining of the foundational grounds of community or *what matters*. In this way, dialogical ethics is also a critique of Mexican society as *not yet* grounded on demands, on *what matters*, on value; by extension, it is a critique of modern society as struggling to sustain a meaningful conversation about this ground. The generation which motivates Portilla's project is an actual generation, irresponsive (and irresponsible) before values, and thus "silent." But it is also the possible future generation, one in which *we* live.

A Human Worry

Jorge Portilla's *Fenomenología del relajo* is perhaps the best example of the existential-phenomenological encroachment or *intervention* in the Latin American world. I call it an "intervention" because in true colonial fashion it forces itself onto the Latin American scene and, in uncharacteristically pragmatic fashion, promises to unconceal the inner lives of subjects despite their historical or political marginality. It promises an unprejudiced interrogation. At a time when neo-Kantianism, neo-Thomism, and positivism seem to have exhausted the patience of the Latin American for philosophy itself, phenomenology *intervenes* and reveals new realms of conversation and analysis previously occupied by the totalizing forces of Western metaphysics. In Mexico, the promise of phenomenology is equal to the ambitions of its practitioners.

Unapologetically situating himself within a tradition that includes Husserl, Heidegger, and Scheler, Portilla appropriates the intervention and develops a rigorous analysis of Mexican subjectivity and culture.[6] His analysis will be situated in the history and culture of Mexico, but this does not mean that it will not concern itself with *universalist* grandeur or concern; it will *tend* in that direction. Portilla realizes that he must necessarily begin from the most familiar (his Mexican circumstance), but he also understands that staying within the familiar will not bring about the kind of (internal or external) change that he seeks. He says: "The individual, as such, is ineffable and the only path to individual knowledge is universal knowledge" [17]. In other words, while the scrutiny of one's immediate circumstance, of one's self or one's cultural habits, provides a most appropriate starting point for philosophical investigations into one's being and being in general, what one discovers through that scrutiny is limited and defined by the immediacy of circumstance, self, or habit. To get at one's being, and at what is common to all—that is, what can ground a practical moral perspective—the investigation must be pushed outward toward the universal. But it begins with the analysis of *relajo*. To paraphrase Ortega, Portilla believes that through the intuition of *relajo* one can communicate with the universe. This is because the revelation of the essence of a seemingly "cultural" behavior like *relajo* is the kind of revelation that transcends human particularity and historical situatedness, and whose intuition, if properly grasped, can lay the groundwork for a prescriptive account of the moral life that can serve humanity in general. For this reason, I insist that Portilla's revelations are meant to go beyond the descriptions of "Mexican national life" and apply to us all—then and now. In this way, Portilla inserts himself into the phenomenological tradition by producing a very unorthodox analysis of a nonorthodox crisis that, nonetheless, has consequences for contemporary orthodoxy. (It has important consequences for modernity, as a critique and a denunciation.)

It becomes evident upon reading the *Fenomenología* that Portilla's idea of phenomenology deviates from the standard interpretations of this methodology or "attitude," as some have called it. Nonetheless, Portilla's method throughout could be called "phenomenological," although there are moments in which this attitude is abandoned as a response to the demands of the theme, namely, the complex phenomenon of *relajo*. Overall, Portilla's descriptive account could be understood as a responsive appropriation of two different strands of phenomenology—one that emphasizes *reduction* and the other that emphasizes *destruction*. Portilla's prescriptive account can be understood as a version of, what I have called here, *dialogical ethics*, a normative approach to human sociality made popular by the Brazilian philosopher Paulo Freire (but unconnected to it).

———◦———

Leopoldo Zea, in reference to his insistence that philosophy must concern itself with the Latin American circumstance, asked some time ago: "Why do we bring to the history of philosophy an interrogation which has never before been posited and, from that, bring about a strange philosophy?" (Zea 1969, 11). My hope is that what has been said in this chapter helps to understand this question and to answer it. The problematic of *relajo*, or of the "suspension of seriousness" of which it is a name, gives rise, indeed, to an interrogation never before undertaken. The theme is not, historically at least, a *philosophical* theme. Portilla himself expresses reservations about addressing it in the beginning of the *Fenomenología*. And the theme demands, as all objects of study, its own method of investigation. Hence, Portilla appropriates the phenomenological tradition in a way that *fits* his need and thus gives birth to a "strange philosophy."

Ultimately, Portilla's represents an "original" profile of Mexican philosophy. It is original in a double sense: its originality is grounded on its novelty—his theme had not been treated before; its originality has to do with its relation to its Mexican origin. The second sense is the most important. It allows us to see Portilla as an original philosoper in the sense that his philosophy arises from the Mexican circumstances, although it aspires to address universal crises of value wherever they may be found. This is the sense of "original" with which other Latin American philosophers, such as Leopoldo Zea, had proposed as a justification for their own philosophical efforts. Zea wrote: "When the Latin American asks himself whether there is an original Latin American literature, philosophy, or culture, he does so only in relation to what the world 'original' means in its widest acceptance: place of origin" (Zea 1992, 4). Upon none of this depends, however, our final estimation of Portilla. In other words, I do not wish to argue for the originality of Portilla's thought, although I think this is quite obvious. Ultimately, Portilla was a phenomenologist, an existentialist, and one of the most astute yet hesitant critics of modernity who has emerged from Latin American soil.

CHAPTER FIVE

Metaphysics of the Subject

The subject is defined by the movement through which it is developed. Subject is that which develops itself. The only content that we can give to the idea of subjectivity is that of mediation and transcendence. But we note that the movement of self-development and of becoming-other is double: the subject transcends itself, but it is also reflected upon . . . In short, believing and inventing is what makes a subject a subject.
—Gilles Deleuze (1991, 85)

Inherent to the Nietzschean dictate to "become who you are" is the suggestion that you are not *now* who you are *supposed to be*. This sense of being *other than* what one is "supposed to be" drives one to fashion one's self according to ideals ready-made for that sort of self-fashioning. In the postcolonial world, these ready-made ideals might take the form of religious, cultural, or political instructions left over from the colonial period: the ideals which dictate the processes of subjectivity are a colonial inheritance. Of course, philosophers will disagree on the extent to which the colonial legacy influences thinking. People on the periphery, they might contend, can make choices completely free of that legacy. Jorge Portilla, for instance, will place a great deal of emphasis on the power of rational deliberation in the construction of Mexican subjects; these will be the subjects empowered to bring about the future of Mexico given its past. He does this by arguing that those instances when a person *fails* to choose, *fails* to express herself, or *fails* to bring about progress is a failure of the rational over the social, or, to put it in his terms, a triumph of a destructive form of collective consciousness over the call of duty (values). The destructive form of collective consciousness manifests itself in *reactionary* acts against both colonial instruction and individual rationality. What we see is *relajo* as "an act of lack of solidarity with the value and with the community that realizes the value" [20]. But although a lack of solidarity, or disassociation, *relajo* nevertheless configures certain senses of identity which are adopted by those who initiate it or participate in it. "In this act," Portilla writes, "the subject is defined as a non-participant in the venture tending toward the incorporation or realization of value" [20]. However, Portilla suggests that the identity of the subject as a "nonparticipant" is no longer an identity, and the subject is no longer a subject, but, as unwilling to participate, a nonsubject. This is the (non)subject who initiates *relajo* so as to suspend a process of subjective construction already underway in the realization of values. In this way, it is *relajo* which suspends the arrival of Mexico's future; it is *relajo* which, as a reaction to established values and seriousness, suspends the ability of persons to become who they are "supposed to be." Portilla's presupposition here is that no one is supposed to be a nonsubject, as nonsubjectivity is subhuman. So he considers *relajo* as a reactionary suspension of reason and destiny, one that defers the emergence of subjectivity, thereby maintaining the postcolonial self in a perpetual state of marginality and silence. We can see from this that the critique of *relajo* is far-reaching, since a cursory glance of our environment reveals the suspension, interruptions, and deferrals of *relajo* at work all around us—even if our language lacks a name to properly capture it.

The objection here might be that "subjectivity," and ultimately, "humanity," is itself a colonial imposition, the standard of which is also a colonial ideal, and, thus, that achieving it does not take us *beyond* colonialism but back to it.[1] The answer to this might be that the idea of subjectivity, and the related idea of humanity, to which Portilla implicitly aspires, is precisely a denunciation of the way in which subjectivity in Latin America *has been* conceived. So philosophers, like Portilla, writing in the mid-twentieth century, will link their notions of "subjectivity" to a modern period to which they belong and whose promises (and dangers) they are helping to realize, not to a colonial period that was out of their control. Less significantly, philosophers such as Portilla will seldom emphasize "subjectivity"; rather, they emphasize "identity" or "personhood." But Portilla's talk of subjectivity suggests that its process is disrupted in the event of *relajo*. Those under the spell of *relajo* or its suspensions are "non ubjects," nonactive spectators to modernity. The nonsubjectivitity of the spectators assumes, as its contrast, a notion of an active subjectivity that participates in the historical drama and in the overcoming of those impediments to human flourishing that history and circumstance may deposit in the everyday and that call for human effort and doing.

The present chapter answers the question: what notion of subjectivity is at work in Portilla's critique of modern culture? This will help us account for the extent to which reactionary acts of suspension are deferring its emergence in Mexico, Latin America, and elsewhere in the postcolonial world, or even *our* world.

Before getting to this question, it is fruitful to consider the context of Portilla's thinking on the matter.

Leopoldo Zea and "*lo mexicano*"

For Mexican philosophers of the twentieth century, questions of identity were questions of subjectivity. Like Charles Taylor forty years later, midcentury Mexican philosophers understood identity as "the ensemble of (largely unarticulated) understandings of what it is to be a human agent: the senses of inwardness, freedom, individuality, and being" which constituted the self (Taylor 1989, ix). The identity they were after was the identity of what they called "lo mexicano," *Mexicanness*. In asking after this identity, they were asking about the Mexican experience, about subjectivity, about the "post"colonial, post-Revolutionary notion of freedom and democracy at work in their circumstance, and about the (unarticulated) ways of life which were specifically Mexicans (their *being*). Driving these interrogations was a desire to discover those emotions, notions, behaviors, or forms of life which were obstacles to self-determination and "authentic" humanity. They sought to expose those "largely unarticulated" understandings making authentic subjectivity impossible. The modern Mexican self, they agreed, would emerge once Mexicans took responsibility for the complexes of value and sense inherited from history and once they affirmed those which allowed for overcoming while denying those which did not.[2] Thus, Mexican philosophers suggested that being "free" is not enough; one must also be *responsible*. Similarly, being Mexican is not enough to bring about the future of Mexico *for* Mexicans; one must also *take responsibility for* oneself *as* Mexican. This knowledge requires knowing more than the *fact* of one's nationality; one must also know the *possibilities* of being a historical *subject* (of course, one situated in Mexican history).

The most recognizable Mexican philosopher of the last century, and the founder of *el Grupo Hyperión*, Leopoldo Zea, summarizes the project in an essay appropriately titled "The Sense of Responsibility in the Mexican" (1949). I quote it at length here:

> What is the Mexican? [*¿Qué es el mexicano?*] Here we have a question to which all of us Mexicans would like to give a precise answer. The question, it is necessary to say, does not emerge due to a simple curious urge. No, on the contrary, with the answer that we give to that question it seems that more is at stake than deceiving that curious urge. Those of us who ask and try to give an answer to the question feel that we are wagering something with more depth, something that lies much deeper in our questioning, deeper than that which we know ourselves to be externally, including our own flesh and bones, something which is deeper and at the same time further away from our limited existence as subjects. We wager our own *being*.
>
> We know ourselves [*Nos sabemos*], aside from being particular individuals with some determinate characteristics which make it possible for us to be persons X, as subjects of a determinate community, history, and cultural characteristics. *We know ourselves as subjects of something which defines us* and gives us personality in addition to our particular being. Subjects of something which makes us *be* Mexicans in opposition to other groups of people we encounter and before which we feel different. What this something could be is precisely what preoccupies us here. (Zea 1952, 172–73; emphasis added)

We notice immediately that the question is not "Who" (*Quién*) the Mexican is, but "What" (*Qué*) the Mexican is. It is a question of essence. But Zea assures us that there is more at stake in answering the "whatness" question than eidetic curiosity. What is at stake is "our own being"— something "deeper" and "further away" than "our limited existence as subjects." This way of formulating the project exposes its duality: on the one hand, the project will be an ontological investigation into the *being* of Mexicans; on the other hand, as the paragraph that follows indicates, it is a hermeneutic interrogation into the constitution of that "limited" subjectivity which is already "known." I say it is an investigation into constitution because, as Zea puts it, of interest is that "something which makes us be [*nos hace*]" subjects, and what is more important, Mexicans. The second horn of this project is what worried Zea and his contemporaries.

In the background of Zea's interrogation is a tension between a Cartesian and a Hegelian conception of subjectivity. There is a "particular being," the Cartesian *cogito*, "in addition to" a personality constituted by "something" other—history, perhaps. Zea's repetition of "*Nos sabemos,*" *we know ourselves as,* harks to Descartes; while the indeterimate "something which makes us Mexicans" harks to Hegel.

Ultimately, there is a move away from Descartes demanded by the project of *lo mexicano* itself, as conceived by Mexican philosophers of the midtwentieth century who found it more valuable to historicize the subject so as to begin a process of recovery and healing. Zea, Portilla, and the rest were, after all, students of José Gaos, who himself was a student of José Ortega y Gasset, for whom Cartesian subjectivity was an empty abstraction. Ortega's famous dictum, "*Yo soy yo y mis circunstancia,*" "I am myself and my circumstance" (Ortega 2000, 45), against Descartes, proposes a historical subjectivity rooted, and immersed, in space and time. Given the presence of Ortega, or the presence of his *oeuvre,* we can conclude that Zea's notion of subjectivity, as Portilla's, is more nuanced than its Cartesian predecessor.

Portilla's Confrontation with Ortega y Gasset's Circumstantial Self

The conception of the self, or subjectivity, that Portilla advocates can be traced to several influences easily detectable in the *Fenomenología.* These influences are, broadly speaking, phenomenological—not surprising, as a cursory glance at the title, *Fenomenología del relajo,* reveals. As mentioned in chapter 3, the first part of this work, the "descriptive" part, is clearly indebted to Edmund Husserl. It is not surprising, then, that Portilla's notion of subjectivity reminds one of Husserl's transcendental, or "pure," accounts of subjectivity in his later works. While not *explicitly* defending a transcendental version of subjectivity, Portilla sets up an opposition between two alternative ideas of the self. On the one hand, he considers, surprisingly, the notion of a figure whose influence on Mexican and Latin American thought and philosophy is immeasurable, José Ortega y Gasset's circumstantialist view; on the other hand, he posits the idea of subjectivity which is *beyond* the trappings of circumstance. Portilla criticizes Ortega's version and upholds the virtues of its alternative, which, I claim, is his own *transcendental* version.

Patrick Romanell, in his classic study, *The Making of the Mexican Mind*, ends a crucial chapter titled, "Perspectivism and Existentialism in Mexico," with the words: "The fact remains that Ortega's perspectivist ideas have been the greatest single intellectual force in the nationalization of the Mexican mind" (Romanell 1952, 184). It is worth examining Portilla's indebtedness and resistance to Ortega, if only to appreciate Romanell's judgment. But there is a legitimate reason, namely, that Portilla's views on subjectivity represent an exception to the totalizing "force" of Ortega's philosophy.

ORTEGA'S EARLY AND LATER VIEWS ON SUBJECTIVITY

In one of his earliest works, *Meditations on Quixote*, published in 1914, Ortega famously identifies the self with circumstance. The self is not a detached substance, floating in thought above the *res extensa*; the self is *in* the world, communicating with and through those things which *stand around*—the *circum stare*. He writes: "Individual life, the immediate, the circumstance, are different names for the same thing" (Ortega 2000, 43). Ortega identifies the self with life and life with circumstance. Thus, his theory of the self has it that subjectivity is an all embracing term designating the totality of the self's absorption in the world. To lose one's connection to the world, to the *circum stare*, is to lose one's self—it is the loss of subjectivity. Having diagnosed the crisis of subjectivity in early twentieth-century Europe as one of loss and homelessness, Ortega points to its recovery: "the reabsorption of circumstance is the concrete destiny of man" (Ortega 2000, 45). We must return to the ground of our being. His point is that human destiny can be fulfilled only if we "reabsorb," take-in, internalize, make ours, and own up to our immediate life-world. This is because, he writes, "circumstantial reality forms the other half of my person; only through it can I interpret myself and be fully myself" (Ortega 2000, 45). Subjectivity thus emerges from the synthesis of self and circumstance. This is the meaning of Ortega's famous statement: "I am myself and my circumstance, and if I do not save it, I do not save myself" (Ortega 2000, 45). We could call this idea of subjectivity "circumstantial."

Ortega's circumstantial self is situated and temporally determined. The "reabsorption of circumstance" required by the crisis of modern Europe is an effort in time and of the future; this is the task of *saving the circumstance*, and it is a task *to be done*. But this act of "saving" the circumstance places the subject in relief. In one of his later works, *Man and People*, Ortega highlights the *labor* that goes into reabsorption and saving the self and circumstance from loss and homelessness, or what he calls there, the crisis of "being besides oneself": "Almost all the world is in tumult, is besides itself, and when man is besides himself he loses his most essential attribute: the possibility of meditating, or withdrawing into himself in order to come to terms with himself and define what it is that he believes, what he truly esteems and what he truly detests. Being besides himself bemuses him, blinds him, forces him to act mechanically in a frenetic somnambulism" (Ortega 1963, 16).

But genuine subjectivity does not come about as a result of merely "withdrawing into" oneself or what Ortega calls "*ensimismarse*" (Ortega 1963, 18). This would mean that subjectivity is found somewhere in the recognition of that *inner life* or *inner certainty* that defined Descartes' cogito. The process of subjectivity requires a movement toward the circumstance, or an act of transcendence, which is typical of post-Cartesian theories of the subject (Hegel, Marx, Dilthey). But the act of withdrawing into oneself is requisite of any transcendence: "*It is impossible to speak of action except in so far as it will be governed by a previous contemplation; and vice versa, contemplation, or being within one's self, is nothing but a projecting of future action*" (Ortega 1963, 23). So subjectivity is not that "place" of withdrawal, but a *process* which includes the "projecting of future action," a transcendence toward the *to-come*. In the 1931 lecture course published as *What Is Knowledge?* Ortega highlights the temporal character of the self: "I would start by defining the self as future, as 'the one who is to be'" (Ortega 2002, 130). (We will see, in the next chapter, that defined in this way, the *relajiento*, or whomever falls into *relajo*, is a nonself.)

Ortega's theory of subjectivity can thus be summarized as follows: to be a subject is to be an *active* participant in the *saving* of that circumstance that constitutes one's life and that grounds the possibilities for the fulfillment of one's *destiny*. In contradistinction to Descartes, he reiterates this point in *Man and People*: "Man's destiny . . . is primarily *action*. We do not live to think, but the other way round: we think in order that we may succeed in surviving" (Ortega 1963, 23). I survive; therefore, I am.

Not surprisingly, Ortega's conception of the circumstantial/historical subject took hold of the Latin American imagination—and especially in Mexico. It is not hard to see why. First, it justifies and validates the existential and philosophical significance of the Latin American circumstance. Second, it emphasizes the unity of the self and the Latin American circumstance and calls for the saving of one for the sake of the other. Third, it promotes a withdrawal into *solitude* as the first step toward transcendence, a move Mexican intellectuals from Alfonso Reyes to Octavio Paz find natural for naturally "melancholy" Mexicans (Paz 1985); hence, it is a move which validates a defining aspect of the Mexican character. And, finally, it is a call for action. If independence, liberation, and progress are values which escape those who exist on the margins of the colonial order, then Ortega's philosophy should find a welcoming home in the margins of this order.

PORTILLA'S IDEAL OF SUBJECTIVITY

Like Ortega's, Portilla's subject is a transcendent subject—not transcendent in any mystical, supernatural, way..but, and *against* Ortega, transcendent in the sense that it is possible for this subject to *project beyond* the circumstance, not just out of its self *to* the circumstance. While the withdrawal-transcendence model Ortega proposes in *Meditations on Quixote* and *Man and People* suggests such a *projecting beyond*, the projecting he has in mind, if he is to remain consistent to his circumstantialism, is limited to the circumstantial horizon which defines the "I." In other words, when I emerge from the withdrawal, I emerge to act on, or "save," my circumstance, through which, he says in his first book, "I communicate with the universe" (Ortega 2000, 41). The circumstance determines the possibility of my projects. Portilla takes issue with this *circumscription*, which, he thinks, limits human potential and, in so doing, progress toward a future freedom.

According to Portilla, there are various ways in which the self takes itself out of its circumstance. One of these ways is humor. There are two types of humor: simple humor [*el humor*] and authentic humor [*el humor autentico*]. In simple humor, the intentionality of the humorous act is not directed to values (in this sense, humor is *not* like *relajo*); rather, the humorous act is directed toward the circumstance in which the value is supposed to be realized, thereby suspending the realization of the value by "disparaging" the circumstance. So, for instance, instead of undermining the value of family (as one would do in iterated acts of *relajo* emerging before family-value), one disparages one's family by pointing out its indecency, illiteracy, ignorance, and so on, which, in consequence, undermines the value of family itself. This is why, according to Portilla, simple humor leads to cynicism [74]. Ultimately, simple humor further ties one to one's circumstance, since by disparaging one's family one does not go beyond it but further commits oneself to it in the now.

Authentic humor, however, "has an intention that is explicitly directed toward freedom. Its starting point is, in general, the negativity of existence; in particular, a case in which this negativity manifests itself strongly, in order to, from there, head toward freedom itself" [75]. This means that authentic humor *begins* with, and goes beyond, the recognition of the oppressive circumstance which circumscribes one and ties one to a determinate space-time. From this ground it aims beyond the circumstances and toward freedom itself. Unlike simple humor, then, authentic humor leaves the circumstance behind and shows instead one's ability to detach and surpass the most oppressive circumstance. Portilla's examples are straightforward, yet crude:

Someone told me on a certain occasion that, on the day of her birth, his grandmother had been stricken with a cancer on one of her toes. It was necessary to amputate the toe to prevent the cancer from spreading. But the cancer reappeared. There was need for another amputation, and the process continued uninterrupted. "When I met her," my friend concluded, "my grandmother was just a bust on the piano and, when she died, she was nothing more than a little lock of hair." This is a real masterpiece of black humor. The story is sinister and yet it shows the possibility of treating it comically, of distancing oneself from the most intolerable situations. [75–76]

This is an example of what Portilla calls "black humor," which is an instance of authentic humor, as the humorist achieves distance and detachment from her misery and her circumstance.

Authentic humor, like irony, does not undermine value; rather, it reaffirms it by showing, for instance, that while the significance of cancer and death—what these *mean* to us in our everyday lives—can be kept in mind and addressed, this significance (the value) cannot be "suspended." At the same time, however, one is able to distance oneself from the situation by showing, through words or actions, that it is not oppressive and that we have not given up hope that it can be overcome—that one is *defined*, but not imprisoned, by it. This is a critical juncture in Portilla's analysis, as it allows him to suggest an overcoming of Ortega's influential doctrine.

> [Authentic humor] shows . . . how man is always already beyond himself and his circumstance; how he can find himself in the most adverse situations and face them as though they were external and alien facts, which cannot overtake him completely. Humor is an attitude in the stoic style which shows the fact that man's interiority, his pure subjectivity, can never be reached or cancelled by the situation, regardless of how adverse this might be; it shows that man can never be exhausted by his circumstance. "I am myself and my circumstance," Ortega y Gasset has said; for the humorist I am rather myself than my circumstance. [75]

Humor is a type of transcendence. Through the comic, one can laugh oneself out of the circumstance while keeping values intact. In the act of making light of an oppressive situation, one floats above it. Of course we, the spectators to the comic, also find relief. We are carried away by the comic and, in this way, are carried beyond what is immediately *around us*—the *circum stare*. What is most important, this reveals a "pure subjectivity" that is unaffected by the circumstance; it reveals that *there is* an inexhaustible interiority which makes up the self which is *not* tied, or determined, by the circumstance, as Ortega proposes.

Beyond Ortega

Portilla reiterates his proposed distance from Ortega y Gasset's circumstantialist view:

> The human person is a being of such a nature that even when participating in the very being of things as a corporal being is able to transcend them. The person is not merely a thing *together*

with other things, but can take those things as *objects*, face them and, in the process, goes beyond them all. The person is capable of proposing ends to him/herself which surpass his/her own situation and the present state of the world, taken as a whole. As a virtue of the form of his/her *being* itself, the person, every person, is always already beyond him/herself and beyond his/her physical contours; beyond the body and the situation. The human being is facticity (body, situation, irrevocable past, etc.) which is at the same time a transcendence, that is, a going beyond all of this, giving it sense through an ownmost project. [60]

Here we see Portilla's faith in the power of the subject to liberate itself from things by "facing" them (*"puede enfrentarse a ellas"*) and, in this confrontation, transcend them. The suggestion here is that presenting one's face in the realm of objects justifies one's humanity before those objects: they are there *for me*, as a resource "ready to hand." In the process of "facing" things, a person is capable of breaking ties with them—they stand *against* me. The person can always dissolve the union of "myself" and "circumstance" which, in Ortega, gives rise to the "I." Moving beyond itself and things in proposals that project beyond the immediacy of the circumstantial now, moreover, the subject reveals its temporality in its projecting beyond the now to the future. This living in the "ends" proposed is a living beyond one's self—again, a transcendence. Hence, neither the objects which oppose us nor the body which encloses us can keep us where we are; transcendence, Portilla concludes, is a condition of our facticity.

Of course, Portilla's project in the *Fenomenología* is in line with the goals of the project of "*lo mexicano*," that is, motivated by the desire to arrive at the "essence" of what it is like to be Mexican. Portilla claims not to have arrived at this essence, but rather at an essential aspect of this essence, namely, *relajo*. But he also claims that this essential aspect characterizes us all, Mexicans and non-Mexicans alike. So, while Portilla realizes that *relajo* represents a *difference* which characterizes some humans from others (thus, not just Mexicans from non-Mexicans), he suggests that this difference is due to a sameness which characterizes us all: a private inwardness which transcends toward freedom. Portilla thus holds a notion of the subject in which the subject *is not* the circumstance; this is a view in which the subject is unified in its interiority, transcends from it, and projects toward liberty beyond circumstance. He describes this view in the following way:

Each individual is a spiritual vortex that polarizes all his or her outline toward his or her center. If we call the imaginary space delineated by this vortex "subjectivity" and if we call the property it has of being a source of actions capable of modifying its shape "freedom," we can characterize freedom as a passage or transfer, a passing from interiority to exteriority, no matter how difficult it may be to establish exact limits between both terms. My freedom is actualized in this passage. It can be said that freedom *is* that passage, that freedom can also be conceived of as a moving from the exterior to the interior in a process of interiorization. In interiorization, we also find an activity of subjectivity, a centrifugal motion analogous to the realization of an action toward the outside. [55–56]

On this view, subjectivity is a pure inwardness that creates movement. It is an inwardness which leaps from itself toward exteriority in an act ("passage") of freedom, a freedom that can be exercised also as an internalization, or a *withdrawal.* So freedom is the movement of subjectivity, and as such, without freedom, subjectivity is impossible.

Like Ortega's, Portilla's theory of the subject can be understood in terms a movement or transcendence, one which *modifies* the world. But, unlike Ortega's, Portilla's theory of subjectivity goes beyond the circumstantialist view in that Portilla emphasizes a space for freedom beyond the horizon of circumstances. This space of freedom is the space of novelty and invention. Hence, he writes: "Subjectivity is the primordial origin of the different meanings that the world can have and it is, as such, an origin, free, since it does not emerge necessarily from the state of the world but rather it is—in the last instance—a source of its meaning and its state" [63]. This is the idea of a world-constituting, sense-bestowing subject. This does not mean that the subject creates significance out of nothing, invents the meaning of things, but rather that the subject finds value within, and makes sense out of, interpretive schemes, value systems, and linguistic structures, which it has inherited from history as past productions of intersubjective labor. This found value and created sense "does not . . . surge from the world" as a gift from the earth, but surges or has surged from subjects themselves. Hence, the subject is the "primordial origin" of what things mean and the value they have; in other words, sense and value are human inventions. (In the next section, and further in the next chapter, I will show how this "theory of the subject" is challenged by the phenomenological revelations of those reiterated interruptions which he calls "relajo," in which not only is sense-bestowal suspended, but also that transit to and from the interiority of the self, which is freedom.)

The notion of a world-constituting subjectivity is not new to Portilla, but is handed down from the tradition which goes back, most relevantly, to Husserl, who greatly informs Portilla's own eidetic phenomenology. Husserl writes: "Every sense which the world has for us . . . both its general indeterminate sense and its sense determining itself in particular details, is, within the internality of our own perceiving, imagining, thinking valuing life-process, a conscious sense, and a sense which is formed in subjective genesis" (Husserl 1971, 83). This is what Portilla means when he says that the subject is the "source of its sense." Husserl calls this "subjective genesis." Another way to say this is that without the subject, things would be meaningless: there would be no one around to find them *meaningful*. "For we are the ones," writes Husserl, "in whose conscious life-process the real world which is present for us as such gains sense and acceptance" (Husserl 1971, 83). Husserl extends his analysis of this "transcendental" subject further and argues for the role that the transcendental subject plays in the constitution not just of sense but of community and the "I" itself. Portilla does not follow Husserl into the realm of transcendental subjectivity, but remains on the outskirts, with a view of the subject as both world constituting and transcendental (or sense bestowing).

Hence, and despite their differences, Portilla shares with both Ortega and Husserl an ideal view of the subject as a maker of worlds, or, more precisely, a maker of meaningful worlds. It conceives the subject as reflective and effective, or creative and inventive. Recently, Gilles Deleuze offers such a view of subjectivity in his *Empiricism and Subjectivity*, which I place in the position of epigraph to this chapter only to draw attention to persistence of this conception. Deleuze's definition of subjectivity emphasizes movement and self-development. To be a subject thus requires more than self-awareness (or self-reflection). To be a subject requires transcendence, a moving out of one's self towards a world; to act upon it. Deleuze summarizes this by saying that to be a subject is to *believe* and *invent*, or, put differently, to think *and* work. So for Deleuze, the subject is more than self-aware and *more* still than circumstance. Subjectivity, both with Ortega and Portilla, is an internal movement (*mediation*) toward otherness (*invention*). The crucial difference between these two thinkers rests with Portilla's insistence, against Ortega, that circumstance does not define the possibilities for the subject. Portilla's view is more in line with Husserl's notion of transcendental subjectivity as meaning bestowing and world making; it is a less situated view. *Relajo,* of course, situates the subject in a determinate circumstance and prohibits the realization of its world-making potential.

Relajo and Subjectivity

When, instead of participating in the democratic process by voting, organizing a community youth group, speaking out against the evils of capitalism, speaking out against the evils of socialism, writing a novel, or volunteering at a homeless shelter—when instead of doing any of these things we allow ourselves to fall into a state of perpetual indecision and meaningless interruption, we have been overtaken by *relajo*—we are *relajientos*. When so overtaken, we have suspended the possibilities of commitment to any of these efforts, and, in effect, suspended the possibilities to the kind of meaningful commitment which induces world-making subjectivity. In order to be who we are—world-making subjects—we must maintain constant vigilance over the interruptions and displacements of our commitments. This requires seriousness. Seriousness, then, is a condition for the realization of "who we are," for the possibility of subjecthood.

To see how seriousness is a condition for the possibility of authentic subjectivity, we must first recognize that every situation has a value; this value demands to be realized every time that the situation presents itself. So voting has a value. When the time to vote rolls around, it demands a response from us: will we answer the demand of our civic duty? The value of voting demands to be realized; that we do it or not is, ultimately, up to us. But it places us, our national pride and loyalty, and, ultimately, our subjectivity, in question. The realization of the value demands a "yes"—yes, I participated. In democratic societies, we say that we have a "duty" to vote. According to Portilla, it is a duty borne in the value of socially responsible participation itself, not out of some legal responsibility. To realize the value of voting is to *be* "serious." The "movement toward loyalty and commitment," he says, "is seriousness" [18]. And what is more loyal than consistent democratic participation?

Affirmatively answering to these kinds of demands is a subject—a subject who thinks about her future, her commitments, and her duty and who, by acting, gives *meaning* to her life. Subjectivity depends on the affirmation, and only the "yes" of seriousness will bring it about. This means that the emergence of subjectivity depends on the self's ability to be serious to its commitments and its values. A similar view of the self is proposed by Charles Taylor in *Sources of the Self*: "To know who I am is a species of knowing where I stand. My identity is defined by the commitments and identifications which provide the frame or horizon within which I can try to determine from case to case what is good, or valuable, or what ought to be done, or what I endorse or oppose. In other words, it is the horizon within which I am capable of taking a stand" (Taylor 1989, 27). If we extend this account of the self to our own, then seriousness boils down to the capacity to take a stand when those commitments by which I am defined demand it. Portilla suggests that *relajo* undermines that capacity and the knowledge of "knowing where I stand."

A person can fall into *relajo*, thereby jeopardizing her status as a subject. This is because being a subject requires an adherence to values that, as Taylor puts it, "provide the frame or horizon within which I can try to determine" my actions. Subjectivity demands that one *respect* and take *responsibility* for the cohesion of those horizons and the values which define that for which I am willing to take a stand. Only when one adheres and structures one's life in accordance with those values can one be authentically subjective. To be a subject, then, means that one knows where one stands and is willing to take a stand when demanded to do so by the values one respects and is responsible for. Nonsubjectivity is a result of a loss of standing, of an unwillingness to answer to demands, to duty, of a falling into *relajo*.

The subject as world constituting is, therefore, also a subject willing and ready to take a stand on its commitments. This is a strong conception of subjectivity, or the ideal of a strong subject. It is a transcendental-ethical self: "Subjectivity is like the dimension of world's profundity; from subjectivity, variations in the way the world appears constantly emerge; subjectivity is like the very possibility of these variations" [63]. We could read Portilla's glorification of subjectivity in two ways: on the one hand, as the Western ideal that seems to be part and parcel of the history of modern philosophy, internalized by Mexican philosophers as a consequence of historical contiguity; or, on the other, as a postcolonial ideal, a desire to be a subject free from the hegemonic worldviews which imprison minds and bodies to purely causal determinations (i.e., to inferiority and insufficiency). In this last sense, subjectivity *is the goal of liberation*; a liberated subject is an end in itself, liberated from colonial restrictions, from history, from the super/base structures which determine our choices and our deeds, our destinies, and our philosophy. That is why subjectivity in this "strong sense" is the "source . . . of that way of seeing"; it is the source of a perspective which is free to search and discover the world's depths. But this kind of subjective possibility is the ideal: we "see" this possibility only through an overcoming of *relajo*.

Subjectivity and Modernity

We could answer the question as to why Jorge Portilla would hold on to such view of the self, when it seems obvious that this view is deeply rooted in the colonial heritage of Mexico, by noticing that this view of subjectivity is the *strongest* view possible. Ortega's subject is dependent on its circumstance—determined by it and *to* it. Portilla's subject is independent, a maker-of-worlds and source-of-sense. This is a powerful subject. Centuries of colonial marginalization and psychological inferiority demand that the subject aspire to such heights if the postcolonial subject is going to positively insert itself into modern history. Portilla finds in this notion of a transcendent subject the path to liberation:

> When I free myself from a prejudice, in other words, when I learn to direct a clean gaze toward things and people—no longer paying attention to the blurred glass [*cristal empañado*] of a stock phrase or of a preconceived notion that I received without knowing when or how I did—apparently, nothing has happened. I have changed my attitude, but everything remains the same. No doubt, there has been a change, but *only* in my interior. *Only* my subjectivity has been altered.
>
> One could think that such a change of attitude is a false liberation and that such changes don't affect in any way the progression of things, that the variations of subjectivity are a value when considering reality and that good intentions ought

to continue contributing to a worsening of hell as a fair punishment for their ineffectiveness.

But . . . it is a fact of experience that a change of attitude in pure interiority can have and indeed actually does have the effectiveness to change the way the world appears to the person who adopts the new attitude; and the way the world appears is not a negligible factor in lucid and effective action. [62–63]

The "blurred glass" of tradition and heritage obscures a proper concept of the self and of self-creation or self-fashioning required for future action. To free oneself from a past that, as Heidegger says, "is always ahead of oneself" in preconceptions and prejudices *about oneself* (Heidegger 1962), and one's future is to liberate one's mind. This kind of liberation, which gives rise to an "altered" sense of self, is a prerequisite for action and the reconfiguration of those "aspects of the world" that demand to, and should be, reconfigured.

Ultimately, Portilla's theory of subjectivity is also a theory of liberation. To be a subject in this *strong sense* of subjectivity is to be free . . . and powerful (a creator of worlds!). The *cure* for what ails Mexican culture, and humanity, is found in this conception. Of course, this is the ideal of subjectivity: the reality of the Mexican subject (and of the *modern* subject generally) is a much different one. To overcome this reality is, Portilla says, the "difficult task into which we are all thrown" [95], that of reaching for an ideal which itself makes possible the constitution of an authentic community which, reciprocally, makes possible the realization of the ideal.

The internal motivation behind Portilla's formulation of this ideal of subjectivity is obviously concern. That is, the very thought that subjectivity is more than the *fact* of belonging to a nation or a community, but, rather, that subjectivity is that which transcends the factual and announces possibilities beyond those history has endowed particular peoples—this thought emerges from a concern for the marginal situation of Mexico and its people in the modern world. The sense of self depicted in the ideal is imagined to pave the way to an overcoming of the fallenness which *relajo* is but an obvious representative. Salvation, or the overcoming of *relajo* and the overall crisis of modernity to which it points, lies in world-making—in constructing one's world in accordance with one's excellences and the full creative forces of one's imagination. But what Portilla finds when he looks around him are not world-making subjectivities but *relajientos*, victims of provocations and interruptions. What he finds are subjects lacking in subjectivity, fragile and fragmented nonsubjects. The *ideal* subject is a subject *in* power, not a subject *of* power.

Ultimately, and while I think Portilla's notion of subjectivity is motivated by genuine concern, my claim is that the reactionary acts of suspension which Portilla criticizes as deferring the emergence of subjectivity are instantiations of a *postmodern* sensibility which has gone beyond colonialism and the kinds of ideologies which marginalize and silence. Thus, Portilla is shortsighted in censuring these acts of disruption simply because he fails to see that in their midst lurks a kind of subjectivity in tune with the demands of our contemporary world (the twentieth and the twenty-first centuries). For this reason, I see *relajo* as more of an expression of our postmodernity. In fact, in *The Postmodern Condition*, Jean-Francois Lyotard writes that "it is important to increase displacement in the games, and even to disorient it, in such a way as to make an unexpected 'move'" (Lyotard 1987, 76). I think *relajo* is such a displacement and such "an unexpected move." Of course, Portilla could not see this. His own dogmas about correctess and seriousness prevented him from seeing *relajo* as anything more than deviant behavior. This suggests that perhaps Portilla's general disillusionment with his own generation was due to a standard of subjectivity that he thought *relajo* made impossible to realize, but in which he saw the salvation of his people and himself.

KOAN

a paradoxical anecdote or riddle without a solution, used in Zen Buddhism to demonstrate the inadequacy of logical reasoning and provoke enlightenment.

CHAPTER SIX

from the Japanese — matter for mystic thought

The Presuppositions of Modernity

> Chaos is the state of always-already-lost 'naiveté' and . . . is also
> a definition of the human condition.
> —Lacoue-Labarthe and Nancy (1988, 51)

A crisis of culture is a crisis of value. The crisis of value is fueled by the devaluations of subjects for whom value, in all of its manifestations, appears as unrealizable or simply not worth the time and effort to realize. The future as promised by established and tested cultural or social norms, or by values which ultimately constitute the better qualities of the culture and the community, is itself negated in acts of resistance or unwillingness.

Relajo is the name given by Portilla to this devaluation—to the resistance and unwillingness. Opposed to *relajo* and the individuals who propagate it, the "spirit of seriousness" represents its antithesis. Individuals possessed by the spirit of seriousness, Portilla calls "*apretados*," or *snobs*. Instead of devaluing and displacing the commitment to values that others might exhibit, snobs embody values and expect others to do the same, to embody their values and their commitments. Those who do not value what must be valued, or commit themselves fully to the realization of the "right kind" of values, are excluded or dehumanized. The *apretada* thinks herself to be upholding that which is right to uphold. Again, she is merely "going along with" the value, but in so doing, she is also willing the continuation of the social structures that created it.

103

"Our colonialist naïveté," Portilla writes, "says that these individuals are 'very British,' and they themselves have a—often self-proclaimed—weakness for what they call 'good English taste'" [88]. This "weakness," I take it, is that conscious or unconscious disposition to accept the objective validity of the "valuable," the "good," the "godly," and so on, simply because these concepts are couched in vocabularies which originate in cultures presumed philosophically (and economically, politically, and historically) rich, that is, English, North American, European. Ultimately, these two poles of subjectivity are marginal to the "ideal" of subjectivity Portilla prescribes as a necessary guideline for genuine humanity and authentic human community (chapter 4). In effect, *apretados* and *relajientos* are "nonsubjects" whose presence demands overcoming.

Portilla ends the *Fenomenología* with the following declaration: "Relajientos and apretados constitute two poles of dissolution of that difficult task on which we have all embarked: the constitution of a Mexican community, of a genuine community, and not of a society divided into proprietors and the dispossessed. [*y no de una sociedad encindida en propietarios y desposeídos*]" [95]. With these words, Portilla burdens *snobs* and, especially, *relajientos* with the full weight of the historical class struggle. These two poles of the subjectivity spectrum embody the consequences of the historical dialectic between the haves and the have-nots, subjects and *nonsubjects*.

The desubjectification of the *relajiento* makes evident that Portilla's critique of *relajo* and the *relajo*-subject (the nonsubject) is rooted in two presuppositions which are worth exposing (or "destroying"):

1. The exemplariness of Socratic seriousness (as reflected in Socratic irony);
2. The infertility of dissident behavior (as reflected in *relajo*).

This chapter aims to deconstruct these two presuppositions. In the process, I propose a reading of *relajo* that uproots it from these presuppositions and reconceives it as an act of defiance before the colonial legacy (of which Socratic seriousness is a manifestation) and against the axiological imperialism which that legacy instituted.[1] This means that *relajo* must be minimally creative. Portilla, of course, disagrees. He writes: "*Relajo*, a conduct of dissidence, can be the expression of a will to self-destruction" [34].

But conceiving *relajo* in this way is paradoxical. Portilla calls it "the conduct of dissidence" in the same breath that he calls it "an expression of a will." But while dissidence may at times be intrinsic to a will to death, it is not always negative (Socrates was a dissident, and so was Martin Luther King Jr.). Dissidence, after all, can be a catalyst to political and social action. That *relajo* is both of these things suggests a tension which perhaps Portilla was not willing to admit—one nestled deep in his own *mestizaje*. That is, Portilla seems torn between, on the one hand, *relajo* as a form of struggle and, on the other, *relajo* as a will to nothingness before the demands, or the requirements, of Western rationality.

Presupposition 1: Socratic Seriousness

Portilla considers Socratic seriousness as exemplary. It is itself a value to which human beings should aspire. It is beyond the pretense of those simply possessed by the "spirit of seriousness" or those without pretense at all (*relajientos*). In a telling passage, Portilla writes:

> Socrates was affirming his absolute relationship with truth. He was making himself infinitely responsible for it. For Socrates, truth was an absolute demand that required an absolute devotion. His irony is founded on a supreme seriousness, since seriousness is nothing other than vocation for and unconditional devotion to a value. In it, this vocation and devotion are not subject to any condition whatsoever, not even to that of living. Socrates could employ irony precisely because he transcended himself and his concrete interests toward truth, beyond the pretenses of his fellow citizens regarding virtue and knowledge, but also beyond his own life. He himself points out *the absolute character of his commitment* when he presents it as a demand of the Deity and he affirms, facing death, its irrevocable character. [69–70; emphasis added]

Socrates' commitment to truth, or to the value, is *absolute*. His case is not one of possession by the spirit of seriousness. He is not a snob who "considers himself as valuable . . . [where] 'being' and 'value' are fully identified in that privileged perspective which he represents" [88]. In other words, Socrates is not pretending to "embody" truth, he seeks its discovery as an "absolute demand." Truth is not what Socrates is; it is what he *does*; that is, it is his "vocation." His seriousness is expressed in his "unconditional commitment" to the call of duty, a commitment which takes precedence even over his own existence. In his seriousness, Socrates transcends the limitations of his own life, of his "concrete interests," and of his *circumstance*. Socrates is serious even *in the face of death*.

Portilla defines "seriousness" as an "inward movement toward loyalty and commitment" [19]. This inward movement takes the form of saying "yes" to duty. In the *relajo*-event, all values are suspended, even the value of life. Fallenness in *relajo* is an expression of a "no" to life, or a will to death, which Portilla witnessed as his own generation, "in the midst of perpetual laughter," gave itself to a "slow process of self-destruction" [15]. The "no" of *relajo* is a rejection of seriousness. The "no" of *relajo* is a refusal of the future. Seriousness demands that "I mortgage my future behavior" [19] to the realization of what matters (value, truth, commitment) predictably in the future. By saying "yes" to the call of Divinity, that is, to duty, Socrates committed himself to the future; his "yes" committed him to the value of truth, and, inevitably, to death. Indeed, Socratic seriousness is required for world constitution, cultural production, and, most important, for the realization my future self, which participating in world making (in affirmations of value), fulfills the ideal of subjectivity.

The virtue of Socratic seriousness is that it guards against the temptations of appearances and allows one to stay on task, to do what matters most in any given circumstance. This kind of discipline is lacking in the *relajiento* who falls victim to the *relajo*-phenomenon at the moment of its manifestation. Portilla suggests, through his critique of *relajo* and the snob, that this fallenness into appearance is the condition of modern humanity: the *relajiento* falls into the appearance of resistance, and the snob falls victim to the way in which he himself appears, and we all fall in one way or another to what *does not matter*. Socratic seriousness is beyond appearance; it is an absolute commitment to value and *what matters* which does not waver, regardless of the temptation or the interruption. Portilla considers Socrates as incapable of falling, since he "is deeply serious, having the genuine seriousness that does not take seriously what is not serious, the appearances that are flaunted with a

no consider on investment in future self

Portilla sets Socrates "seriousness" apart as a truth

pretense for recognition by men" [70]. In this way, Socratic seriousness is a "liberating act" [71].

We have to ask if Portilla's glorification of Socratic seriousness is an uncritical bias inherited from history. Is Nietzsche on to something when he associates seriousness with the one-dimensional rationality of Western asceticism? Nietzsche writes: "No longer should every person who is serious by nature become a Don Quixote, since he has better things to do than to grapple with such would-be realities. But he must in any event take a close look, and every time he discovers a mask he should shout, "Halt! Who goes there?" and rip off the person's disguise. How strange!" (Nietzsche 1995, 117). And this is what Socratic seriousness *as* irony accomplishes: it rips off Euthyphro's mask and exposes his ignorance. Seriousness as a will to truth rips off disguises. What is "strange" is that seriousness is elevated to the level of *aletheia*. Only seriousness can unconceal. Portilla's glorification of seriousness suggests that he did not see anything "strange" about it or that he *could not* see anything strange about it, that, perhaps, he could not see *beyond* this aspect of his colonial heritage. To think of Socratic seriousness as strange is to be open to the possibility that there might be other ways of *being* which are truth seeking—or that there are other ways of realizing values.

Portilla also says that *relajo* "cancels the *normal* response to value" [19; emphasis added]. So not only is Socratic seriousness *not* strange, but it is "normal," or as Nietzsche says, "natural." Of course, the criteria for normality are cultural and historical inheritances. In Mexico, these inheritances are tied to other inheritances, namely, colonial, oppressive values and value systems that still linger in the Mexican, and Latin American, life-world. That Portilla did not consider this influence on his notion of "normality" should explain his blindness to *other* ways of world making besides the ironic seriousness of Socrates. Therefore, we ask: could we not imagine that *relajo* is a suspension of a "strange" practice and, as such, *truly* resistance?

Presupposition 2: Fecundity and *Relajo*

Presupposition 2, the presumed infertility, or infecundity, of *relajo*, is related to the first presupposition in that both operate with a creative concept of "seriousness" which is then opposed to *relajo*. Portilla writes: "*Relajo* is a negation that founds a pseudofreedom that is purely negative and thus infertile [*infecunda*]" [71]. In other words, the *relajo*-event is sterile, unproductive—it brings about *no-thing*. Nothing emerges from the "time" of *relajo*. There are no decisions, no revisions, no ideas, and no plans for action. In fact, *relajo* effectively kills action. Portilla puts the matter dramatically: "Not only does it render effective action difficult or impossible, but also, with its negativity, it erases the motivation of the action itself: value. *Relajo* kills action in its crib" [85]. The dramatic in *relajo* is evident in that in the process of destroying one's attachment to value, or that which motivates action, *relajo* "kills" action. The *relajo*-event seems to be consumed by silence and uneventfulness. From the uneventfulness, or inactivity, of suspension, there is no movement, no passage, and thus no exercise of freedom; at this time, values are left unrealized. If "[v]alue is . . . a horizon which absorbs me towards my possibilities in the future," then, as a consequence of *relajo*, there is no future [35]. Thus, Portilla argues that *relajo* destroys the future. "The *relajo*-individual [*hombre de relajo*] effects a profoundly irrational movement which consists in the suppression of an entire regulated future. There is in *relajo* a certain turning-of-one's-back [*volverle la cara*] on the future so as to bring about a simple act of negation of the immediate past. The future is thus deprived of its power of attraction. Every instant of the immediate future is lived as a mere possibility for the negation of the present" [39]. Put differently: the future is suspended, the past is negated, and the present is governed by "profoundly irrational" decisions. *Relajo*'s negations of the past, in the form of negating established values, suspend the arrival of the future, which comes in the form of an accomplished expectation; it is a suspension of fulfillment and realization which is *to-come*, or *por-venir*. The future is thus annulled, and the individual is trapped in the repetition of the "now," in the repetitive process which cancels the eventuality of the event, killing action in its crib, and deferring all meaning to an impossible future.

But are these events, these "acts," these *suspensions, possible* at all? Is Portilla not describing *relajo* as some would describe death, namely, as the limit of the possible, or as the impossibility of the possible (of the future)? Portilla's description of *relajo* echoes Marcus Aurelius' description of that ultimate finality, where this is the "cessation of an activity, the ending of an impulse and a thought" (Aurelius 1983, 91). In this sense, *relajo* is the death of all future thought and impulse, if not death itself—that is, the dreamless sleep of Socrates. In the phenomenological tradition, in which we find Portilla, Heidegger's notion of death as the

suspensions

"uttermost possibility" and the "end of Dasein" (Heidegger 1962, 303) signals the possible impossibility of the future (Thomson 1999, 32). At the same time, however, for Heidegger, this impossibility is constructive. In other words, "without death, there would be no futurity" (Thomson 1999, 33), which suggests that, if *relajo* is the impossibility of the possible, as Portilla makes it out to be, then *relajo* should be that "event" which we both avoid and are perpetually anticipating. Death would be the last *relajo*.

This interpretation makes sense in light of Portilla's characterization of the event of *relajo* as the limiting horizon of thought and action. And it also reveals Portilla's presupposition; the "why" he portrays *relajo* as death—as the ultimate source of infertility and nothingness.

Portilla presupposes the truth of *instrumental reason*. Plainly, instrumental reason is that form of rationality that privileges means over ends. It is the rationality of power and capitalism—the rationality of economic exchange (it measures "cost-effectiveness"). This presupposition is also coherent with Portilla's Marxist leanings (Michael 1996; Reyes 2003; Hurtado 2006), a philosophy which depends on the *fact* of instrumental reason, namely, Marx's notion of "use value," "social use value," "commodificaiton," and so on (Marx 1999). To reason instrumentally is to assume the normativity of the production-producer dyad. It is natural, then, that instrumental reason finds its limit in death, since death is the end of production. For this reason, instrumental reason is seen by some as a colonial "mechanism of power, of domination" (Quijano 1993, 145). It is, furthermore, an outgrowth of modernity—or "modernization" (Quijano 1993, 146). And, as I have been suggesting, a belief in the value of "modernization" is a reason for Portilla's *critique* of *relajo*.

The historian Claudio Lomnitz suggests that Portilla "believed that Mexico could only modernize if Mexicans succeeded in organizing the purposeful collective actions that were being undermined by the nihilism of *relajo*" (Lomnitz 1992, 10). This belief, I want to suggest, is grounded on the promise of a progressive liberal philosophy to which Portilla, the occasional Marxist-humanist, subscribes, and on the colonial influence which Portilla does not fully recognize, a lack of recognition perhaps due to, as Anibal Quijano has recently put it, "the colonization of the imagination of the dominated" (Quijano 2007, 169) by a persistent colonial presence which advertises instrumental rationality as the means to liberation, progress, and the good life (Quijano 1993, 146). Not surprising given that, as Quijano has brilliantly concluded, "The colonizers

. . . imposed a mystified image of their own patters of producing knowledge and meaning" (Quijano 2007, 169).[2]

We do not have to dig very deep to see that Portilla is clearly working within the framework of an instrumental rationality in which *relajo* is *like death*—the end of work, the end of efficiency, the undesirable interruption of production, and a wrench in the mechanism of progress. The logic of instrumental rationality is central to Marxist labor theory and to the familiar work ethic of capitalism which it criticizes, a work ethic which is memorialized in the libertarian credo that "to each according to what he and the instruments he owns produces" (Friedman 1962, 161–62). According to this logic, even a physical death is desirable over *relajo*, as death symbolizes an opportunity for the employment of another, while *relajo* announces a wasted resource.

However, as I see it, even if we assume that it is inevitable that, in our time or Portilla's, one reason instrumentally, *relajo* is not the last refuge of the useless or the sterile. There may be life in the chaos of *relajo*. The chaos, that is, may be productive. Commenting on the motif of chaos in romantic literature, Philippe Lacoue-Labarthe and Jean-Luc Nancy said it best: "Chaos is . . . the locus of possible generations, of potential production; and since Descartes it is in reconstructing the world from a primitive chaos that the subject . . . constitutes itself as subject" (1988, 52). Portilla's countryman Fernando Salmerón echoes this view in his 1951 essay, "Una imagen del mexicano," urging Mexicans to "make from chaos a cosmos full of meaning, it is the most human of all the creations and the most creative of all the human endeavors" (Salmerón 1951, 178). It is thus possible, and even foreseen, that a subject that brings about the *relajo*-event (the "chaotic pleasure" (Lomnitz 1992, 10)) is affirming its own subjectivity in the process. This "bringing about" is already an act of creation and production. As Portilla puts it above, the "*relajo* individual effects," or brings about, the irrational movement. That is, the *relajo*-individual wills—even if his willing is perceived as a will to nothingness.

That the *relajo*-individual is able to insert herself in a situation and bring about its suspension further shows that she is not powerless before the demands of value. Perhaps death would describe those that fall into the event once it is initiated, if those that succumbed actually did *nothing*. But those who fall also contribute to the interruption; it is up to them to turn a simple interruption into the "event" of *relajo*. Unlike death, *relajo* is both possible and the possibility of the possible. The suggestion here is that *relajo* is creative, productive, or world-constituting *in some sense*. But in what sense? Not the sense that Portilla has in mind. Not in the sense that would realize the *ideal* of subjectivity. But *relajo* is creative in a triple sense: it re-creates itself ("repetition" is part of its essence); it creates a polarizing event that constitutes its participants in the affirmation of the negative; and it is a creative response of the marginal in their marginality, whose resistance to value is, truly, an act of defiance.

This is my point. The dissidents who in *relajo* manifest a will to nothingness are trapped in a dialectic of power which they are impotent in overcoming otherwise. And, while *relajo* is not, as Portilla suggests, the means through which Mexicans will throw off the yoke that binds them to their colonial past and move forward into a postcolonial modernity, I nonetheless see it as life affirming, a valuation that inverts that which is other to the status quo. At the same time, it is an expression of a difference characterized as inferiority that colonialism has nurtured through the imposition of values and value hierarchies representing the seriousness of imperialism and the influence of coloniality, values of sobriety and order and progress, which are serious values inherited from colonialism and kept alive today as a power that itself colonizes. *Relajo* is thus both an expression of surrender and an expression of resistance.

These two presuppositions, (1) the exemplariness of seriousness, and (2) the infertility of *relajo*, underline Portilla's "moral" evaluation of *relajo*. Revealing them allows us to look beyond them and to see if there are positive aspects of the phenomenon that Portilla simply overlooks.

Postseriousness

We can say without much exaggeration that Portilla presupposes the truth and validity of a Western ideal of what it means to be subjective. It assumes that the event of *relajo*—the suspension of seriousness, the rejection of values, the displacement of attention, the invocation to indifference—is itself a nonevent when opposed to the productive, worthwhile, and life-affirming event of Socratic irony, with its constitutive seriousness, commitment, attentiveness, and possibilities of disclosure. The two types of subjectivity constituted by *relajo*—*relajientos* and the "spirit of seriousness," that is, *apretados*, respectively—are marginal subjectivities, and, hence, nonsubjectivities, due to the distance they represent to the *ideal of subjectivity* which Portilla embraces, one he thinks to be the form of subjectivity capable of extracting Mexicans *out of* the "Nietzschean generation" in which they might find themselves.

But what does it mean to say that the *relajiento* and the snob are *nonsubjects*? In terms of the snob, whose nonsubjectivity is a result of a complete immersion in values thought to be "higher" or "normal" or "divine," his desubjectification is merely intellectual. That is, in society, the snob appears as fully constituted in community: he votes, he pays taxes, he *possesses* [87]. In this respect, the *apretado* is a subject and what is more important, is *treated as* a subject. We only have to think of the religious fanatic who embodies his values and detests those who do not, but who is neither marginalized nor oppressed by our social and political institutions. Her voice matters, despite the extremity of her positions. However, the *relajiento*, whose commitments are spurious, who deflects any attempt at embodiment of values, and who surrenders to the nothingness of the *relajo*-event whenever it arises, is marginalized in thought and practice. *Relajientos* do not vote, do not meaningfully participate in the constitution of community, speak without commitment, and, when they speak, interrupt and silence the committed; for this, they are marginalized in both thought and deed. They do not count. Opposed to the snobs, *relajientos* are the real nonsubjects.

But what is the nature of this nonsubjectivity? And is it truly the negation of meaningful being human as Portilla suggests? Could the nonsubjectivity of the *relajiento*, in fact, mirror the diffused and detached subjectivity prevalent in our information-saturated, technologically constituted, age? Put differently, does not the diffused and detached nonsubjectivity of the *relajiento* better prescribe the kind of human being required to navigate our postmodern, postcolonial, and post-911 world?

The nature, or essence, of nonsubjectivity rests on the initial relationship that an agent establishes, or fails to establish, with the values that define his or her context. Portilla insists that values are "guidelines" or criteria for self-constitution, or self-construction, and that their negation negates the possibility of realizing the construction of self.

> It is evident that if value is a guide for self-construction, the systematic negation of a value is a movement of self-destruction, at least at the level of the personality that could only be configured by an internal and responsible relationship with whichever value may be the case. In this way, *relajo* is, inexorably, a

self-negation. In addition, one of the effects of this self-negation is a fragmentation of the subjective temporality of whomever adopts negation as a permanent style [of behavior]. Based on this fragmentation, we understand the figure of the relajiento as an individual without projects, one who has fallen into the present instant (ab-ject), and who, precisely because of this, is incapable of giving unity to more or less long periods of objective temporality. [41]

The temporality of a negated subjectivity can be understood as a "fragmentation of subjective temporality," which means simply that the *relajiento*, as a nonsubject, has divided his or her temporal life into fragments of the past (which is negated), the now (which is dispersed in the event), and the future (which is impossible). In other words, the nonsubject, as a fragmented temporality, is a fragment of subjectivity, and as such, an accident to an ideal subjectivity, or nonessential to the ideal of humanity. Fragmented, accidental, and consequently marginal to the ideal of authentic human being, the nonsubject's temporal shortcomings contribute to her inability to find her proper place in life and the world and, consequently, to her inability to "take a stand" once that place is found—if ever (cf. Taylor 1989, 27).

In addition to temporal fragmentation, the nonsubjectivity of the *relajo*-individual can be characterized by marginality and powerlessness. That is, the *relajo*-individual embodies the marginalizations which constitute his place in the world. We can see this from the fact that the act of *relajo* is an act where a subject refuses the demands of a value which is *imposed*—an imposition that hides, or so thinks the *relajo*-individual, an authority or power that is established and centered. The *relajo*-individual embodies this mistrust, and, in turn, this *being-on-the-fringes*. But the persistence of *relajo* also announces the powerlessness of that kind of being. Thus, it is easy to characterize the *relajiento*, powerless and against the ropes (the margins), as a tragic hero, an "underdog" whose only weapons against the force of power are jokes and banter. According to Diana Taylor, this underdog "reverses the colonialist insider/outsider configuration, embracing those who get the joke and excluding those left wondering what it is all about" (Taylor 2003, 129). Taylor's suggestion is that the *relajiento/a* accomplishes what history itself cannot, namely, a victory in the class struggle. However, the reversal of the colonialist configuration is a provisional victory. The order is reversed only for the moment after the joke is told and while laughter, vulgarity, and so on run their course, after which things return to "normal." This is why Portilla considered *relajo* infertile, because in his eyes it accomplishes nothing. Ultimately, Taylor is overly romantic, attributing to the *relajiento* the character of a tragic hero whose best offense is an unintelligible joke. But Portilla does not think that the *relajiento/a* is an underdog or a tragic hero. Rather, Portilla describes the subjectivity of the *relajiento/a* as diluted and fragmented, one which is weakened by marginality and expresses itself in frail attempts to disrupt power.

Notwitstanding Taylor's misunderstanding of Portilla's characterization of the *relajiento*, I see the point as attributing some power to the individual who intitiates or brings about *relajo*. The *relajiento's* only offense is not an obscure joke that some get and some do not; but neither is the disruption of seriousness meaningless and infertile. That is, we cannot call this diluted subjectivity a negation of meaningful human being. Taylor is right in one respect: as infertile as it may be, *relajo* is an act of resistance to power. We could, anachronistically, say that *relajo* is a perfectly crafted expression of "postmodernity," if we define this with Lyotard as "an incredulity toward metanarratives" (Lyotard 1987, 74), that is, metanarratives which take the form of established values and value schemes. Portilla describes the resistance represented by *relajo* as a "refusal" to "engage in behavior which is expected of me" [38]. But to refuse the metanarrative is to assert myself, to "take a stand," so my refusal to participate asserts my humanity and validates the processes of self-fashioning that I have chosen to shape the various senses of subjecthood to which I may feel entitled.

Taylor, and with her the common view, also fails to grasp Portilla on the notion of *relajo* itself. Taylor says that *relajo* is "an act of spontaneous disruption" (Taylor 2003, 129). But the acts of refusal and assertion, interruption and provocation, are rather reflexive acts undertaken by an agent who refuses to participate in the construction of his or her own subjectivity, who *suspends* subjectivity in that act. This does not mean that the individual premeditates and lays out the process of disruption before she arrives at a situation; but neither does it mean that the *relajiento/a* just interrupts or displaces, as if instinctually like a frightened animal or a person suffering a neuropsychiatric disorder (e.g., Tourette Syndrome). While *relajo* is not premeditated, it is *mediated*. It does not simply erupt out of nowhere, as it were. Language, culture, habit, history, and trauma, for example, mediate the appearance of that initial act that will become *relajo*. Hence, the person who initiates it comes to the situation prepared, if the opportunity arises, to disrupt or interrupt it. Whether or not this agenda has been fully worked out, the person does not arrive on the scene ready and willing to realize its value(s), as would a serious person. Put differently, the *relajiento* does not come to the symposium convinced that he will listen to the speakers and partake, intelligently, in the discussion. His or her presence already represents the *possibility* of *relajo*. Sure, the inopportune joke or the sudden laugh that initiates the stream of vulgarity that materializes into *relajo* may seem as though it *came from nowhere*, but this seeming hides a *will to relajo* that is not a nonwill. What appears as the "spontaneity" of *relajo* is merely its unexpectedness in a social setting that was previously held together by expectations and the scaffolding of some value or another. *Relajo* is thus mediated. As infertile as it is for Portilla, he insists that *relajo* "is not an originary or direct act, but derived and reflexive" [20], hence, it is mediated. Later he says: "*Relajo* is a self-destructive movement. It is an attitude that is precisely contrary to the *normal, spontaneous* attitude of human beings confronted with values when those values act upon consciousness like a guide for self-constitution" [39; emphasis added]. Put differently, self-destruction is a process, mediated by refusals themselves mediated by world-views and historical conditions of which I might not be fully conscious. Again, *relajo* is not spontaneous.[3]

Despite its infertility, temporal fragmentation, and mediations, the act of *relajo* validates one's human being in virtue of the fact that it is a kind of direct and immediate *affirmation*—a negative affirmation, but an affirmation nonetheless. It is a *standing out* (*existere*) in the world, or a standing against. As a refusal to participate, it is to take a stand against taking a stand. It is an affirmation of one's primordial being-there. It is to take a stand on the moment and say "no" to what is demanding the right of realization. Portilla, who says that the *relajo*-individual "lose[s] the guide of affirmation and become[s] blind to value" [41] nonetheless describes this individual as a force to be reckoned with: "Their mere presence is a foreshadowing of the dissolution of any possible seriousness. Their mere appearance unleashes a light breeze of smiles and the atmosphere is transformed into a condescending expectation of a shower of jokes that will dissolve the seriousness of all topics, reducing them, literally, to nothing. In the colloquial language of Mexico City, this type of individual is designated with a horrible yet adequate word: This individual is a 'relajiento'" [39]. The picture here is of a strong figure whose approach is welcome, yet feared. One who provokes anxiety and expectation. The *relajiento*, in fact, *creates a future* by merely being somewhere: everyone is *waiting* for the *relajo* "to arrive." Everyone waits for the chaos that is sure to ensue. Of course, what transpires is what is expected (the future "arrives"): the suspension of value and the release of commitments. Those present fall into the scene without resistance and perpetuate it by contributing to its demise. But, even as unproductive as it is, it is a spectacle, and it is created by an individual who is, according to Portilla, a nonsubject. The regret is, however, that were this strong figure to hold on to value and commitment, Mexico's future would be secured, and modernity would, at last, claim a hard-won victory in Latin America. Portilla's foregone conclusion is that the *relajienta/o* is wasting her talents.

Failing to place the *Fenomenología* in its proper (Latin American) context, allows one to miss something obvious about it, namely, that it might be a description of the way in which colonized peoples rebel against systems of social control that have existed since the conquest. Seen in this context, seriousness (in either sense described by Portilla) proves to be the most corrosive form of obedience (to values), leading, ultimately, to what Samuel Ramos called an "inferiority complex" (Ramos 1962). According to Ramos, one of the main causes of this inferiority complex is an "exalted idea of the self" held by the colonized coupled with an inability to realize this idea (or *ideal*) (Ramos 1962, 8). This inability to fully live up to an ideal, or to fully *go along with* the value, results in a sense of inferiority and resentment (Ramos 1962, 103). Seriousness can thus be characterized as the attempt to *fully live up to* ideals imposed, so to speak, from the outside, to go along with what the dominant discourse proposes as valuable, and thus to perpetuate an oppressive self-interpretation; thus, negatively put, to be serious is to willingly, or dogmatically, uphold an established interpretative scheme which ultimately distorts an individual's sense of self and circumstance.

A Critic of Modernity

Highlighting the above presuppositions has the obvious consequence that it lets us see Portilla as a *critic* of modernity, where modernity is "associated with (1) a certain set of attitudes towards the world, the idea of the world as open to transformation by human intervention;

(2) a complex of economic institutions, especially industrial production and a market economy; (3) . . . a complex of institutions—which unlike any preceding culture lives in the future rather than the past" (Giddens 1988, 94). The tell-tale signs that Portilla's target of criticism is modernity, rather than a simple everyday behavior witnessed in modern Mexican life, are the various ways in which he criticizes the *relajiento* as unproductive, lacking a future, and oppressed by her own behaviors. "Modernity" is a consumer-driven, future-oriented, existential-political condition grounded in market capitalism and industrial production, where what's important is *productivity*, *efficiency*, and *individual freedom*. If modernity has given rise to the *relajiento*, then maybe there is something wrong with modernity.

This, of course, is a possibility that Portilla could not have considered: the subjectivity of the *relajiento*, as a nonsubjectivity, or better yet, a *fragmented* subjectivity is perfectly in line with twenty-firstcentury postcolonial, postmodern, or post-911 schizophrenia. In other words, his is not only a criticism of modernity, but it is also a prediction of its failure. Portilla does not suggest that the *relajiento* is especially capable of navigating the labyrinths of our post-911 world, as we still need commitment and seriousness to accomplish that task; what he suggests, rather, is that the *relajiento* is an expression of that world and those anxieties, and she can survive the angst and terror through acts of suspension which might, possibly, as for the ancient skeptics, bring *ataraxia*, or tranquility.[4]

In the event of *relajo*, the individual suspends the moment of commitment. It is this time-out-of-time that the construction of subjectivity through loyalties and commitments is itself suspended. The suspension of subjectivity here signifies the possibility for other identifications prohibited by the situation which the *relajo* event has infiltrated. In other words, the *relajo* event offers the possibility to postpone subjective constitution for a future time. *Relajo* might be death, but death only of the demand to be who one is *expected* to be at a particular time. The future is suspended, but only in the form of a suspension of the future as expectancy. It is to withhold judgment on what may come next, and, as such, a way to take in reality as it really is, without the mediation of values and their demands.

The demands of our modern information age—its values and duties—are not absolute. It is expected that we will switch the channel when a show on television loses its appeal; we are expected to navigate the internet, aimlessly at times, in search of our pleasures, and to continue navigating even after we find what pleases us; we are expected to be unfaithful to our product "brands"—modern advertising depends on our infidelity. We are expected to change our minds on every commitment, from the most trivial (our Facebook profiles) to the most serious (our spouses). Consequently, the time of the *relajo*-event is a time for suspension of all commitments, a time to withdraw into the chaos of the moment, and allow ourselves a future time for commitment. After all, commitments will always have to be made—except of course, in death or *relajo*.

These considerations raise a further, yet perhaps the most important, question: considered as a human social phenomenon, is the fragmented subjectivity, or the nonsubjectivity, of the *relajiento* the exception or the rule? Again, the idea here is that *relajo* is not a social phenomenon limited to the Mexican experience, but a social phenomenon manifested everywhere, but oftentimes lacking a name. As Zirión tells us in his magnificent *Historia*, "Portilla does not commit the stupid mistake [*torpeza fácil*] of saying that his object of study is [anything other than] a way of being human" (Zirión 2004, 302). This means that *relajo* and its processes are generalizable to the modern world. If so, then today we may find *relajo* manifested in every culture of the planet, where suspending seriousness might be the most appropriate way to cope with the speed and availability of information, the persistent and irrational demands of technology, and the overabundance of values that all of this creates. Hence, the answer to this, most important question, is that *relajo*, understood as a suspension of serious commitment to value and duty, *is the rule*, not the exception (in our times as it was in Portilla's).

Portilla was a critic of modernity—in the form in which he found it and in the course he saw it take. It is clear that he, like his Latin American counterparts, desired the promise of modernity: the fulfillment of the ideal of modernization, tied as it is to the ideal of subjects as self-creating and world making. But what he found, instead, was *relajo*—*relajo* as the reflection of what modernity had become, a space-time of fragmented, uncommitted, irresponsible nonsubjects for whom world making was not as important as rejecting the demands of value through disruption and interruption. A future for modernity was made impossible.

In this sense, Portilla is the most prescient and realistic philosopher Mexico, and Latin America, has produced. The failures of modernity are captured in his frustrated descriptions and desperate appeals for overcoming. His prophetic vision is that we will all become marginal, fragmented, and victimized by *relajo*, in whatever form it comes and whatever name it bears, whether ushered in by strong personalities which interrupt lectures or forced by the constant bombardment of mass media messages in emails and television screens. The solution is Socratic seriousness. But I doubt that Portilla *seriously* considered the possibility that we (Mexicans or not) would ever achieve such discipline.

Concluding Remarks: Portilla and Mexican Philosophy

We are brought to a point in which we must recognize a certain *difference* between Portilla and the tradition in which he situates himself. For instance, we have to recall that Husserl's phenomenology, Heidegger's ontology, and Scheler's axiology are responses to the *crisis of European culture* to which most European thinkers (e.g., Oswald Spengler, José Ortega y Gasset, Edmund Husserl, to name but a few) were responding at the time. It would be a mistake to say that Portilla was, either when he emerges as a recognizable figure in Mexican thought in the late 1940s or when he wrote his *Fenomenología del relajo* (published posthumously in 1966), responding to a European crisis. What Portilla was responding to, what he was addressing, was a Mexican problem. However, Portilla's address has consequences to that European crisis, and more generally, to the crisis of modernity which has gripped the globe. Portilla's *Fenomenología* aims to draw attention to that crisis, one represented by the proliferation of *relajo* as a resistance to a general condition of "seriousness" toward values, a condition which is historical and, thus, rooted in centuries of exploitation, alienation, and value-imperialism (the forcing of values by imperialistic means). The crisis continues today, exacerbated by demands placed on our liberty by technology, social networks, and the mass media. To break the bonds of seriousness is to break the bonds of an oppressive system of values that are, in the long run, inevitable and unbeatable. Seen in this way, *relajo* is thus truly a "behavior of dissidence," or, we can say, the conduct of dissidents.

But the dissidents are fragmented, fragile, and marginal. Portilla points to their impotence. However, *relajo*, while an expression of impotence, is simultaneously an expression of power—the power to defy and suspend the seriousness of culture, a tradition, or a project. This power to resist totalization arises, I would like to suggest, from a will that longs to defy and deride values it has internalized as oppressive and demeaning. In Mexico, or elsewhere on the fringes of modernity, these would be the colonial values which represent an oppressor who, through a history of violence and paternalism, has nurtured a culture of passivity and inferiority.

As a *suspension* of seriousness in the act of detraction from otherwise established versions of the Good Life, *relajo* is an act of *resistance*. As an act of resistance before the status quo, *relajo* is an act of *defiance*. However, Portilla insists that this liberatory aspect is only an *appearance*. It so appears that *relajo*—as an act of suspension and value inversion—is a manifestation of human freedom; it appears in the realm of what the human being *can do*. But it is an expression of *negative* freedom—one in which all is fair, and irresponsibility is the rule. But one must be held responsible for *relajo*. What exactly is one responsible for? If *relajo* is a manifestation of a will to nothing, then the answer is straightforward: nothing. Consequently, Portilla, the humanist, is critical of *relajo*, since this attitude signals the end of responsibility *for* value. He writes: "Indeed, the degradation of value is something threatening. The *fact* of the degradation of value opens up the horizon of a possible universal degradation of all values and even of the absolute extinction of value" [47]. The insinuation here is that a culture in which there is a "universal degradation of all values" will be a value-less culture, a lost culture.

But before we end this investigation, one more presupposition must be considered. In the now classic *The Cage of Melancholy*, Roger Bartra suggests (indirectly through his critique of the philosophy of "lo mexicano") that "relajo," as conceived by Mexican philosophers, that is, Portilla, is a "myth" created to perpetuate the oppression of Mexicans by the intellectual elite (Bartra 1987; Sáenz 1999). *Relajo*, in Bartra's structuralist critique, could be a concept developed to name a way of being that the superior moralities deemed inferior but desirable for the inferior classes; the intellectual elite then legitimize the concept in the process of naming it. In other words, Portilla's naming of *relajo* further marginalizes Mexicans.

The trouble with Bartra's critique is that it is a particularization that is overly focused on a critique of Mexican intellectual elitism and thus remains "ambiguous" in its understanding of the texts it is critiquing (as pointed out in Sáenz 1999, 152–63). Bartra, that is, cannot get beyond the structuralist critique to appreciate the significance of the philosophical effort he criticizes. But this sort of criticism also overlooks the fact that Portilla is naming a phenomenon of *human life*, which just happens to have a name in Mexico—a name, or a "code" (Barthes 1970), given to the phenomenon not by the intellectual elite, but by the common people. This is why I claim that Portilla is a critic of modernity, and not just a critic of a specifically "Mexican" behavior.

After all is said and done, the normative scrutiny to which Portilla subjects *relajo* is ultimately mired in the specifically Western prejudice that seriousness is the way to truth and progress. In the end, Portilla contrasts *relajo* to irony via an appeal to Socrates whom he describes as one who labored for truth from the depths of seriousness and responsibility. He goes on to conclude that because Socrates's negations where ironic and not meant to suspend seriousness, then *relajo* is "infertile." The charge of infertility is consistent with the view that *relajo* is an expression of a will to nothingness. But this same charge also holds a more stubborn commitment, namely, that the progress of a people is tied to a certain view of rationality and responsibility which is particularly *Eurocentric*. Following the Socratic example, to be serious is to be responsible. But perhaps Portilla missed Ortega's remark that "we owe innumerable things to the Greeks, but they have put chains on us, too" (Ortega 1962, 30). On the cusp of breaking through the Western paradigm and to an idea which we could call "postcolonial," Portilla flinched at the thought that perhaps *relajo* was a particularly anti-Western form of liberation, a *reaction* to colonial seriousness. He opted for the traditional prejudice favoring the wisdom of Western rationality.

But perhaps I am just reading too much into his hesitation. Nevertheless, if we attend just to the phenomenological *givenness* of *relajo*, in which this behavior is given *as* defiance and resistance, then we see that Portilla does fail to see that the imputation that *relajo* breeds infertility and irresponsibly is itself an *extra thought*, perhaps one arising from commitments to literary and philosophical values to which he feels himself responsible. My suggestion, of course, is that Portilla's hesitancy might also indicate something more seductive, namely, that *relajo* as an act of resistance and defiance is necessary in order to usher in an age beyond seriousness, one in which options are always open and nonconformity is the norm—or perhaps that that age is already here, and we are living it.

Appendix

Jorge Portilla, *Fenomenología del relajo*

Translated by Eleanor Marsh and Carlos Alberto Sánchez

What follows is a translation of Jorge Portilla's *Fenomenología del relajo*, first published by Ediciones ERA in 1966. The following translation based on the 1984 Biblioteca Joven edition, *Fenomenología del relajo y otros ensayos*. Méxíco D.F.: Fondo de Cultura Economica. Carretera Picacho-Ajusco 227, C.P. 14738, México D.F. This Edition consists of 750 copies.

I thank my co-translator, Eleanor Marsh, for her tireless efforts. I also thank the Fondo de Cultura Económica for permission to publish this essay.

PHENOMENOLOGY OF *RELAJO*

Translated by Eleanor Marsh and Carlos Alberto Sánchez

Introduction *[13]*[1]

The present essay is an attempt to understand a fact that all of us are familiar with in our everyday lives. It involves understanding [the phenomenon of] *el relajo*, that form of repeated and sometimes loud collective mockery that emerges sporadically in the daily life of our country [Mexico].

123

But why should we think precisely about this subject? It seems that approaching it implies a lack of seriousness. Talking about *relajo* seems like something frivolous, especially in these times in which the human situation[2] has acquired such seriousness that it is resistant to even the most subtle humor.

Nevertheless, no subject is too insignificant for reason, and this is not because thought itself is something that conveys its own seriousness to any subject but rather because of deeper causes. Within the entire realm of reality, there is nothing that can be considered absolutely isolated and lacking in meaning. Nothing is completely outside the web of meanings that links things to each other, uniting them into an intelligible world. From the pack of cigarettes that sits on my desk there emerges, like a spider's web, a system of relationships that transports me on the one hand to the totality of the physical universe and on the other to the human world of labor, industry, and science. Human labor, the science of nature, and the sciences of the spirit are all present in its humble presence. My imagination can lead me, with the stimulus of its presence and with no need for reflection to evoke the struggle between capital and labor or between imperial powers and colonial peoples; it can serve as an example to distinguish between contingent being and necessary being, between being and entity, and so on.

In the same way, a form of consciousness so incidental and transitory as mockery or laughter can serve as a key to understanding essential characteristics of the human condition or to penetrate the spiritual structure of a people; because of the spontaneity and the lack of [14] reflection that usually accompany it, it can do this even better than other, more respectable forms of consciousness such as politics and art.

But none of this can be, or is, the reason that led me to fix my gaze on the subject of this essay. My intention is not, of course, to describe neutrally and objectively a form of expression of the [Mexican] national character in the way an entomologist studies the life of insects, among other reasons, because people are not insects, although some may behave as if others were.

The spirit of a people (allow me to use this expression for lack of a better one) is not something that is there, once and for all, like a stone. It is the whole of forms and styles adopted within time by the history of a freedom marching toward its liberation; and if in the course of this liberation, one finds permanent configurations of [national] character, it does not mean that these cannot be affected by the flow of the nation's life, to the point of disappearing completely or of changing their meaning.

In this way, the purpose of this work is not analogous to that of a physician who offers a diagnosis, but rather to that of a person who begins a dialogue. It is an attempt to bring to full consciousness an aspect of Mexican morality on which I don't attempt, by any means, to say the last word. Other writers in the past have made valuable contributions to this issue, and others in the future will undoubtedly say wiser and more correct things [about it], if they condescend to take seriously subjects that are not that serious. Any work directed toward attaining self-consciousness and clarity is not a solitary endeavor; it is (in a way that I don't quite see very clearly yet) a collective venture that can only be achieved through dialogue.

Indeed, it [the search for self-consciousness and clarity] can only be achieved individually and in the state of withdrawn concentration on work,[3] but in a dialogic state of concentration that points toward communication and in which thought can find an echo, and with it, its own true path: the path that advances toward a community.

In light of these ideas, allow me to situate autobiographically the origin of this research, which on the surface could only precariously aspire to another type of justification: its purpose is simply to gain—for myself and for those who may find it useful—the greatest possible clarity regarding the subject.

I belong to a generation whose best representatives lived for many years in an environment of the most unbearable [15] and loud irresponsibility that could be imagined; in spite of this, I unfalteringly consider them the best representatives of that generation. Some of them were men of talent, others of a noble and generous character; all of them seemed absolutely incapable of resisting any occasion for releasing a stream of coarse humor that, once flowing, became uncontrollable and continuously thwarted the emergence of their better qualities. It was as if they were afraid of their own excellence and as if they felt obligated to forbid its manifestation. They would only bring their excellence out when in conversation with a friend or when in a state of inebriation. I almost never witnessed them taking anything with real seriousness, even less so, their own capabilities and their own destiny. They were—I can see it clearly now—a Nietzschian generation *avant la lettre* that, in the midst of perpetual laughter, lived dangerously, devoted in actual fact to a slow process of self-destruction.

I find it a bit uncomfortable to add—due to the suspicions of romantic imagery that this could raise—that many of the members of this generation died tragically, or disappeared, swallowed up by the most extravagant varieties of vice.

On the other hand, I confess that I would not be able to establish a necessary or clearly visible link between these facts. In any case, I am trying to understand something that caught my attention more and more, as the frustration suffered by those who exhibited it so insistently before my eyes became evident to me.

An awareness of the facts themselves was already pointing toward a possible philosophy of *relajo*, no matter how funny this expression might sound.

I believed that it was worth it to examine this issue, not so much because of a Pharisee-like desire to warn youth of the dangers of the lack of seriousness, but rather because of the desire to understand—to the limits of my means—an issue that is alive and well in our community and—so to speak—to take philosophy out into the street (which is its natural place) by stripping it as much as possible of the "technical" shell that sometimes conceals it.

But the aspiration toward clarity is not simply a subjective aspiration based on personal experience. Clarity is an obligation for both the philosopher and the nonphilosopher, for the intellectual and for the *other*, as Ortega says. But for the philosopher, it is a double obligation.

On the one hand, to the degree that the philosopher is interested [16] in the most universal and traditional subjects of metaphysics, clarity means a clear consciousness of the historical condition of philosophizing, of the incidences of the factual, of social class, of nationality, of character, and so on, on thought. On the other hand, clarity is the very task of the philosopher, if one considers philosophy a specific function of the culture of a community. From this point of view, philosophy has the function of promoting reason in a specific society, of clearly putting before the collective consciousness the ultimate base of its thinking, of its feeling, and of its acting.

Philosophy, to the extent that it is a "logos" on humankind, performs an educating and a liberating function. Through it, what is concealed

and tacit becomes present and explicit, and something can be transformed by its enlightening action. A person is not exactly equivalent to
him- or herself before and after being understood. The person cannot be
[the same], because the power of the word has transformed him or her.
I cannot be the same person before and after knowing that, in a sense,
the designation "petit bourgeois" applies to me. The word situates me;
it creates me like a "fiat" pronounced by others which makes me emerge
before myself with a new appearance that I barely recognize but that I
cannot reject outright either.

But, just as the word integrates me into a whole that overwhelms
and alienates me, it can also put me at that ideal distance from myself
that is freedom, or at least one of the conditions of freedom. It allows me
to adopt different attitudes in relation to myself, and it hands me over
to my own decision: it allows me to choose, with full consciousness, a
behavior that is not necessarily deducible from the situation in which I
find myself. The word can pull me out of the magma of the situation and
allow me to act in a manner contrary to the objective currents of obligation that flow from it. In a direction opposite to that of psychological habit, tradition, class interest, and so on, the truth sets me free, and
perhaps the ultimate sense of all authentic philosophy is this liberating
operation of "logos" and not the creation of a framework of concepts
as a mirror of reality.

In Mexico, nothing seems more necessary than this liberating action
of "logos." In Mexico, where the dominant spiritual attitude seems to
be a reflection on the sense of our own history within the framework
of universal history, [17] since, granted that a large part of what is currently being written here [in Mexico] points tacitly in this direction,
not little of it ends up being a mysticism of the land analogous to the
emotional backdrop of a certain sector of our film industry, coarse self-
complimenting, or a confused self-denigration.

However, the honest will for self-understanding cannot remain content with an unfurling of more or less rational justifications of a feeling
of self-satisfaction or self-disgust, although it might never reach total
completeness in this respect.

Reflection directed toward the unequivocal establishment of being
itself necessarily fails. The individual, as such, is ineffable, and the only
path to individual knowledge is universal knowledge. Just as the structures of the self are not reachable by direct intuition, it is probable that
the essential structures of a national spirit are not either. Just as I cannot

see my "self" in a direct way in reflection, and I am only capable of looking at it with stolen glances and out of the corner of my eye, in contemplating my states and actions, a national character is accessible to me
only with the same marginality when I examine some specific aspect of
that character or of the historical actions that marked its birth. I cannot
see "Frenchness" in a pure state as I see these trees on the other side of
the street, but I can see it sideways, as a style, as an atmosphere that is
not directly graspable, found in the characters and actions of a novel, in
a treatise on civil law, or in the work of a philosopher.

I. PHENOMENOLOGICAL DESCRIPTION OF *RELAJO*

Notes for a Definition

In Mexico, what is designated with the term *relajo* is not, obviously, a
thing but rather a behavior. More than a noun, one can say it is a verb,
since the expression denotes the unitary sense of a complex behavior, of
an act or a set of acts performed by a subject, to which the subject itself
grants a nonexplicit yet precise meaning.

I say "sense of a behavior" and not simply [18] "a behavior" because
behavior—if considered a mere set of acts abstracted from its sense, precisely "lacks sense." A series of actions such as gestures, bodily attitudes,
words, laughter, or unarticulated sounds does not mean anything if it
is abstracted from its sense. But there is no totally insignificant human
action. Every action is composed of both physical movements and the
meaning that holds together these movements from the inside. The error
of behaviorism is exactly not conceiving the meaning of a behavior as
a constituent part of that behavior, to suppose that the meaning of a
behavior can be separated from it without radically altering the behavior, or to consider the sense of the behavior an extrinsic factor or as
supervening within the group of acts that manifests that sense.

A behavior is understood through its sense. What is being referred
to when [a behavior] is named is exactly that which "gives sense to it"
and not a merely imagined series of movements only thinkable of in the
abstract, outside of their sense.

The sense or meaning of *relajo* is the suspension of seriousness, that
is to say, suspending or annihilating a subject's adherence to a value
proposed to his or her freedom. It is not simply to provoke laughter

or, simply, to laugh, no matter that such a suspension often—although not necessarily—presents itself as a stimulus for laughter. *Relajo* has a certain relationship with the comic, but it is not the comic alone; there are comic situations that do not involve *relajo*. The comic, whose precise relationship with *relajo* we will attempt to determine later, is not an essential characteristic of this phenomenon but rather, at most, something concomitant and secondary [to *relajo*].

All value, when grasped, appears surrounded by an aura of demands, endowed with a certain weight and with certain gravity that brings it from its pure ideality toward the world of reality. The value solicits its realization. The mere grasping of the value carries with it the fulfillment of that demand, of that call to its own realization in the world; and in order for this demand—which appears in the objective realm of the lived experiences of the value—to be realized, the subject, in turn, performs an act, a movement of loyalty [to the value] that is a kind of "yes," like an affirmative response. This is the first outline of what, when grasped reflexively, we call "duty." This answer, this "yes" that corresponds—by means of the subjective aspect [19] of the grasping of the value—to the objective demand with which it presents itself, is an intimate movement of loyalty and commitment. This is seriousness.

When, in an immediate and direct (nonreflexive) way, I pronounce that "yes" inside myself, when I give an adequate response to the demand for actualization inherent to the value, I tacitly commit myself to a behavior, I mortgage my future behavior, making it agree beforehand with that demand: I take the value seriously. Seriousness is the intimate and deep commitment to which I make a pledge with myself in order to maintain a value within existence.

From now on it is necessary to distinguish between what I call seriousness and what is known, especially in recent French philosophical literature as "spirit of seriousness," with which I will deal later on. The spirit of seriousness is pure gesticulation, an exaggerated exteriorization that tends more toward showing one's own excellence and toward underscoring one's own importance than toward the realization of the value. The spirit of seriousness is reflexive; seriousness is pure spontaneity; the former projects outward, while the latter is "intimate"; the former is a behavior toward others;[4] in [the case of] genuine seriousness, I am alone with myself before the value.

The sense of *relajo* is precisely to frustrate the effectiveness of this spontaneous response that accompanies the grasping of the value. *Relajo* suspends seriousness; that is to say, it cancels the normal response to the value, freeing me from the commitment to its realization.

The behavior whose sense is designated by the term *relajo* consists of three discernible moments in abstraction. In the unity of a single act, these three meet: in the first place, there is a displacement of attention; second, the adoption of a position in which the subject positions him- or herself in lack of solidarity with the proposed value; and finally, an action in the proper sense of the word that consists of outward manifestations of gesture or word that constitute an invitation to others to participate with me in this lack of solidarity.

There is, in fact, in the first place, a displacement of the subject's attention that moves from the value being offered for his or her acceptance either toward the "external," purely factual circumstances in which the value appears or toward something completely alien to the circumstance itself. A [20] case in which this displacement is more clearly visible is that of the extemporaneous comment that interrupts a ceremony or a performance to call attention to some physical characteristic of those taking part in it. The displacement of attention already begins to appear on the background of an expressed negation of the corresponding value, but it is not yet negation itself. This does not prevent the pure displacement of attention from being essential to this phenomenon. *Relajo*, in reality, always implies the characteristic of "digression": it is always a certain "deviation from something." It is not an originary and direct act but rather one that is derived and reflexive. It requires an occasion, which is to say, the appearance of a value that offers itself to the subject's freedom and from which a dissent can begin. In this way, the displacement of attention is like the axis around which the entire moral meaning of *relajo* revolves: it is the basis of all the meanings that constitute this behavior.

However, the displacement of attention does not imply an "effort of attention" in the common sense of those words. It is only a change in the intentional object of consciousness and not a deliberate act in which the subject will "concentrate" on a new object. The ray of attention is likewise displaced when, with a distracted gaze, I look at things around me without "paying attention" to any particular thing: the perceptive consciousness slides from one [thing] to another without any mediation whatsoever by the voluntary purpose of exploring any of them "attentively." In this way, attention here simply means the directing of intentionality toward an object and not "attention effort" in a psychological sense.

Second, an intimate act of negation is a constituent component of *relajo*. This is not a direct negation of the *value* but rather of the essential link that unites the subject to the value. It is an act of lack of solidarity[5] with the value and with the community that realizes the value. In this act, the subject is defined as a nonparticipant in the venture tending toward the incorporation or realization of the value. The subject rejects the behavior that would allow the unfurling of the value within reality.

It is evident that this type of negation implies an ambiguous appreciation of the value. In other words, the subject—in operating within his or her own situation in relation to the value—does not leave the value totally [21] untouched. The negation of the value can be a negation of the value as such, the negation [of the idea that] the proposed value is actually valuable, the negation of the proposed value as inferior or not pertinent relative to a superior value, and finally, it could also happen that the value simply ends up in parentheses.[6] In this case, the value ends up out of play, neutralized in the indifference of a subject that is limited to evading the commitment in such a way that one cannot speak of an appreciation of the value as such. In any case, what is essential is not the implicit appreciation of the attitude of *relajo*, which could manifest itself in some other way. What is essential is the intimate decision to not make a commitment regarding the demand that flows from the present value.

Finally, constitutive of the essence of *relajo* is the ability to manifest itself in actions of the most varied nature. These can range from the most imperceptible facial expression to the formulation of perfectly coherent and rational positions [regarding the value]. In the middle of this range there are bodily attitudes, words, shouts, noises, and so on, that imply a call to others to adopt the negation of the proposed value. This characteristic constitutes an action per se, an external act that leaves a mark on the surrounding world, in contrast with the "intimate" nature of the two previous ones.

However, it is necessary to underscore the concrete and unified character of *relajo*. From the demands imposed by the process of description—which must go step by step—one should not infer that *first* there is displacement of attention, *then* the subject deliberately decides to abstain from commitment when faced with the value, and *finally*, as a last chronological step, the subject comes to express his or her decision externally.

Gestural or verbal externalization *is* at the same time a displacement of attention and *is* also the intimate decision to not participate in behavior that will support the value, in the way that the qualities of a thing *are* the thing itself to perception. The acts that tend to provoke the transformation of a serious situation into *relajo*[7] necessarily imply that adoption of a position [regarding the value] and that lack of attention. Also, this does not mean that when reflecting on this phenomenon we discover in another subject an interiority that is concealed to us [22] and evident to him or her and that we will suspect that lack of attention and disassociation from commitment as individual acts that are "lodged" in that subject's psyche. The external acts themselves, because they are meaningful, point back in retrospect, in an essential manner, to those "internal" movements. In other words, the displacement of attention and the self-positioning engaged in by the subject are not reflexive or deliberate actions, but simply unities of sense that emerge parallel to the corresponding acts of behavior and that make themselves visible on the subjects' intentional horizon.[8]

In acts of *relajo*, the value appears to the subject of *relajo* as a "value to be put out of play by the action itself." *Relajo* is an action in the world and not an introspection in which the subject takes as an object his or her own states or decisions.

The characteristic of "action," essential to *relajo*, points back in turn to another essential element: *relajo* can only present itself in a horizon of community.

The acts that contribute to constituting *relajo* are acts that presuppose an immediate communicative intention. If *relajo* is an attitude toward a value, it is also, in parallel fashion, an attitude that indirectly alludes to "others" [23].

It is true that all human activity takes place in this horizon of community. The artist that works in the solitude of her workshop, isolated from any form of company, when facing the material transformed with her work, is referenced in a mediating manner to all the possible viewers of that work. Even the solitary person who endures or searches for solitude in isolation is engaging in nothing other than a deficient mode of "being with others," which is a constitutive dimension of the human condition. But in "*relajo*," this reference to others appears in an immediate manner, so direct, almost as in a conversation or in a greeting. *Relajo* is an invocation to others present. Concurrent with the negative intentionality toward the value, there emerges a "lateral" intentionality toward others, which is as necessary as the former to constitute the essence of the phenomenon of *relajo*.

Relajo in solitude is unthinkable, or, I should say, unimaginable. Following the guiding thread of the expression "echar *relajo*" [literally, *echar relajo*

"to throw *relajo*],[9] it can be said that in solitude, there is "nowhere" to "throw" it. The existential space in which *relajo* is created [literally "thrown"] is limited by the community of those present. There is a double intentionality in *relajo*: It is constituted both by my lack of solidarity [with a value] and by my intent to involve others in this lack of solidarity, which creates a common environment of detachment before the value.

The invocation to others is not, we insist, something accidental, but rather an essential constituent of *relajo* that is concomitant with all the other characteristics. The subject of *relajo* does not first do the "intimate" actions previously described to attempt afterwards to catalyze his or her own attitude in other people by means of gestures or words. To the contrary: gesticulation, attitudes, and words *are* at the same time both those internal movements and this invitation. With his or her own action, the active subject creates a certain void around the person or situation imbued with the value, and thus, he or she prevents the value from fully acquiring substance in reality. That being said, the void is not created only in the pure subjectivity of whoever promotes it; it is not a localized void, but rather it extends throughout an environment: the intersubjectivity of those present.

Thus, it is equally unimaginable for *relajo* to emerge between two people. Within a dialogue, the negation of one of the subjects in relation to the other can very well exist in a thousand different forms such as contradiction, lack of attention, lack of comprehension, or misunderstanding. But this negation will never be able to assume the form of *relajo*, precisely because in this case, that dimension of depth, that quasispace in which *relajo* [24] can proliferate like parasitic vegetation, is lacking. In the case of a dialogue, the nonsolidarity of one of the speakers with the other could lead to a weakening of the communication relationship and, at the extreme, to the suspension of the dialogue itself, but not to *relajo*.

To the previous characteristics it is necessary to add that of reiteration, which is derived from the very sense of the behavior of *relajo* and which refers directly to the active nature of this phenomenon. *Relajo* is a reiterated action. A single joke that, for example, interrupts the speech delivered by a speaker is not enough to transform the interruption into *relajo*. The suspensive interruption of seriousness must be repeated indefinitely whether or not the agent [of *relajo*] achieves his or her purpose. It is necessary for the interrupting gesture or word to repeat continuously until the dizzying thrill of complicity in negation takes over the *disruptive*

group which is the most paradoxical of all communities: the community of noncommunicators, as a negative backdrop that makes the activity of the value's agent impossible or useless.

Nevertheless, in order for there to be "a *relajo*" it is not necessary for this contagion to actually take place. For the behavior [called *relajo*] to be outlined in its essential characteristics, it is enough for an individual to exhibit the repeated action that signifies an ambiguous negation of a value through a lack of solidarity [with it]. The characteristic of repetition, on the other hand, highlights its essential character when examined in light of the relationship between pure value and the behaviors tending toward its realization.

Indeed, the value always presents itself as something to be realized [made real]. It offers itself to my freedom, calling on my support in order to enter into existence. A single act is not enough to eliminate or to sufficiently reduce this invocation. When an act goes from my negation to the required behavior, the value's call appears again. A new act of suspension [of seriousness] can show once again the possibility of neglecting the value, but immediately after, the value's demand will reappear, and so on, until my negation is supported by other negations that establish a continuity of negations with no gaps. In this way, others' solidarity with my lack of solidarity [with the value] creates an atmosphere in which the realization of the value is definitely thwarted [25].

The relationship of the value, in its pure ideality, to reality also makes understandable the noisy character of certain forms of *relajo*, although noise is not essential to it. Silence is the most adequate environment for the manifestation of certain values, and perhaps to the extent that the value is of a higher level, silence is, in parallel fashion, an indispensable condition for its appearance. Such is the case, for example, of the careful search for a truth in meditation, not to say of the higher forms of the emergence of the sacred. "The sound and the fury" are perhaps the way par excellence of thinking a world that is absolutely not valuable.

In the noisy *relajo* that invades the field of emergence of the value, there is something akin to a flood that drowns the value itself and muddies the atmosphere in which it would reveal itself. Like a barrier, noise interferes between the value and the consciousnesses of those called to support it; it obstructs the pathways of behaviors directed toward this end and makes it impossible.

Gibberish floods the human quasispace through which the value was to insert itself into reality and expels it from this realm; it leaves it "outside," in its neglected pure ideality. Once [this process] is initiated, it is necessary to prevent—by any means necessary—the return of silence, in which the value could once again shine like the sun after a rain storm, appealing to our generosity.

The essential characteristic of repetition and the accidental one of the increasing noise, that raising of voices and disordering of gestures that so often accompany it, become understandable in light of the essence itself of *relajo* that we have tried to specify so far.

To summarize, *relajo* can be defined as the suspension of seriousness toward a value proposed to a group of people. This suspension is performed by an individual who is trying to make others commit to it by means of repeated acts with which he or she expresses his or her own rejection of the behavior required by the value. With this, the behavior regulated by the corresponding value is substituted with an atmosphere of disorder in which the realization of the value is impossible. By extension, *relajo* is a term also applied to the real situation provoked by the intentionality that has been described: "achieved" *relajo*, the state of things produced by an individual that has achieved his or her purpose of making the incorporation of the value [26] impossible by means of those acts that, without further clarification, we have called a "suspension of seriousness."

I must insist one last time on what has already been pointed out previously: This is not a deliberate attitude or an action that is deliberate, voluntary, or reflexive. The proposed definition [of *relajo*] is derived, simply, from the immediate meaning of the events such as they occur in a spontaneous action, before any reflection. The promoting of the described situation is not necessarily the result of deliberation, but even in the case of mediation by a reflexive act, and of the behavior being deliberate, this behavior will also have the specified meaning, and at the very instant of being put into action, the reflexive attitude will have been abandoned entirely.[10]

RELAJO, MOCKERY, SARCASM, AND TEASING

We have said that *relajo* is the sense of a behavior. That said, a behavior is composed of acts that have a meaning, which points toward an end, although this end may not be proposed by an act of deliberation. The purpose or sense of *relajo* manifests itself in an action; it is concurrent

potential
← vs →
action

with the acts that constitute it. Having expounded upon the sense of *relajo*, the nature of the acts that carry that meaning must still be clarified. To do so, let us first note some characteristics of actions in general.

In the first place, following Jean-Paul Sartre, we distinguish between a merely mental action, such as the action of doubting, meditating, or making a hypothesis, and actions that modify the structure of the world, such as "playing the piano," "sawing wood," or "driving an automobile." Both types of actions have a [27] characteristic in common: that of being transcendent to consciousness. They actually distinguish themselves from the consciousness that points toward them. Both reveal themselves to reflection as intentional; that is to say, through them, consciousness is directed toward ends that transcend the action itself. The purpose is the peculiar form adopted by the intentionality of active consciousness. It is a type of intraworldly intentionality that precisely allows one to distinguish between action in the actual sense of the word and lived experience. If I suddenly run into an unexpected situation, I try to overcome my surprise by speculating about the causes that have made the situation appear. In this case, my conjecture is not an action but rather a lived experience; there is only the spontaneous consciousness of the conjecture imprinted on my consciousness of the world. But if I try to solve a detective-like problem, for example, my conjecture is then an action; it is then a case of the "endeavor" of speculating.

The actions that imply a modification of my surrounding world always have the character of action per se, the character of an endeavor. But in any case, action is always intentional; that is to say, action is always directed toward an end.

Relajo is not merely a lived experience, but it isn't a pure mental action either. It possesses the double transcendence of action as such. It is immediately visible that, even given this, it isn't action toward things, as in the case of the previous examples; this notwithstanding, it is also—with an equal amount of evidence—action in the world, since it is the provoking of a "state of things" among people. It is the modification of a situation and even the creation of a situation. It is the arranging of the surrounding world in a certain order. My intentionality prolongs itself in the world and makes it change its appearance by means of the active body.

The expressive function of the body, assumed in the intentionality of *relajo*, allows the action that constitutes *relajo* to be pure mimicry. The most perfect example of this active function of bodily expressiveness is the total suspension of seriousness manifested in some of the manner-isms of Mario Moreno.[11] There is no situation, no matter how serious, that is not completely defused by the demolishing expressiveness of this great mime. The action that constitutes *relajo* can thus be a series of merely "Cantinflas-like" characteristics, so to speak. [28]

But the action that constitutes *relajo* can consist of uttering a word, or even less; a noise or an unarticulated scream can suffice. During a screening of a film version of Shakespeare's *Julius Caesar*, in the scene in which Cassius falls pierced by his own sword, the expectant silence in the movie theater was broken by a long groan that invincibly provoked laughter among the audience. It is true that the performance did not collapse into a case of *relajo*, but had such joking expressions from the viewers continued, between the mocking attitude of some and the indig-nation of others, disorder and confusion could have proliferated, putting an end to the aesthetic situation.

The prolonged groan was not, evidently, produced in its author by the suggestive power of the events unfolding on the screen. It was, no doubt, an intentional act directed toward the dissolution of the aesthetic complex "drama performed before an audience."

Finally, the action [that constitutes *relajo*] can consist of isolated words, but words that are geared also toward the neutralization of the value, or toward mockery or jokes that are openly directed against the person, or persons, or situation that embodies *relajo*.

Mockery, as such, is an action that tends to subtract or to deny the value of a person or situation, but that, when considered in isola-tion, does not yet constitute *relajo*. Not even a series of repeated acts of mocking is enough to make *relajo* emerge. It is possible for repeated mocking to occur between two speakers, one of whom systematically makes fun of the other, without the situation having to be branded *relajo* because of this. Mockery, and its frequent instrument—the joke—main-tain an instrumental relationship with *relajo*. They can be dominated by the specific intentionality of the latter: to suspend seriousness in a community. Within this intentionality, the joke and mocking appear as moments articulated according to that intention. In that case, *relajo* is the transcendent unity of sense toward which acts of mockery—be they oral mocking manifested in jokes or mocking consisting purely of bodily gestures—are directed.

Mockery, on the other hand, cannot manifest itself in isolation; it is always subject to intentionalities that go beyond its own specific intentionality of subtracting value from people or situations. Nevertheless, these intentionalities, which transcend mockery, can vary substantially. For example, mockery—with an instrumental sense—can be found in irony, a topic with which we will deal [29] at a certain length later on.

There is a form of mockery that cannot be assumed instrumentally within *relajo*: sarcasm. Sarcasm is offensive and bitter mockering. The corrosive intent of sarcasm is directed totally toward a specific person, and its devaluing purpose is subordinated to the purpose of offending. *Relajo* creates a void regarding the value; sarcasm eats away at a person. Sarcasm creates a stigmatizing relationship: it points like a sword to the heart of a person in a strictly interindividual relationship, with no need for witnesses and, so to speak, in a low voice. *Relajo* is environmental, collective, and occasionally noisy. *Relajo* may provoke laughter; sarcasm can provoke an atmosphere of uncomfortable expectation that is full of threats of violence, like an insult or like a slap in the face. Sarcasm paralyzes; *relajo* is an invitation to chaotic movement; their respective intentionalities cancel each other out. The two cannot cross paths, nor can one be assumed inside the other in an instrumental relationship or in any other type of subordination.

On the other hand, sarcasm is an individual act, like mockery. A single sarcastic remark is already full and total sarcasm, while *relajo* does not exist without the repetition of the acts that constitute it.

Sarcasm is closer to teasing than to *relajo*, granted that teasing is less caustic, more playful, and less tense than sarcasm. The relationship with others in teasing is inter-subjective, as in sarcasm, although incidentally it can occur before a group. The individual that "teases" another presents him or herself as value; deep down there exists in this individual a will to show his or her "superiority" relative to the other individual in a game of wit that is essential to this form of mockery; in teasing, mockery likewise manifests itself as a means of showing someone's nonvalue, but in this case it is subordinated to the intention of showing the supposed superiority of the agent.

Teasing [*choteo*] is not distinguished from *relajo* in that, as the latter, it is repeated action, but the intentionalities of teasing and *relajo* are radically different. Teasing demands the stability and the preservation of the relationship between the subject and his or her interlocutor, since only in this way can the presumed superiority of one over the other manifest itself, such that *relajo* always [30] ends up totally neutralizing the people or situations that are its object, and it ends up directed exclusively to itself, to the maintaining of an atmosphere of disorder and detachment. In teasing, the agent is interested in holding the attention of a possible spectator on its object; teasing lacks the intentionality of deviation that we have signaled as an essential moment of *relajo*. On the other hand, the individual who teases presents him- or herself as, and turns into, a focus of attention, as the one who can, as one who surpasses the other in wit, one who totally transcends the other. Thus the teaser draws a bipolar and linear field of communication in contrast to the three-dimensional nature of the quasispace inherent to *relajo*.

The fact that teasing can occur—and often does—before a group of spectators does not alter this structure in the least. The spectator of teasing is simply that: a spectator; he or she is passive and limited to witnessing the events. Incidentally, in the case of teasing, the spectator can come to play the role of the chorus but never the role of the actor, since the individual who does the teasing is precisely interested in keeping the spectator in the role of a mere witness of his or her own activity. In contrast, the agent of *relajo* is "humble," tending to disappear and to hide behind the environment he or she has created, and this individual's action is an inciter of the others' action. The agent of *relajo* wants everyone to be an actor. The one who teases jumps into the arena like a cock ready for a fight, and this makes him or her a bit fearsome and a bit ridiculous because of the intention of receiving recognition and because of the vacuity of this ingenious game.

Let us note, finally, that teasing requires a certain skill; its mockery is necessarily ingenious. The one who teases needs to know exactly whom to tease, why, and how to do it, since he or she especially takes advantage of double entendres and plays on words, making them function within a specific situation. In order to do this, the one who teases needs to have full consciousness of the elements and the articulation of the situation, as well as of the ambiguity and the multiplicity of meaningful nuances of words. In contrast, *relajo* does not *necessarily* require these elements. It is also possible to have a coarse, obtuse, and simply noisy form of *relajo* that achieves its goal with no instruments other than noise and screams devoid of any meaning [31].

Value and *Relajo*

A central point remains to be examined: the way in which value manifests itself in *relajo*, in other words, the way in which value manifests itself to make it possible to face it in the attitude of *relajo*. Indeed, so far we have looked at things by adopting the point of view of the subject who promotes *relajo*, but we have left the object of *relajo* somewhat in the shadows: that is, the value and the forms of its manifestation—and which could be opportunities for the emergence of *relajo*—and the acts by means of which value is put out of play.

As a general principle of this investigation, at least in this first descriptive part, it must be established that all the descriptions presented refer to the spontaneous attitude of active consciousness, to the world of lived experience in general, without allowing for the incorporation of any reference to a theory of values as such. We are not interested here in what might be the ontological status of value. We do not care here whether values are ideal entities similar to numbers or concepts, or whether they are merely a specific form of the life of consciousness.

What matters is to find out the way in which a value manifests itself in spontaneous consciousness, independently from its ontological or metaphysical quality and independently of the relationships that might be established a priori among values themselves, among them, hierarchy, subordination, relationship of polarity, or foundation. In this sense, it interests us little to know whether values are entities that float beyond being or if they are endowed with a *sui generis* being that precisely would be "to have value." Neither do we need to consider the problem of whether values are something akin to entities in an other-world in the way of Plato's ideas. Such problems can only emerge with regard to philosophical reflection directed toward such entities, be they conceived of as things in and of themselves or as unities of sense that constitute a specific region of reality, as in the case of Max Scheler's and of Nicholai Hartmann's work. Before such reflection, it is evident that values are something assumed or presupposed in the natural attitude of humans, who are turned toward the world and devoted simply to the task of living.

What interests us is to clarify the way in which value gives itself in daily life, before any [32] speculation about its essence, its hierarchy, or its polarity.

Let us say, for the moment, that all human life is steeped in value. Wherever we turn our gaze, value gives sense and depth to reality. Lived values are not those essences that are presented in philosophy manuals, like pearls of meaning organized hierarchically beyond being. Value underscores and organizes the things in the world. The coolness of the water I drink on a hot day is a value. The gracefulness of the woman that one crosses paths with in the street is a value. The softness and the good design of the armchair in which I sit down to rest are values. The intelligence of this friend or the good humor of that one is a value.

Value is a quality of the world, and even when value founds a duty for me, this duty seems to me imposed by reality itself; "Justice" is "justice that is to be realized in the community."

My valued action, when it exists, starts out by tracing itself on the backdrop of the conditions of my situation. There is an appeal by things themselves to my action, for the world to finish perfecting itself and to reach a certain fullness; whether it is accessible or unattainable is of little importance. In the most modest of the realities that surround me, there is also—like a small void—the outline of value as a demand, as something that things themselves are lacking, as something requested by them. Bookcases that must be organized, suits that must be ironed or any other small tasks that must be completed are likewise forms in which value appears in the very heart of the world that surrounds me.

But value can also appear as a demand, as a need to fill a void in the very center of my existence. It appears then as a norm of my self-constitution, as the perpetually elusive and evanescent indication of what *my* being ought to be. My personality in the world is like a precipitate remaining after me in my perpetual yearning to fill that void.

There is not a single act in the life of human beings that does not owe its first warning signs to the demand of value. We all run dizzyingly after ourselves, directed always by those indications that foreshadow and allude to the fullness of our own being. Value attracts us like a whirlwind [33] in the center of which our own self appears, illuminated by value's aura. All of our acts are ordered toward the realization of some value.

Getting dressed hurriedly in the morning, drinking a cup of coffee in a rush, walking down the street in long strides, and, perhaps running, distressed, after a bus that barely stops to let me get on—[these] are nothing but the external signs of my determined (intentional) pointing toward the constitution of my own "punctual being." If after all of this, I finally do arrive on time to the office at the hour stipulated by a set of rules, and breathe a sigh of relief, then, *am* I punctual yet? It is evident that this is not the case. It is simply that today I got to work on time.

Value has escaped me once again. I have not succeeded in incorporating value into myself, in constituting my being definitely, nor will I ever achieve this. I have not succeeded in adopting value into myself in a permanent and secure way; the value continues being a guide for my self-constitution. I will never be able to stabilize and ensure my valued being, because my being can never finish conflating itself with value, which continues to be, according to Kant's ideas, simply a direction and a limit of my transcendence.

My punctuality is but the ideal unity of all my actions geared toward it, and it will only acquire body and solidity when, after my death—that is to say, once every possibility of my being late has been cancelled— some generous soul points out the magnificent fact that I was never late anywhere. But before the unfortunate event of my passing occurs, I will have to laboriously take hold of my own reality, to make it transcend, always newly, toward the ideal limit of absolute punctuality that I have chosen as my possibility, a limit that, likewise, I can abandon at any moment. My punctuality depends on and is a creation of my freedom, since my freedom draws the outline of my person in the world. It is a possibility of my transcendence (and my transcendence toward the world is precisely my freedom). Thus, value always hangs on freedom; it emerges precisely because of it, or I should say, freedom is a perpetual surging toward value. Because of this, value is rooted in the very structure of existence; it is an essential component of that structure; in that sense, it is consubstantial to human beings.

We have already said that *relajo* is a suspension of [34] seriousness and that seriousness is nothing less than freedom's response to the call of value. This being so, how can one say that freedom is an emergence toward value. If freedom is an emergence toward value, it doesn't seem possible to conceive of any attitude in which freedom negates a value or deviates from it. But, on the other hand, if such attitudes of free deviation or free negation of value are possible, can one still speak of freedom as an emergence toward value?

Later, we are to approach the problems that freedom presents as a condition that makes *relajo* possible. Let's point out, simply, that there exists the possibility that freedom can be the source of behaviors geared toward freedom itself as a formal value and not toward concrete or material values. On the other hand, let's note briefly that *relajo*, as a deviation from values, could very well be a formula for self-annihilation, just as the previously described behavior is understandable as self-creation or self-constitution. *Relajo*, a conduct of dissidence, can be the expression of a will for self-destruction.

In any case, what is now important is not to give an interpretation of that behavior, but rather to continue with the description. It is necessary to find a way for value to manifest itself such that it makes *relajo* possible. The path to finding this way is very clear. Value doesn't manifest itself only in that practical, immediate dimension in which I live it as the liminal and ultimate meaning of my own actions. We have already said that value can also appear as a dimension of something real, and in that case it presents itself to us in the present. Thus, I don't live it as a meaning that pulls my own being from the future but rather as a thing that presents itself to me head on in a special type of perception. Value thus appears linked to a receptacle that can be a person or a thing.

In the previously described example of "punctuality," I don't "face up to" the value; I don't even face up to myself as a repository of the value, but rather I go after a "myself" that *is* valuable and that I never attain, that always runs ahead of me like a prow of a ship that cleaves the future. This is surely not the only way in which value manifests itself, nor is practical behavior my only way of being [35] in the world. Value is not only a horizon that absorbs me toward my possibilities in the future. There is also a multitude of cases in which value presents itself to me head on, in which it is not merely the distant and wavering outline of my being, but rather it acquires the stable massiveness of things. This is what happens in the previously enumerated examples: the flavor of a fruit, the coolness of water, or the kindness of a friend.

Let's note, incidentally that the passage from one of manifestation of value to another can seem at first glance as a progression on the order of firmness, and, in a certain sense, this is so. But [this happens] correlatively in that the relationship of a value to the subject that faces it, the "reification" of the value, is parallel to its fragilization. Paradoxically, the more personified value appears to be, the more incorporated and endowed with a firm and stable being, the less power it exerts over the subject that perceives it. The value to be realized by me immediately, in my practical life, exerts an infinitely greater power over me than the beauty-quality of a woman's face, the flavor of wine, or any other "thing-value" which I may run into in the world. This first case is the form par excellence of the manifestation of value, no matter how rarely we may take note of it. This direct and nonpositional form of manifestation of a value presents it to us as an essential component of the structure of existence. It gives [the value] to us from inside, like a presence that is out of reach and that, nevertheless, permeates the totality of existence.

Relajo is not possible in these two forms of manifestation of value. The negative response of *relajo* is not possible in any of these styles of manifestation. In [the case of] value incorporated within the total interiority of a personal project, such a response [*relajo*] is impossible because there is no room for any "response" whatsoever. The subject finds him- or herself wholeheartedly embarked on the venture of making the value real. He or she can abandon such a venture out of disappointment or tiredness. But just as the task of realizing the value had been assumed into pure interiority, the project is abandoned in this very same interiority and in the silence of pure subjectivity.

Neither can the negative response of *relajo* occur in the case of the "quality-value" nor the "thing-value," among other reasons because this form of manifestation does not constitute any call whatsoever from freedom. The coolness of water or a man's intelligence can go unnoticed; they can even be negated, but this negation or this lack of attention [36] cannot assume the form of *relajo* because such values do not need any freedom as a support. The coolness of water, or the delicate flavor of a fruit has no other base of support than the water or the fruit. They are constitutive elements of the things themselves, just as color or consistency finds its support in the irrefutable corporeality of matter. In the first case, value, which fully permeates freedom, manifests itself as a supreme dynamism and power. It is identified with the very emergence of freedom. In the second case, value appears as an inert good, independently of my freedom. In neither of the two cases can value be the object of a prereflexive and active negation as in the case of *relajo*. This negation is not possible, in the first case, because I find myself fully committed to the endeavor of the realization of value. In the second case, I can negate the value, but this negation does not reach the value because the reality of value does not depend on my adoption of it.

In order for *relajo* to take place, it is necessary for value to manifest itself in such a way that it partakes in both styles of manifestation. On the one hand, it is necessary for the value to appear as an object in the midst of the world, but at the same time as something requiring my acceptance and my action for it in order for it to attain its fullness. Such is the case when the value appears under the charge of a repository and at the same time within a communal context in such a way that the gathering of the community is indispensable for the realization of value.

The most obvious example of this possibility is in performances. For example, the gracefulness of a male dancer is something almost tangible, but at the same time it requires the attention of an audience to be able to unfurl itself in the fullness of its possibilities. It requires the attention of one or two people who anticipate the graceful movements as something expected, necessary, and "logical," and which nevertheless surprises [them] as an absolute creation, as an absolutely unpredictable novelty. Gracefulness, undoubtedly, rests on the dance technique—learned laboriously by the performer—but also on recognition by the spectator. In a certain sense, it is a collective endeavor directed from within by a tacit agreement between performer and audience. It emerges, precarious and vulnerable, like a burgeoning that lays root in the field of harmony among dancers, musicians, and spectators, and it survives as something definitive, prefect, and stimulating in the [37] memory of all these groups. This gracefulness cannot attain the stability and solidity of the "thing-value." Its evanescent reality has required the support of multiple generosities, and it rests on this support. Just as the value pursued in the self-constitution of existence, the value never comes to attain definitive being; but in contrast to it, [this gracefulness] can almost be touched in a perception that partakes in the evidence of things and of the transparency of the purely meaningful, of the etherealness of consciousness and of freedom.

Approximately the same thing occurs in the university lecture, in the ceremony, in orderly and creative conversation, and in the fiesta.[12] In the case of the university lecture, we find the same structure serving as a support for the truth-value. The same occurs in the religious ceremony with certain spiritual values, [and] with civic values in the academic ceremony or in the purely civil or political ceremony. In the intelligent and lively discussion among a group of people, one also finds this polarity between performance and audience. A person talks, and others listen with their attention directed toward the truth of the topic being discussed.

In all these cases, the situation is one of a contest of freedoms dedicated to the task of supporting a value whose repository can be a person—as in the cases of the Socratic conversation and of the university lecture, or an institution, as happens in a ceremony or finally in a situation, as in the case of a fiesta.

In the fiesta, the situation cannot necessarily be divided into the polarity between performer and spectators, although sometimes an analogous polarization may emerge, as in certain peasant festivals centered on collective dance under the observation of a director. In any case, in the fiesta, value is attained by means of the situation and not by means of a person or institution. Here, the repository of the value is the situation itself, a situation that has a stable structure—although it may not be as immediately discernible as in the case of a ceremony.

At the fiesta, the value to be attained is joy. [The fiesta's] sense is to make joy real, the joy to communicate precisely in joy and in rejoicing. The fiesta is perhaps one of the privileged forms of communication. That said, in order for there to really be joy at the fiesta, it is necessary for the [38] participants to maintain a behavior regulated by that vital value [joy]. It is necessary that no one adopt a behavior that will turn him or her into an *aguafiestas*, a killjoy. In this sense, the fiesta is something of a ceremony, [but] in which regulation is less rigid, less precise, and less meaningful. But granted that in the fiesta, regulation is freer and spontaneity finds a wider margin and a greater freedom, it is no less true that it is, as in the ceremony, subject to certain rules, the violation of which implies a failure of the fiesta as such.

A ceremony is a more rigid and stable set of collective behavior in which the reality of an institution is expressed. The life and the sense of a university, for example, are expressed in the ceremonies for initiating and closing the academic term and in those ceremonies for the conferring of degrees. In these ceremonies, solemnity appears as an expression of the rank of the spiritual values toward which university life is directed and of the "superior" level that institution occupies in the community. All the gestures and expressions of the people who participate in a similar ceremony are totally incorporated into being, in the way of "quality-values." That said, the gesture of the one who occupies the central place in a ceremony can be expressive of anything one may want, but it is also a call to recognition by me. It invites me to observe the behavior adequate for the circumstances. And "the circumstances" are nothing other than the insistence on making visible, through certain conventional means, the high rank that the university holds in the community and the elevated hierarchy of the values believed to be fostered in this institution. Having said that, I can refuse to engage in the behavior expected of me, and I can provoke a *relajo* in the previously described way, thus making it impossible for those values and situations to fully attain body in the ceremony. Likewise, I can spoil a fiesta, a university lecture, or a conversation by preventing the manifestation of value and dismantling the situation that would allow it.

In general, and not to extend these reflections too much, we can say that *relajo* is possible only when value appears embodied in a repository or agent that can be a person, an institution, or a situation, and at the same [39] time, the value calls on my support in order for it to acquire full reality.

On the one hand, the value must be almost a "thing-value" that is locatable in the present world, and on the other, a pure solicitation to my freedom, a guide for my self-constitution.

The value pursued in the creation of one's own "self," implies the performance of a behavior that is regulated, directed, and organized. The behaviors we have previously described—directed by the pursuit of a certain "punctual *being*"—mean that the actions of the individual that performs them are predictable and outline a comprehensible future based on the realization of a value-filled self.

Relajo is a self-destructive movement. It is an attitude that is exactly the opposite of the normal, spontaneous attitude of human beings faced with values when those values act upon consciousness like a guide for self-constitution.

The *relajo* individual performs a profoundly irrational move that consists of turning one's face against the future to realize a simple act of negation of the immediate past. The future is thus stripped of its power of attraction. Each instant of the immediate future is lived as a mere possibility of negation of the present.

In certain individuals, this structure of time acquires a stable character that turns these people into veritable incarnations of *relajo*. Their mere presence is a foreshadowing of the dissolution of any possible seriousness. Their mere appearance unleashes a light breeze of smiles and the atmosphere is transformed into a condescending expectation of a shower of jokes that will dissolve the seriousness of all topics, reducing them, literally, to nothing. In the colloquial language of Mexico City, this type of individual is designated with a horrible yet adequate word: this individual is a "relajiento."[13]

A "relajiento" is, literally, an individual without a future. The "relajiento" lives perpetually turned toward that very close past from which the present has just emerged, to laughingly negate its content. He or she refuses to take anything seriously, to commit to anything; that is to say, a "relajiento" refuses to guarantee any of his or her own behavior in the future.

The "relajiento" assumes no responsibility for anything; he or she doesn't risk doing anything; he or she is simply a good-humored witness of the banality of life. Thus, there is nothing strange in the fact that this

individual lacks [40] a future. Relajiento individuals destroy it themselves by considering their own projects as an object of mockery, and
this symbolic destruction is projected onto objective time, transforming
the relajiento into an individual lacking a future.

The temporal structure of this attitude can adequately be described
as an indefinite sum of moments connected to each other by relations of
negation. It is an endless rosary of negated moments.

This temporal fragmentation and its stigmatizing intentionality
toward the moment of *retention* make the "relajiento" an individual of
reduced seriousness, an individual who "does not guarantee" anything,
but they also turn this individual into an excellent companion, in general, who is much more generous than what his or her sometimes fearsome wit would perhaps suggest.

For certain, the "relajiento" "has no future," but this means that he
or she could hardly threaten anybody else's future. The relajiento is a
good instant comrade who dissipates the seriousness of life and makes
us laugh heartily. He or she is, undoubtedly, good company. With a
"relajiento" time goes by.

Since the form itself of the relajiento's interiority is to "make time go
by for someone," the time does indeed go by, and we all thank this person for it. Really, the function that the relajiento assumes—to expel each
instant toward the past, thus distracting us from being attentive to the
future, [which is] the place of worry—is worthy of being appreciated.

The relajiento does not bring about preoccupation but rather unoc-
cupation. He or she is an unoccupied person perpetually bent on the task
of being unoccupied, of emptying one's consciousness of all seriousness
and of all commitment.

The relajiento may not be lacking in talent and is almost always
very intelligent, but this individual's function of dissipating seriousness
doesn't make anyone inclined to trust him or her too much. Because of
this, although the relajiento might have been able to "come a long way,"
he or she hasn't made it anywhere. The relajiento's way of moving in
hops traces no defined trajectory in the world. A relajiento is at the same
spot he or she was many years ago. A jovial and bitter person, the relajiento can be understood as having a life which is a series of accidents
that coagulate together to endow him or her with a friendly and amor-
phous personality. However, the relajiento is not totally a failure since
he or she does not believe in victory. Thus, he or she is "human," and
everyone, sometimes rightly, suspects that a good heart is hiding behind

that smiling and carefree mask. The relajiento's lack of ambition fore-shadows the generosity and the genuine humility of individuals capable of laughing at themselves.

[41] Relajiento individuals laugh at themselves because their continuous neutralization of value operates from the very center of their interiority, and the first object of their demolishing attitude is their own self. This also explains their deep melancholy that is only revealed in secret confidences as if it were a hidden sin that is hard to confess, since this makes one serious and thus vulnerable even to one's own attitude. This fragile seriousness can only be entrusted into the hands of a friend, of somebody who has proven to be generous and endowed with enough flexibility of spirit to guarantee that he or she will not annihilate this seriousness with mockery.

This also explains the possible nihilism disguised as good humor, into which the relajiento falls without wanting to, dragged by the mechanicality of his or her negation. Accustomed to the movement of deviation and of a neutralizing indifference toward values, relajiento individuals end up losing sight of the fact that such deviation and indifference have their origins in their freedom and that these are but personal options contingent among other possible ones. Relajiento individuals end up believing that the negation has its origin in the things themselves and in the things' incomplete and negligible character. Relajiento individuals lose the guide of affirmation and become blind to value. This process can reach deep layers of the relajiento's personality; the process can lean toward an acute sense of failure as something inevitable and determined from without, and can thus open relajiento individuals to the possibility of resentment and to all forms of suicide.

It is evident that if value is a guide for self-construction, the systematic negation of a value is a movement of self-destruction, at least at the level of the personality that could only be configured by an internal and responsible relationship with whichever value may be the case. In this way, *relajo* is, inexorably, a self-negation. In addition, one of the effects of this self-negation is a fragmentation of the subjective temporality of whoever adopts negation as a permanent style [of behavior]. Based on this fragmentation, we understand the figure of the relajiento as an individual without projects, one who has fallen into the present instant (ab-ject), and who, precisely because of this, is incapable of giving unity to more or less long periods of objective temporality. That is why we say that the relajiento has no future [and] lacks a time to come.

This individual's negative attitude presents a double pathway: on the one hand, it is self-destruction, and on the other, it is a fragmentary temporality, a flicker of presents without direction and without form, of negations of the immediate past [42].

RELAJO AND LAUGHTER

We have spoken about *relajo*, teasing, sarcasm, and mockery. On the horizon of such issues we cannot avoid perceiving a close or distant relationship of *relajo* with another topic: that of laughter and the comic.

All of us know that *relajo* has some elements of the comic. Whoever has experienced any of the previously described situations knows of the presence of a sometimes uncontrollable laughter that goes off when a serious situation is suddenly suspended with the intervention of a joke or of mockery. In the general majority of cases, *relajo* manifests itself accompanied by hilarity. Whoever provokes *relajo*, laughs; whoever participates in it laughs, and incidentally, whoever is its victim laughs.

In order to complete our description of *relajo*, we must account for the presence of laughter in the issue at hand. Unfortunately, in order to clarify this, we have no other choice but to make a very brief incursion into the slippery and difficult territory of the meaning of laughter and of the comic. I say *unfortunately* because dealing with the issue implies an indispensable discussion of a much explored and equally confusing topic. To this day, a truly satisfactory examination of this slippery issue does not exist.

The most serious philosophers have dealt with the subject of laughter and the comic, and in any of the works devoted to this, one finds impressive lists of illustrious names associated with it: Plato, Aristotle, Cicero, Descartes, Pascal, Hobbes, Kant, Hegel, Schopenhauer, Spencer, Renouvier, Bergson, [and] Freud have all said something about laughter, without the need to consider any of their theories definitive. On the other hand, the bibliography on the subject is incredibly extensive. Some researcher has noted the existence of more than ninety theories about laughter, and the sum of books and articles devoted specifically to this subject exceeds two hundred.

The difficulties are raised a notch when one takes a look at things themselves, because laughter does not always present itself with a univocal meaning. One can laugh with joy, and one can guffaw at something comical. There is laughter provoked by a joke and laughter provoked by a real comic situation. There is pathological laughter, "hysterical laughter," and the "physiological laughter" provoked by physical stimuli such as [43] laughing gas or "tickling." There is the smile, which isn't only [a type of] incipient laughter. There is no continuity between the smile and the guffaw. A smile is not a weak guffaw, nor is a guffaw, obviously, the culmination of a smile. There is naïve laughter and malevolent laughter, the "little nervous laugh" and the serene smile, the pious smile, the courteous smile, the ironic smile, and so on.

On the other hand, almost all the thinkers who have said something on this issue have been content with explaining it, trying to determine the essence of the comic and have left up in the air the question of the relationship between laughter and the comic. In general, they take for granted that the comic provokes laughter in the same way that heat causes objects to expand, which could be false. They take for granted that the comic is a *cause* of laughter, no less. This implies a presupposition regarding the relationship between consciousness and its object, a given which is far from justified. The comic does not necessarily induce laughter. The synthesis of the comic and hilarity is not a causal synthesis; it is a free synthesis, since between the comic and hilarity, there is a relationship of a consciousness to an object. Proof of this is that not everyone laughs in the same way or at the same forms of the comic. A joke or a comic situation that can make a person crack up can leave another unmoved. There are "strata" of the comic that can be understood by means of the degree of education or the nuances of the esteem in which social classes, professional groups, and nationalities are held. All of us know the meaning of the expression "German joke" [*chiste alemán*],[14] and we have witnessed scenes in which this expression contrasts the irritation of one person with the uncontainable laughter of another.

Laughter, then, is not an automatic reaction or causal effect of the comic. It cannot be, because laughter is a particular form of consciousness, exactly like an emotion or like an intellection, and it cannot escape the universal law of consciousness, which is intentionality. To say that laughter is an effect of the comic is just as absurd as saying that study is an effect of science or that rage is an effect of evil or of some other *cause*. Laughter, like any emotion or like the acts of intellection, is a form of direction of consciousness toward an object. It would seem, rather, that laughter is a way of *designating* the comic. More than designating, perhaps we should say "intending" [44], "pointing to," or "alluding," since the peculiar form of intentionality that is laughter is not exhausted in a mere designative function. Let's say, then, that laughter is the peculiar form in which consciousness is directed toward the comic. With regard to this intentional relationship, one can set up any theory about its origin and its significance. It can be said, for instance, that laughter is a collective or individual defense reaction to some threat, as does Bergson, for whom laughter is a form of defense of the social group against the intervention of the mechanical in the creative current of life. Laughter would then be a kind of revulsive agent against the stratification and the automatization of the life current, a way for the vital impulse (that Bergson supposes is the metaphysical foundation of human society) to violently expel from it all the moments tending toward mechanical repetition [and] toward automatic rigidity. The comic would be precisely that intervention of the mechanical into the living, and laughter would be like a punishment against the agent of that intervention executed by the social group that is defending itself from the danger embodied in it. Laughter can also be explained as liberation of energy accumulated in the simmering cauldron of the unconscious, à la Freud, whose theory on the relationship between jokes hinging on equivocation and the unconscious is very widely known.

In both cases, it becomes obvious that laughter and the comic are only pretexts to show the workings of a metaphysical doctrine. And no doubt both doctrines "work" well, on the condition that one does not pay too much attention to laughter itself and to the comic. After studying [these two theories] carefully, we will have learned a lot about the "vital élan" and about the social function of laughter, about libido and the unconscious, but we will not have clarified too much that very same issue about which we were supposedly going to be instructed, that is to say, about what *is* laughter, about its essence, the description of which ends up concealed in the name of an "explanation" geared toward the confirmation of a previous theory (that is also alien to things themselves). [In Bergson's and Freud's theories] there is no penetration into the phenomenon that one is attempting to clarify; this phenomenon ends up obscured rather than illuminated.

This lack of attention to things themselves is more visible[15] in older theories, which on the other hand, have the virtue of not ignoring the bodily character of our phenomenon; granted that they also fall into assertions that at the current level [45] of psychological research—opened up by phenomenology—seem frankly comical.

Such is the case of Kant. Kant is right in asserting that laughter is an emotion, thus ridding himself of the tendency in his time to consider laughter an issue of the understanding. "Laughter," he tells us, "is an emotion born of the sudden annihilation of an intense wait." But when trying to explain the pleasurable character of such an emotion, he affirms that it is derived from "the alternating tensing and relaxing of the elastic parts of the intestines."

This notwithstanding, Kant, in treating laughter as a part of his theory of pleasure, doesn't neglect to note the double nature—both spiritual and bodily—of this phenomenon, and he explains it ultimately as a bodily pleasure obtained by means of certain manipulations of concepts; that is why he classifies the joke as a "game of thoughts" alongside the "game of chance" [gambling] (with which he does not deal because he does not consider it a "beautiful game") and alongside music, which he considers another drawing room game: a "game of sounds."

As a final analysis, perhaps the most penetrating theory about laughter comes from Alfred Stern.[16] Stern says that "laughter is a value judgment, a negative value judgment concerning a degradation of values." With this formula, Stern opens up a path full of suggestions and possibilities for a theory of laughter, although it is very far from providing a definitive solution to our problem.

For instance, it is evident that laughter is not a judgment. It is not a value judgment nor a judgment of any other nature, neither affirmative nor negative. Perhaps Kant was closer to the solution when he asserted that laughter is a pleasurable emotion. However, Stern has hit upon an important point in affirming that one can discern a degradation of values as the ultimate sense of the laughable. His correctness is limited to postulating a theory that can give the ultimate reason for the comic, but there is still the need to clarify why the comic *provokes* precisely this style of intentionality called laughter; and one must also clarify the sense of the markedly bodily character of this type of intentionality [46].

Stern says "the comic is any incident and any action that displaces our attention from a value to a nonvalue or from an intrinsic value to an instrumental value. The two cases are equivalent to a degradation of values that *provokes* the instinctive negative value judgment that is laughter."

As one can see, Stern considers the problem of the relationship between the comic and laughter resolved in taking for granted that the comic—understood as a degradation of values—*provokes* laughter; on the other hand, he frees himself from the study of laughing as a special type of intentionality by declaring it as a judgment.[17]

We have all noticed the mysterious disappearance of the *vis comica* of a joke or of a situation that has made us laugh until our jaws hurt.[18] If laughter didn't have a certain ability to beget the comic, it could never happen that the comic could cease to be comic; on the other hand, if this creative capacity of consciousness were absolute, there would be no rule for the comic, nor would there be any possibility of sharing laughter. At this point is where the ambiguous character of the relationship between consciousness and the world presents itself with greater evidence. Everything happens as if laughter were partly created by the comic (in whatever manner one may conceive of the comic) and at the same time the comic was created—or rather, sustained—by laughter. My laughing is a continuous recreation of the comic. It does not matter that upon reflection my laughter appears simply as an automatic reaction to the joke or the situation. If we add to this the verisimilitude that the essence of the comic involves the degradation of values discussed by Stern, laughter could be interpreted as the consciousness of this degradation, a consciousness that does not limit itself to being a reaction to the degradation but at the same time is an interpretation of it that implies a special form of relationship of consciousness [47] to the totality of the world.

Indeed it seems that in any possible comic situation and in any joke one can discern a degradation of values. Both Bergson's theory and those of the absurd (being perhaps the theories that have most closely approached the exact determination of the essence of the comic) can be subsumed into the idea of a degradation of values. A "logic" of jokes that would examine the totality of the structures of the comic would surely allow us to emphasize as its fundamental sense the degradation of values of which Stern speaks. Then laughter could be interpreted as a peculiar emotion, in other words, as the pleasurable emotion of the harmless character of that degradation, as the sense of being safe [from the degradation], of being free, out of its reach.

Indeed, value degradation is something threatening. The *fact* of the degradation of a value opens up the horizon of a possible universal degradation of values and even of the absolute extinction of the value. Perhaps laughter can be interpreted as a form of consciousness that, while alluding to that degradation, at the same time would affirm the "local," limited character of the degradation itself, thus causing the pleasurable feeling of being safe, for both the consciousness of the one who laughs as well as for the totality of the world of the valuable; laughter, thus, would be like the emotion of freedom facing possible degradation and like the pleasurable feeling of the "ultimate" stability of the world of the threatened value. This last point would render comprehensible, on the one hand, the pleasurable character of laughter, and on the other, the tendency of laughter to remain within existence, to prolong itself, to re-create itself while at the same time sustaining its object before the gaze of consciousness, that is to say: the unitary concept of the comic. Laughter would then be a form of consciousness that, faced with the degradation of the value and precisely *because* of this degradation, would try to secure for itself its [own] freedom with respect to such degradation and, at the same time, to ensure the invulnerable character of the world of value in general. The intentional structure of laughter would be that of a "yes . . . but" expressed with a bodily violence whose ultimate sense would be that of enjoying with one's own body the stability of the world of the value. It would be a lived experience analogous—although inverse—to that of enraged individuals who "feel," in the cenesthesia of their rage, in the contraction of their bowels, the hatefulness [48] of their enemy or of the offense. Enraged individuals, in effect, *sink into* their rage; they let it flow like a current of bodily sensations that manifest the hatefulness of what provoked the rage; they *let themselves be led* by the rage precisely to make the abominable [aspects] of the motive more embodied and more tangible—which serves at the same time as a legitimization of the violence of their emotion. The same thing happens with suffering: emotional individuals who suffer hang on to their suffering; they re-create it; they incite it in order to make it more real, to lose themselves in it and, in a certain way, to achieve a paradoxical liberation, by handing themselves over, without measure, to emotion. This is nothing other than the sense of the liberating and pacifying power of tears and of other such violent expressions of pain. In the same way, laughter wants to condense itself infinitely; it wants to turn into "laughter-in-itself," [into] an infinitely dense pleasure of the infinite certainty of the rational and of the value faced with the threat of the absurd and the possible degradation of values.

A sample of the explanatory effectiveness of Stern's hypothesis would be the simple example of the solemn man who slips and falls. The king of creation suddenly becomes a part of creation, subject, like a mere stone, to the laws of gravity. Here is an evident degradation of the value of free personality, attained by the regularity to which the most humble and negligible realities are subject. Not everyone laughs at such an incident, surely. A person who is aware of the axiological hierarchy, or who has a strong sensitivity for the human condition, will experience, rather, a sense of embarrassment and an accentuation of consciousness regarding his or her own vulnerability. But a person who is not bothered by such considerations probably will laugh willingly, feeling safe from such contingencies [and] affirmed by the soothing conviction that, deep down, nothing serious has happened. His or her laughter will be, for that person, a bodily perceptible guarantee that nothing has happened to him or her and that the little incident doesn't profoundly alter the stability of things. The laughter of the one who suffers the accident can never have the same transparency and the spontaneity of that of the spectators. The victim cannot avoid feeling "hit." In his eyes, the degradation of his own value will be accompanied by a feeling of vulnerability; in this case, the characteristic of liberation [49]—which I consider essential to laughter—cannot take place and will prevent the manifestation of laughter. If, perhaps with some laborious effort, the victim is able to laugh, his laughter will be simulated, wanted, like a reflexive affirmation of his freedom, and the bodily pleasure of such a freedom will prove difficult.

The examples could be multiplied by analyzing the most complicated jokes and those with the most delicate comic structure. There will always be a backdrop of degradation of values that, although not absolutely adequate as an "explanation" for laughter, does have the advantage of universality and of the ability to encompass all the theories formulated about it.

From all that has been said previously, one can clearly surmise the sense of laughter in the case of *relajo*. Since *relajo* is a refusal to support a value, the value in question ends up degraded, in a certain way, since its striving for full incorporation ends up unfulfilled. The actor is its victim; he ceases to be an interesting character, [only] to turn into, for example, a small, pot-bellied, or stuttering man. The solemn official who embodies a respectable institution is reduced to the role of the man who cannot control a situation. The anniversary party turns into a pandemonium in which those attending attack each other with all kinds of projectiles. The performance, the ceremony, or the party turns into "*relajo*."

Nevertheless, comedy is not essential to *relajo*; it doesn't always accompany *relajo*, and this is due to essential reasons. Whoever has seen a group of "relajientos" in action knows that the laughter provoked by this action is always precarious. On occasion, there appear indeterminate possibilities of unpredictability and of fear that prevent frank laughter.

Indeed, *relajo* is, in a certain sense, an imaginary destruction of a value that, in general, only reaches the level of a mere degradation of the value. But from the imaginary destruction and the degradation, one can go to real destruction or to the loss of the value, even if this loss and destruction do not necessarily affect the value that has now been put out of play.

That being said, a *loss* of the value is not comic, but rather it involves pain. The higher the lost value, the more serious the pain, until this correspondence culminates in that annihilation of superior values called tragedy; and tragedy does not make one laugh but rather cry. Certainly, the movement [50] from imaginary destruction to real destruction is not necessary. Nevertheless, it is very often possible, and the mere possibility creates an atmosphere of anxiety that, more than provoking laughter, prevents it. The occasional cases of destruction of bullfighting rings or sports parks that have sometimes been reported in our newspapers serve as evidence of this possibility to go from "enthusiastic clapping" to the jubilant setting of galleries and rows of seats on fire. Municipal authorities in Mexico City have on some occasions seen themselves forced to forbid performances or meetings—innocuous in and of themselves—that often culminate in acts of destruction; these acts cannot be understood by dubbing them with names that constitute only a moral condemnation (which is probably justified) but that don't make intelligible the event itself, much less so the means of preventing it.

II. MORAL SENSE OF *RELAJO*

With the rigor allowed by the informative purpose of this essay, we have attempted a phenomenological description of *relajo*. Such a description implies a double demand. In the first place, that the description be precisely that: a description, in other words, the abandonment of an explanatory attitude that would attempt to understand it [the phenomenon] from an external point of view. Second, it is indispensable for whoever undertakes the task of describing to adopt the point of view of the subject and perform the described act in order to bring to light meanings that are inherent to it. In the previous descriptions, we have placed ourselves in that "internal" position relative to the issue that we are studying, and we have adopted an exclusively descriptive attitude, that is to say, a totally neutral attitude with respect to all attempts at explanation (of "external" understanding) that would have been able to come into our heads.

That being said, it is evident that the possibilities of intelligibility of our issue are not exhausted by the information brought to light by mere description. There are still many things left to find out. We do know, more or less, *what* relajo is, but we don't really know anything yet about its moral significance or about its origins, or about its function in the totality of events, norms, uses, habits, and social demands that form the spiritual environment of our country [Mexico] [51].

Certainly, something of all of this has been suggested throughout our exposition, but only in a provisional sense and more like a negative aid which has been useful to determine what *relajo* is not. Thus, we have seen how it is not merely a case of mockery, how it is not irony, or satire, or teasing; we have seen how laughter is not an essential component to it. But we have not seen positively what the relationship of *relajo* is with all these things and with others of greater importance.

In order to do this, we must abandon the "internal" point of view that we had adopted, and we must position ourselves at a vantage point that will allow us to understand *relajo* in relation to other facts of moral life. Seen from a higher and thus more universal point, the essence of *relajo* will become clearer to us and will acquire a deeper sense.

By abandoning the descriptive attitude and initiating an interpretation [of the phenomenon], we could say that we abandon the territory of the certain to enter that of the probable. Let us shift from the key of "is" to the key of "perhaps"[19] to continue our reflections. Nevertheless, recognizing the importance of such a shift, we will try not to ever lose sight of the information brought to light by the process of description, a process that, on the other hand, we will not abandon completely, so that we may give the greatest possible solidity to the probabilities we are going to explore.

Freedom

The concept from which we will take the necessary support for clarifying the moral sense of *relajo* is that of freedom. The concept of freedom will allow us to understand, from the roots up, this complex bundle of behaviors seemingly regulated by the idea of nonregulation, of disorder.

Indeed, if we reflect on our exposition so far, we see that *relajo* manifests itself as a behavior of "deviation." The response to the constrictions imposed by the value is a "no." The response to a demand by the value is an escape. *Relajo*, then, appears as a form of liberation. On the other hand, freedom also appears on the horizon of *relajo* as a condition of its possibility, as occurs—except for certain differentiating nuances—with any behavior or human action. Attribution presupposes the idea of the freedom of human beings, to whom we can attribute responsibility for their actions [52] because we live "always already" in the atmosphere of freedom.

No doubt, it is evident that the operation of attributing or imputing also occurs when we speak of natural phenomena, as when we say that a hurricane decimated the coasts of the Gulf of Mexico or that the atomic bomb leveled Nagasaki. But this is only a way of speaking. Within nature, there is no action per se, and when we say that yellow fever killed so-and-so, not only do we "want to say" something different than when we say that Mr. Such-and-such killed Mr. So-and-so or that alcohol killed Mr. So-and-so. In each case, we perform a radically different operation of adjudication.[20]

These observations allow us contemplate vaguely the idea that *relajo* is a possibility of freedom: that freedom has something to do with all this. But seeing clearly the nature and the form of the internal relationship between both terms [*relajo* and *freedom*] will only be able to be accomplished after some reflections on freedom.

It is necessary to make explicit, even in the most succinct manner, some of the ways in which freedom offers itself immediately to our experience, and to avoid—to whatever degree possible—letting ourselves be influenced by philosophical theories, even if they might be the clearest and the most profound ones, that have emerged on [the subject of freedom]. Once again, the intention is to attempt a description that will make it easier for us to intuit the relationships between freedom and *relajo*, in order to gain a deeper understanding of the latter rather than presenting a summary of theories on freedom.

In general, freedom is lived in many ways, which [53] means that it also manifests itself in many ways. One can grant a greater importance to one or another of the expressions or forms in which freedom intervenes in social and individual life. To decide, for example, that foundational and radical freedom is how we understand "political freedom" does not invalidate the fact of the multiplicity of its other forms of expression that can be found in a pictorial style, in a bodily gesture, or in a habit, for example.

Because freedom is so inextricably intertwined with all aspects of human existence, discerning it with clarity is not an easy task. We cannot see freedom how we see a thing and—when trying to grasp its reality—we only obtain some anxiety-producing evidence that it is impossible for freedom to be represented. There is nothing so difficult to represent as freedom, perhaps because it is inherent to action rather than thought and [because] it evades reflection all the more obstinately, the bigger the effort to grasp it is.

When we raise our hand to point it out, freedom has already disappeared, and all that remains present for us is a sentence or a thing; this does not prevent us from continually having an obscure yet firm consciousness of being free. This omnipresent and at the same time omniabsent character of freedom opens up the possibility of theories that aspire to rid the world of freedom's so often bothersome presence.

But if freedom cannot be grasped in a formula like any other concept, this simply means that it is not a concept or that it is not merely a concept but rather something that occurs, in some way, in human experience. What we can do is pinpoint the experience or experiences in which freedom shows itself with greater exactitude.

In general terms, it can be said that the most universal experience among those that founded the notion of freedom is the experience we humans have in living ourselves as the *origin* of certain actions that we face in the position of *authors*. In this type of action, one experiences a centrifugal movement, in contrast to processes of the opposite type, in which the subject is in the position of *patient*. Artistic creation and illness, almost getting ahead on their own, are the most immediate examples of these two possibilities.

Nevertheless, being absolutely a patient or absolutely an author would be only two purely ideal extremes of this [54] polarity of freedom. There can be no experience—no matter how privileged we assume it to be—in which a person experiences him- or herself as an absolute author of an act; indeed, a person of "flesh and blood" is unavoidably affected by a facticity (a body, social situation, etc.) that imposes itself on, and conditions him or her and that—if not entirely determinant—cannot be completely eliminated.

But if each of the extremes cannot exclude the other, and therefore we cannot ever legitimately consider the human being as mere body or as pure spirit—granted that the immediate experience of freedom as a capacity for origin doesn't cancel the contrary evidence that reveals our rootedness in facticity and in the realm of absolute determination—it is no less true that this experience of freedom exhibits a certain "radial" structure of the person that allows us to speak of centrifugal and centripetal movements and, paradoxically, prevents us from considering the person as a *real* point in a straight-linear causal process.

When we understand a human action by means of the hereditary, social, economic, and educational, and so on history of its agent, all we are doing is establishing a series of convergent lines—in and of themselves incapable of causing the given action to emerge or of explaining it. This action will always be attributable to a person. It will always be an event that is *understandable within a biographical outline* that is personal, internal relative to the person, and not simply a link in a chain of events that are external relative to each other. Between the lines of force that we drew from the circumstances and the action that we want to understand there is always a hiatus: it is like the external and negative side that freedom shows to our attempt to offer an external and causal explanation. Freedom resists being eliminated. No matter how overwhelming the volume of information we contribute to transform our subject into a pure *patient* or to turn our subject into a link in the series, we will never be able to strip this person of his or her character of author, unless we strip this individual of his or her human quality, something which is, in principle, impossible.

Freedom, as a *capacity of origin* is not, however, something absolute that can manifest itself in a pure state, as evidenced by the efforts of certain aesthetic doctrines to perform a "gratuitous act," efforts that are inevitably doomed [55] to failure because freedom in its pure state is an abstract, imaginary entity. Freedom, when it emerges, makes its own motivations and purposes. An action without a motive or without a purpose is an unthinkable and unrealizable action. To affirm its possibility is to play with empty concepts and to accept the naïve notion that freedom is an absence of motivation. But if it [freedom] cannot be found in a pure state, neither can it be negated without immediately falling into a contradiction with universal experience.

Moving our example forward, the virtualities of freedom—in which its meaning for the personal structure of human nature and for what certain literature has come to call "human dignity" are rooted—will become clearer.

A person who has committed a criminal act can have a legitimate interest in getting his or her lawyers to present him or her before the judge as an irresponsible being, in other words, someone who cannot be positioned at the origin of his or her own actions; as a result of chance intertwinements of natural conditions or of others' actions [or] in the way of a mushroom emerging from the putrid floor of a badly organized society. It is possible that, by this means, this person gets exonerated. All this can very well be done, and nobody has anything to object to [in] it. Such things happen daily in all the criminal courts in the world. But this person can vindicate full responsibility for his or her actions. This person can reconquer the responsibility that the defense lawyers had the intention of taking off his or her shoulders by transforming him or her into an excrescence of the circumstances. [In reconquering responsibility], this person can thus recover the famous human dignity. To the extent that this person becomes responsible, he or she becomes free, and, to the extent that this person becomes free, he or she affirms him- or herself as a human being. The person assumes the way of being of a human being and moves away from the way of being of things. Only "someone" and never "something" can be responsible and free.

This example, then, makes visible the internal connection that exists between the notions of freedom and of responsibility. This connection is founded, precisely, on an "interiority" that cannot be suppressed; it [interiority] makes the human being an entity with a "radial" structure—an entity that cannot be inserted into the chains of linear processes that are, perhaps, the form par excellence of nature's intelligibility.

Each individual is a spiritual vortex who [56] polarizes all his or her outline toward his or her center. If we call the imaginary space delineated by this vortex "subjectivity," and if we call the property it has of being a source of actions capable of modifying its shape "freedom," we can characterize freedom as a passage or transfer, a passing from interiority to exteriority, no matter how difficult it may be to establish exact limits between both terms. My freedom is actualized in this passage. It can be said that freedom *is* that passage, which can also be conceived of as a movement from the exterior to the interior in a process of internalization. In internalization, we also find an activity of subjectivity, a centrifugal motion analogous to the realization of an action toward the outside. A well-known process of this type is the acquisition of class consciousness, in which a worker internalizes, in other words, makes actively his or her own, a situation that before was entirely meant to be endured and external [to the person] and that, when internalized implies a certain liberation. The same thing happens in the case of an illness, a physical insufficiency, or any experience of failure. To the degree that I learn to take into account such eventualities, that is to say, to the extent that I make them *mine* with full clarity, I free myself from them. They only confuse me and torment me if I resist integrating them into my behavior just as they are, if I refuse to take them into account. Then I suffer them passively as something external, not inherent to my personality that, however, determines my personality from "the outside."

Freedom appears from a different perspective when we understand it as a condition of the possibility of normativity in general, when we confirm that the existence of any imperative implies the existence of freedom. All imperatives presuppose and recognize freedom, since an imperative—be it legal or moral—can only be directed toward a being that does not perform a fatally predetermined behavior and of which it is presumed that he or she can engage in behavior dissonant with the imperative itself, that he or she cannot fulfill the imperative.

By means of the fact of the law, the need for freedom is revealed to us; this need appears as what makes possible the existence of law. To say it using Kant's terminology, law is the *ratio cognoscendi* of freedom; freedom is the *ratio essendi* of law.

But freedom as seen through the law offers us only [57] an external image of itself. Certainly, when we direct our gaze toward the world of imperatives, we take charge of freedom, but we see it, so to speak, in a mirror. We see it projected outside ourselves on the screen of the objective spiritual world, without attaining it in its metaphysical significance, consequently, the scant influence of speculations of a purely judicial nature surrounding freedom and the vulnerability of the apologies of freedom that seek to derive it merely from law.

Freedom as a virtuality of the world of culture acquires, however, a formidable significance when we consider it as political freedom. From this point of view, freedom vindicates for itself all the privileges of its phenomenological, judicial, and metaphysical significance, and it manifests itself as a truly active sense of human existence on all its levels: as a foundation for what is human as such, as a motor of history, as an aspiration of personal life and of the life of the community. Political freedom is, at the same time, external and internal; it is a condition and an end of action. In its political meaning, freedom acquires the character of the End par excellence.

Political freedom can adequately be described as the situation of a human community in which the development of each individual as a person to the maximum of his or her possibilities is not obstructed either by other individuals or by intermediary entities located between the individual and the State, such as the family, [social] classes, professional or faith-based associations, and so on; it is the situation in which this maximum development of the person not only is not obstructed but guaranteed and protected by the institutions through which sovereignty is expressed.

Aristotle believed that the State was the most perfect of all communities because it is a form of association that allowed one to attain superior values unattainable at the level of family or of clan life. Superior values, inherent to the intellectual or moral life of the individual, could only become possible, according to Aristotle, in the context of human relationships, a context which, seen as a whole and externally, we call the State. His idea of the State was subordinated to what the Greeks called the "good life"; this "good life," in turn, was conceived of by Aristotle as the realization of the superior values of justice [58], wisdom, and so on, that presuppose a harmonious and perfect development of the person and the source of which can be none other than freedom.

This notion of political freedom as a condition for human personal fulfillment can be found—with more or less important differentiating nuances—at the bottom of almost all the political doctrines that have governed the history of the Western world, including Marxism, in spite of its current manifestations that would induce one to think more of a sacrifice of freedom and of the person for the benefit of the State, adopted as an end (subordinated to the total liberation of human beings in a classless society but, in any case, as an end that is independent and external to the individual person).

From this perspective, universal history can be thought of as a progressive realization of political freedom operated by the different human communities by means of successive removals of the obstacles—both internal and external to society—that oppose the total process of deliberation, be it through violence or by a continuous and progressive effort. Thus it can be said that the history of a people, and even of humanity, is the history of a freedom (in a metaphysical sense, as ultimate origin of actions attributable to human beings and as a condition of a possibility of action) that marches toward its liberation (toward the total elimination of the societal and natural barriers that prevent the full realization of the virtualities of the person and of the group).

In the eighth proposition of his *Idea of a Universal History from a Cosmopolitan Point of View*, Kant asserts that "one can consider the history of the human species as a whole as the realization of a hidden plan by Nature to produce a perfect political constitution on the inside and, at the service of this end, equally perfect on the outside; this is the only state of things in which Nature can *completely develop all the dispositions it has placed on humanity.*"

That said, this complete development of human dispositions (even if planned by "Nature") is subject to human initiative, and, because of this, it turns out to be a creation of freedom understood as autonomy of the will. It is the realization of a liberation that presupposes a freedom capable of adopting it as an end. The third "proposition" [59] of this same work, which already conceives of the totality of history as *feat of freedom*—in spite of the fact that its author is thinking of the horizon of the eighteenth-century idea of Nature—states thus: "Nature has wanted humans to bring out eternally from themselves all that transcends the mechanical operation of their animal existence and that does not partake of any other joy or perfection that is not one which they themselves have created for themselves, independently from instinct, by means of their own reason."

Political freedom, however, even extending the radius of its meaning to the point of being able to be constituted as a fulcrum of a possible philosophy of universal history, presupposes all the other notions of freedom, not only as a condition of its own possibility but also, even, as a motor of its advent and of its actualization within reality. But this [point] is precisely its privilege and its importance: it allows us to accept that freedom is not only an attribute of individual subjectivity but also a task and an objective direction of the march of history to which the volume of sacrifice and the effort that humans have made or suffered in its name lend a great seriousness.[21]

Freedom in a political sense—in spite of or precisely because of its seriousness—cannot be the fulcrum that we seek in order to understand the sense of *relajo*, which [60] is our only purpose here, although perhaps it would not be entirely irrelevant in order to understand the true relationship between *relajo* and revolution, or, in general, between *relajo* and politics, a relationship so deeply misunderstood by those who would wish to discover superior values in all manifestations of Latin-American life, even in the most abject ones. It was important to us, however, to point out that freedom can be the end of an action and not just a condition for its possibility or a metaphysical characteristic essential to human existence.

Political freedom is the form par excellence of freedom as the end of an action. Researching the implications of this privilege can, nonetheless, give way to a deep conceptualization, both of the sense of what is human and that of universal history, but it is not the only form in which freedom offers itself to us as an end. There are many other possibilities of the end-freedom that appear in an immediate way in the innumerable experiences of *liberation*.

The notion of *liberation* reveals another possible form of manifestation of freedom, to which the idea of obstacle is inherent and which we will attempt to clarify next.

Humans are beings of such nature that, even if by their corporality they participate in the way of being of things, they are capable of transcending them. A human is not just one more thing *alongside* other things, but one which can give things to him- or herself as an *object*, which can confront him or her, and in so doing, move beyond all of them. Humans are capable of setting goals that can go beyond their own situation and the present state of the world, taken as a whole. By virtue of the form of his or her being itself, a human, each human, is beyond him- or herself and his or her physical boundaries, beyond his or her body and situation. A human is a facticity (body, situation, irrevocable past, etc.) that is at the same time transcendence, in other words, a going beyond all of this, thus giving him or her meaning through a project of him- or herself.

This structure of the being of humans is a condition for the appearance of something akin to an obstacle and of a possible liberation. Only because I project myself as a philosopher or a humanist, because I can be—in any way whatsoever—beyond my present ignorance, the absence of the teaching of Greek, of Latin, or of world literature in our secondary education system can appear to me as an obstacle, but also, by virtue of this transcendence [of mine], I can free myself from my [61] ignorance by studying them on my own. It is a cliché that prison walls are only a prison for those who are capable of pursuing their ends and completing their projects beyond those walls, and they are not a prison, perhaps, for the homeless person who only within those walls can find sustenance and rest.

Experiences of liberation certainly do not exhaust the content of the notion of freedom, but rather they constitute, perhaps, the most immediate and most frequent form of experiencing freedom. Hegel would say that they are not the "truth" but rather the "phenomenon" of freedom. Freedom would then be experienced for the first time with the arrival of the first consciousness of an obstacle, and [freedom] would be realized for the first time by overcoming it.

That said, since transcendence is an essential characteristic of the being of humans, the sense of human existence would be postulated as a sequence of successive liberations; and the course of personal existence could be conceived of as the history of a freedom that marches toward its liberation and, therefore, toward its humanization.

In any case, what is important to us is that when an obstacle is overcome "a characteristic spatiality" opens up, according to the beautiful expression coined by Romano Guardini. There is a form of manifestation of freedom that consists of living the overcoming of an obstacle and that carries with it the obscure consciousness that a space is opening up in front of us. There is a way to live freedom that implies a liberation, and this experience is founded upon the essential structure of human existence.

In order for this experience to be possible, it is not necessary for the obstacle to be external to the person; also a physical insufficiency or sufficiency, a passion, a resentment, a prejudice, can be kinds of obstacles that confine me within nonfreedom.

It is evident that resentment, just as a prejudice, operates as an obstacle that forbids access to a whole sector of reality or of values. A physical insufficiency, such as ugliness or short stature, can come to be an insurmountable obstacle to a normal communal life for some individuals. But the same thing occurs in the opposite case: there are those who cannot transcend their own intelligence, their good taste, or their social status, and who spend their lives showing these, imposing these on others. One can live in [62] perpetual reference—literally stuck—to one's own nose, as a permanent exhibit of a beautiful profile. Passion makes the miserly person powerless to go beyond the elemental significance of money as a source of security and power, without ever being able to reach full satisfaction. The miserly person takes pleasure in making a spectacle of giving it [money] to him or herself, as an infinitely firm incarnation of that security, power, etc. The overcoming of such attitudes is, evidently, liberation.

The intuition of freedom, which shines through from the depths of such experiences of liberation, brings us closer to the notion of freedom that we are searching for as a basis to understand the moral sense of *relajo*.

Indeed, freedom in general can be actualized in two clearly discernible ways. It can consist of an external liberation that implies the removal, destruction, or overcoming of an obstacle that is really present in the world, as occurs in the case of an individual who comes out of prison or in the case of a political change or a revolution. Freedom is here an end and a result of an action actually performed on things or situations. But it can also consist of a pure movement of interiority. It can consist simply of a change of attitude. There are possibilities of freedom that have no need of actual transcendence of consciousness, possibilities, that do not require the creation of a new real order of the world but that are free variations of attitude within pure interiority.

When I free myself from a prejudice, in other words, when I learn to direct a clean gaze toward things and people—no longer paying attention to the steamed up glass of a stock phrase or of a preconceived notion that I received without knowing when or how I did—apparently, nothing has happened. I have changed my attitude, but everything remains the same. No doubt, there has been a change, but *only* in my interior. *Only* my subjectivity has been altered.

One could think that such a change of attitude is a false liberation and that such changes don't affect in any way the progression of things, that the variations of subjectivity are a value when considering reality and that good intentions ought to continue contributing to a worsening of hell as a fair punishment for their ineffectiveness.

But, leaving aside the eventual ineffectiveness of good [63] intentions, it is a fact of experience that a change of attitude in pure interiority can have and indeed actually does have the effectiveness to change the way the world appears to the person who adopts the new attitude; and the way the world appears is not a negligible factor in lucid and effective action. Things vary quite a lot if we look at history through the glass of progress or of decadence. The action of an individual or a human community will be different in one case or another, and how the world appears will prove decisive for the individual's or community's action, and thus decisive for the appearance the world may acquire after this action.

Certainly, nothing changes in the world with my change of attitude but I myself. But to the degree that I am part of the world and that I am essentially in reference to reality, my change can be the beginning of a change in the world.

But, no matter whatever may become of all this, it is important to point out here that a variation in the *appearance* of things corresponds to a certain variation in my subjectivity. Subjectivity is like the dimension of depth in the world; from subjectivity, variations in the way the world appears are constantly emerging; subjectivity is like the very possibility of these variations. It is not then a romantic depth, in the sense of a growing overcoming of distances full of mystery or as a perpetual evanescence of its origin, but rather as an always latent possibility of changing its sense. Subjectivity is the primeval origin of the different meanings that the world can have and it is, as such, an origin, free, since it does not emerge necessarily from the state of the world but rather it is—in the last instance—a source of its meaning and its state; a source, even, of that way of seeing in which the world appears shackled by pure causal determinations.

The free variations of my subjectivity, the changes of attitude in pure interiority—some of which can be characterized as liberations and that produce a concomitant change in the appearance of the world—in operating this change of appearance open up several different possibilities for my behavior. This is what interests us here. To this type of event, of attitude variations, belong those difficult-to-grasp human realities which we call irony, humor, seriousness, and spirit of seriousness. The examination of their meaning and of their reciprocal relationships[22] [64] regarding the backdrop of the notion of freedom will clarify—we hope—the moral sense of *relajo*.

IRONY

Irony, like *relajo*, can be understood in light of the relationship between consciousness and value. We have said that it is a possible variation of a subjective attitude. We must also say that it is a noteworthy and not very frequent attitude that human beings can, however, adopt freely. It is not imposed by any circumstance external to consciousness. Thus, as a given, it is characterized as an attitude of a consciousness or of a human being. But this is evidently not sufficient for a more or less complete intellection of its absence and its value. Our assertion is only an initial step, since irony as an attitude already contains a series of possibilities of behavior, in the way an attitude or bodily gesture indicates a whole series of movements and concurrent actions. In order to show clearly the essence and sense of irony, we will begin by directing our gaze toward the vague notion we all have of irony, before any theoretical reflection, and we will try to corner it using successive approaches in order to achieve a more or less clear intuition of it.

The first thing that the word "irony" suggests is a certain dissonance, a contradiction. It is ironic—we say—that a person knows what justice is and that he is not just. It is ironic that a person believes he or she is wise and does not behave wisely, that he or she purports to possess a "superior" knowledge and has an inferior behavior.

Irony seems even to dominate long-range processes, like a contradiction that suddenly emerges: it is ironic that humans have spent two centuries deepening their voices to speak of progress and of technology and that technology, like a sinister mouse, has given birth to the atomic bomb.

Irony seems to *be* [located][23] not only in a human being, in those who internally consider themselves wise while their external behavior shows them as stupid or evil. It seems also to emerge as a sense of an entire historical development. That said, if we observe these contradictions more closely [65], we will see that they do not seem ironic simply because they are contradictory. What is ironic is not that there is contradiction or dissonance in them, no less, since nonironic contradictions can exist. A person's failure at a long-sought-after endeavor is not necessarily ironic; no matter how much there may be a dissonance between a purpose and an achievement. In the failure of an endeavor permeates a contradiction that could be tragic, without any mix whatsoever with irony. In order for there to be irony, there is a need for something more than pure and simple contradiction. Our examples manifest a contradiction between a "self-assumption" and reality. A person assumes he or she is wise but acts with ignorance. A historical period assumes it is in possession of the key to human happiness, but in furthering its concepts, it produces an instrument of destruction that sows anxiety among humankind. This is what we call irony and it is, really, ironic. But what is ironic here? Certainly not the contradiction taken purely and simply as such but rather the contrast between the assumption of possessing any certain value (wisdom, justice, infallible effectiveness of a means toward achieving human happiness) and the reality of what is actually achieved. On the other hand, this contrast must be made manifest in light of the value in question.

That being said, a contrast is not a real thing that can be found alongside other things. A contrast is a relationship, and relationships—no matter how objective and concrete they may be—are not real attributes of things but rather references established between them by consciousness. Irony is, then, immanent to a consciousness that judges and that notices the distance between the possible realization of a value and its supposed realization by someone with a pretense of fulfilling it. It is, so to speak, the adequate response to the "self-assuming person."

Irony can manifest itself, on the other hand, as inherent to thought itself. It also has to do with the logical structure of thought, or I should say, of the proposition [66]. There is within irony something of a logic game: it is a dialectic. When Socrates tells Euthyphro, "You, admirable Euthyphro, are the only one of us who knows what piety is," all of us *see* that Euthyphro knows nothing about piety. What has happened here? What has happened is that, at the very instant when Socrates says this, we know that he means to say exactly the opposite. The meaning of the proposition "You know what piety is" remains the same, but its sense has totally changed; this has happened at the very instant in which the proposition was made, because the proposition is found within an ironic context. Based on Socrates' ironic attitude, precisely because of that attitude, the figure of Euthyphro has changed its sense, and that of a sentence has been inverted. Because of its purely designative content, Socrates' utterance was destined to reveal Euthyphro's knowledge, but irony made it reveal exactly the opposite: his ignorance.

This shift in sense has occurred because the utterance lives in a mobile, dialectic atmosphere. The utterance itself is alive; it is animated by an intention of Socrates, who, for his part, is moving within the living unfolding of the conversation with Euthyphro. On the one hand, Socrates' attitude is what is ironic, but we see that it is an attitude capable of inverting the express sense of a proposition. Irony is something that can penetrate into logic and into reality; it also causes the sense of the figure of Euthyphro to change, transcending the consciousness or the psyche of Socrates. How is this possible?

Irony is the attitude Socrates holds toward Euthyphro, but he directs himself toward Euthyphro to the degree to which the latter is in relation to a value; he addresses "Euthyphro who knows about piety." By means of irony, Socrates shows that he doesn't limit himself only to saying it, but rather he makes it visible: he *shows* that this Euthyphro knows not one word about piety. Socrates makes us catch him red-handed in his not-knowing about piety. He undresses Euthyphro of his pretentions in such a way that we almost feel a little pity for dear Euthyphro, who is there, before our eyes, trying to cover up his nakedness with some rag of thought. Irony has suddenly transformed Euthyphro the wise into Euthyphro the ignorant.

Irony is thus an attitude, but it is also an action, an endeavor. One can speak, with fairness, of an ironic smile. There is an irony-consciousness, but there is [67] also, as in Socrates, the irony-endeavor, at the end of which it will have been made clear that Euthyphro knows nothing about piety. But irony is not only this.

There is irony-consciousness, which is an ironic attitude and which can manifest itself in a smile; there is irony-action, and also the irony inherent to an ironic proposition. Looking at things well, irony is not a logical quality of the proposition, since the proposition in its pure logical value is sufficient for itself. Irony appears when the proposition is seen in relation to its object with what is meant by it. The logical structure of the proposition, in contrast, is immanent to the proposition itself and doesn't take into account at all the relationship of the proposition to its object. That being said, a proposition is ironic when it reveals exactly the opposite of what it is affirming. Irony—the ironic proposition—is not a paradox. A paradox is a proposition that contains a countersense in spite of which it is true. In an ironic proposition, there is no internal contradiction of the proposition itself, without which the paradox is inconceivable.

The contradiction that exists in irony can be discovered by turning one's gaze to the object of the proposition. Irony is a way of denoting "backwards." Just as [in bullfighting] one can speak of putting *banderillas* on the bull "by dodging it" [*al quiebro*],[24] one can also speak of denoting "backwards." This way of denoting is that of the ironic proposition. The ironic is not, then, found in the proposition but rather in the relation between the proposition and that alluded to by it.

The ironic is also not in things. One speaks of the ironies of life only by analogy. Irony is found more in the way of seeing things, a way of seeing them that underscores or pays attention to contradiction. But contradiction could not be found among things as such either. Contradiction is imposed by human beings. "As such," there is no contradiction between black and white, or between a feather and a piece of lead, or between two locomotives that collide head-on. But there is contradiction between what people say or think, or between what a person says and what that person does, because human doing is a form of speaking, and vice versa. And if there is contradiction between what a person expects and what he or she obtains, this is because all things human are imbued with "speech," with "logos": contradiction is something inherent to the spirit [68].

The ironic consciousness "sees" the contradictions and the vanities of existence and, by naming them, destroys them. But it destroys them by underscoring them, insisting on them by means of the artifice of naming them backwards. [The ironic consciousness] destroys them by condensing their contradictory essence until it explodes and clears open a path for us. Irony calls vanity "knowledge," so that vanity will be such vanity that it will disappear in its own total vanity. Socrates' words do not destroy Euthyphro, but they destroy his vanity for us, making it volatile by condensing it. They make it disappear, if not as a real psychological quality of Euthyphro, as a screen that obstructs the path toward knowledge and virtue.

However, in order for there to be irony, it is not enough to discover contradictions or to annihilate vanities. It is essential to have a will to truth. Socrates doesn't limit himself to bothering Euthyphro or to showing his superiority over him. Socrates isn't "teasing" Euthyphro; Socrates wants to know what piety is, and he wants to know it because he is ignorant of it, and he knows that he is. Euthyphro, in contrast, is a technician of piety; he simply doesn't know what piety is, and Socrates needs this knowledge most urgently, not only to fill the void of his ignorance but also because he considers it indispensable for the good functioning of the city.

Socrates, the father of philosophy, also invented irony. In him, irony is not only the destruction of a vanity by means of the brilliant roundabout of calling it knowledge or virtue, but also a will to truth. Also, [it is] the sharpest, most direct, and passionate will to truth that any human being has ever had before. Plato has him say, "Nothing pleases me if it is not at the same time truth," in a formula that expresses the motto of all genuine philosophy and of all superior humanity.

This will for truth and this rectitude, inherent to Socratic irony, are essential to *irony*, [in general] no less. If it were otherwise, irony could be confused with mocking, with sarcasm, with teasing, and even with *relajo*—attitudes that are purely negative or that tend, at most, as in the case of teasing, toward an affirmation of the individual who adopts them.

Irony, thus, manifests itself, on the one hand, as something demolishing. It is a negation. But, on the other hand, it is a constructive affirmation. In a certain way, it annihilates Euthyphro, but with this, it contributes a liberation for us. It opens to our [69] gaze the path, the space that leads to the essence of the sacred and that, before, had been obstructed by Euthyphro, by his vanity and his ignorance.

Socrates' irony manifests itself as a way of freeing oneself of an obstacle that is in opposition to our knowledge: Euthyphro's authority. We can say, then, that Socrates frees us completely and opens up the path toward truth for us, through an act with which he frees himself—by means of irony—from Euthyphro's illegitimate authority—which at the same time seems illegitimate only after Socrates' irony.

In Socrates' irony, something is also at stake for us; we, who in a certain way are his contemporaries because we are interested *with him* in the truth about the sacred or of the good, of beauty, of justice, and so on. Socrates' attitude is not only an ailment of his interior; it is truly a source of perspectives of the world, and his liveliness is capable of altering those perspectives. The world blocked off by Euthyphro has turned into a world open to our questioning. Socrates' irony, by transforming the world, is in a sense the foundational act of a community: that of disciples, the community of those who seek the truth.

Neither is Socratic irony a mere game, a form of agility that he exercises like a dialectic [form of] fencing in order to show his own importance. In Socrates, irony is an act of liberation; it is distancing oneself from mere appearances in order to adequately direct the pursuit of truth. In irony, one transcends an obstacle toward the truth. This transcendence toward truth is realized in two stages.

Socrates was affirming his own ignorance. With that affirmation, he was saving himself from stock phrases and from formulas of a knowledge that had degenerated, transformed into pure appearances. But with this, Socrates was affirming his absolute relationship with truth. He was making himself infinitely responsible for it. For Socrates, truth was an absolute demand that required an absolute devotion. His irony is founded on a supreme seriousness, since seriousness is nothing other than vocation for and unconditional devotion to a value. In it, this vocation and devotion are not subject to any condition whatsoever, not even to that of living. Socrates could employ irony precisely because he transcended himself and his concrete interests toward truth, beyond the assumptions of [70] his fellow citizens regarding virtue and knowledge, but also beyond his own life. He himself points out the absolute character of his commitment when he presents it as a demand of the Deity and he affirms, facing death, its irrevocable character.

Then, the figure of Socrates shows us the ironist as a person whose calling is truth itself. This person's ignorance is a will to truth; it is honest, good will in opposition to the Sophist, who conforms to an appearance of truth and who shows off as a master of the art of worldly success, moved deep down by a will to power, like a charlatan. Sophists are expressly preoccupied with appearances. They are careful about their solemn physical appearance; their behavior, destined for the eyes of others, is an exhibition of their own importance and of the excellence of their doctrine.

Plato shows us Protagoras strolling along an inner courtyard, accompanied by eight or ten disciples who are obligated to perform the strangest maneuvers to not end up positioned physically in front of him, so they can regain their spot behind the master every time he "with great elegance" turns around and retraces his steps. Socrates doesn't worry about things concerning him. He is a poor man; he declares in his defense before the Aeropagus that he doesn't care for being honored publicly; he affirms "not having had any authority whatsoever outside that of an advisor" and having neglected "what others care so much about: becoming wealthy, economics, generalships, leadership positions, etc."

He doesn't consider himself, nor does he want to be considered anybody's teacher, nor does he aspire—this less than anything—to be treated externally with signs of respect, like the Sophists. With the Sophist, who loudly proclaims the excellence of his own knowledge, the philosopher [Socrates] contrasts, with his irony, the silence of his vocation for truth. His gaze sees beyond appearances, and, with ironic action, he makes the distance between appearances and truth, manifest itself—the chasm that separates the contingent from the value in all its purity. But he is only capable of acting in this way because he previously made himself responsible for value. Because in reality he is deeply serious, having the genuine seriousness that does not take seriously what is not serious, the appearances that are flaunted with a pretense for recognition by people. The ironist takes the weight off appearances in order to throw over his or her back that of genuine value. In doing this, he or she removes from the shoulders of others the weight thrown [71] on them by those who aspire to pass for representatives of value. The ironist's liberating action takes place, thus, against the backdrop of seriousness and of responsibility. It is evident that, in Socrates, the will to truth doesn't mean knowledge. He affirms an absolute commitment to truth, to which, certainly, all of us human beings are obligated, but not an "absolute knowledge." He doesn't present himself as the possessor of a totalitarian system of knowledge. He has no pretense of knowing what he himself has shown that others do not know—which is exactly what the Sophist does. Socrates doesn't affirm himself, but rather he frees his interlocutor and his listeners and frees us by opening up for us the path toward truth. He would badly have been able to undertake this liberation if he had had the intention of imposing *his* knowledge on us. In affirming his ignorance, he affirms a negation, but it happens that this negation is the same one that all human beings have inside. Irony is, in the last instance, a negativity that—because it involves an absolute commitment to value—is capable of founding a community; in other words, it is capable of opening up a perspective for communication of some human beings with others in a constructive task: the investigation and establishment of truth.

Irony, then, does not exclude seriousness. Irony and seriousness appear as correlative attitudes in the *interior* of freedom and of responsibility. In this way, the meaning of irony begins to outline itself in contrast to the fundamental attitude of *relajo*. The latter [*relajo*] is a suspension, pure and simple, of seriousness, which is equivalent to irresponsibility. Irony is a liberation that founds a freedom for the value. *Relajo* is a negation that founds a pseudofreedom that is purely negative and thus infertile.

HUMOR

In the previous example, we have seen how value always transcends its contingent actualizations. An act of punctuality does not make me punctual. Value and being do not seem to ever be able to unite in a definitive manner, or, at least, there doesn't seem to be any experience or object in the area of our human experience in which this coincidence occurs fully. The sweet flavor of a fruit or the coolness of water is not "sweetness" or [72] "coolness" as such, fully realized. Values in themselves always are beyond their possible manifestations; they are not exhausted in any of their realizations. This transcendence of a value, we have said, is what makes irony possible, [since] irony is nothing other than the form of consciousness that makes it [the transcendence of the value] obvious when someone has the assumption of constituting him- or herself as the full incarnation of some value.

We can find another attitude in certain closeness to irony; this is an attitude that, at first glance, is similar to it but that rests on very different foundations: humor. Humor can be defined, in comparison to irony, as transcendence toward freedom. In irony, there is transcendence toward the value. In humor, one simply makes evident that freedom is the transcendence of existence as a whole.

When speaking of experiences of liberation, we had somehow shown how such experiences are only possible thanks to that essential characteristic of the structure of human existence that contemporary philosophy calls transcendence. The latter, for its part, manifests itself to us as a founding freedom, as a freedom that makes liberation possible. Irony then turns out to be liberation toward a value. Humor, in contrast, is liberation toward freedom. Irony has its starting point in a concrete person, to then leave a value wide open. Humor, in contrast, leaves wide open the opening of transcendence itself. What is transcended by irony is existence itself, and what the movement of the humorist transcends is the opening of freedom.

We have already noted in our previous reflections that value and being never coincide completely. On the other hand, we have characterized value—because of its living function within human existence—as a "guide for self-constitution," in other words, as a certain orientation or guide of human existence that can never be manifested absolutely within it. The world suffers from a peculiar form of lack of focus. The worlds of being and of value, although they are in a certain way "the same world," never finish uniting fully in order to show us a clear and unified profile that could offer us the identification of one with the other. Things always seem to us as if we suffered from metaphysical strabismus [73]. We always see them as we see an image being projected by a badly focused projector. Constantly, with an effort, we have to correct the image we have in front of us, precisely to recognize it as an "image" of this or that idea; of this or that value; of this or that mental outline. Outlines are weak, or they pile up on each other; values unfold beyond the drawing, and vice versa. Art offers us, on privileged occasions, an image of what a world would be like in which *being* and *value* would correspond to each other with a correspondence of identity, and not of simple inherence, as occurs in our daily lives. Art offers us a world in which what exists has all the brightness of value and in which value appears already enfleshed, endowed with all the solidity of being. But art only gives us an image, that is to say, an imaginary realization of this lost unity. Religion, for its part, reaches the unity of value and being in the liminal experiences of music or in the eschatological idea of a renovated world, as in the idea of Saint Paul's "new creation" or in the otherworldly worlds of certain schools of Buddhism.

Thus, the value-being unity occurs *as if* it were already realized in art, while religion affirms a real unity of the terms, accessible in an extraordinary experience in which few human beings can participate, or in a unity to come in an indeterminate, yet imminent, future. Outside of these real or imagined exception experiences, we, regular human beings, find ourselves inevitably stuck in what—to us—is the unsurpassable blurriness and fading offered by existence.

Within this view, irony is an act that shows the insurmountable transcendence of value. Irony, we have said, directs one's gaze to the distance that separates what exists and value toward which what exists has directed itself.

Irony smiles when uttering a *no* with its gaze set on a negativity that cannot completely dominate existence.

The noncoincidence of value and being persists when the value in question is a negative value. The horizon of irony is the transcendence [74] of what exists relative to negative values. Irony frees us *toward* a positive value; humor frees us *from* a negative value, from an adversity.

The ironist lives on the horizon of the value's ideality. The humorist lives on the horizon of the negativity of existence. The ironist smiles when faced with a pretense of excellence, the humorist when faced with the powerlessness of adversity to completely dominate human existence. One and the other live in perpetual reference to that essential incompatibility between the value and being that we have pointed out. One and the other show the distance between existence and its meaning, but while the ironist is oriented toward transcendence of the value, the humorist is oriented toward freedom itself to show that the latter ends up abolished by the finiteness and the adversity of existence.

That said, given the fact of the finiteness of human existence and that of the negative tone, which so frequently predominates in it, the humorist is a person perpetually oriented in the direction of what we could call human wretchedness. The humorist discovers the contemptible motivations behind great doings or the despicable origins of great prestige. For example, the story of the man who is acclaimed for having saved another who was drowning, declares he is only interested in knowing who threw him into the water, is a humorous story. But this is only one possible direction for humor: it is the one that shows the insufficiency of the realizations of the value, not by direct reference to the value itself, not *from above* like irony—which makes obvious the value's purity and transcendence—but rather from *below*, by highlighting the presence of the despicable with and within the valuable. Humor, in this sense, appears also as a moderator of human assumptions of recognition of their own value, and it carries out—in a different direction—the same function as irony. In humor, the explicit direction of intention is not oriented toward the value itself but rather toward the circumstances of fact that cast a shadow over its realization.

But this negative critical aspect does not exhaust the possibilities of humor. If humor were to be exhausted in it, it would be merely a type of negative and bitter irony, a skeptic irony, in other words, a frustrated irony, which is almost equivalent to a nonirony. It would be purely and simply moral skepticism: cynicism. Genuine humor, in contrast [75], has an intention that is explicitly directed toward freedom. Its starting point is, in general, the negativity of existence; in particular, a case in which this negativity manifests itself strongly, in order to, from there, head toward freedom itself. Thus it shows how human beings are always beyond themselves and their circumstance, how humans can find themselves in the most adverse situations and face up to them as if they were external, alien acts that cannot get to them completely. Humor is a Stoic-style attitude that shows the fact that the interiority of human beings—their pure subjectivity—can never be reached or canceled by the situation, no matter how adverse this situation might be; humor shows that human beings can never be exhausted by their circumstance. "I am me and my circumstance," said Ortega y Gasset. To the humorist, I am rather me before my circumstance.

This meaning of humor is made particularly visible in so-called black humor, which highlights human transcendence not only when facing one's facticity in general but especially when faced with the painful, somber, or sinister aspects of existence. Someone has said that Mexico is the land of choice for black humor, and this is true to a certain extent. In Mexico, black humor is a common thing, and Mexicans put this attitude into practice sometimes with blood-curdling skill. Posada's drawings are a well-known testimony to this. For example, there is black humor in the story that tells of the exchange between the doctor and the man whose chest is pierced with a knife. "Does it hurt a lot?" asks the doctor. "Only when I laugh," answers the patient. There is also humor in the story about the man who leaves a party in a Mexico City neighborhood with the purpose of buying "*menudo*"[25] and along the way, he gets into a fight and stabbed. Upon returning, he barely is able to tell the hostess: "Please forgive me, *comadre*[26] the only *menudo* I was able to get was my own"; and he falls over dead with his intestines in his hands.

Someone once told me that, on the day of her birth, his grandmother had been stricken with a cancer on one of her toes. It was necessary to amputate the toe to prevent the cancer from spreading. But the cancer reappeared. Another amputation was necessary, and this process continued [76] uninterrupted. "When I met her," my friend concluded, "my grandmother was just a bust on the piano, and, when she died, she was nothing more than a little lock of hair." This is a real masterpiece of black humor. The story is sinister, yet it shows the possibility of treating it comically, of distancing oneself from the most intolerable situations.

In all these cases, comedy is the sign of liberation. One can laugh only if one distances oneself from what one is laughing about. A person, under certain circumstances, can seem comical to others, but not to him- or herself, as we have already indicated. While the others laugh, this person may feel shame or pain. But if this person is able to back off from his or her own situation and position him- or herself in the role of spectator, this person can laugh at him- or herself. In doing this, the person externalizes his or her transcendence-freedom. This capacity for distancing oneself is humor, and, when circumstances are atrocious, we call the situation "black humor." But the individual can only perform this gesture of detachment because freedom makes it possible. Humor is, thus, the externalization of this freedom and the capability of using it in the sense described. My capacity to laugh at myself is in direct correlation to my capacity to assume the possibility opened up a priori by this "internal" freedom.

The polarity within which irony takes place is that of "facticity-value"; the polarity of humor, that of "adversity-freedom"; the regulatory and explicit presence of freedom at the heart of humor allows humor to exert a "beneficial" influence, not only on those who put it into practice but also on those who witness the appearance of the humorous; humor provokes in its witnesses a peculiar feeling of ease and liberation that everyone loves and admires; that is why a person "without a sense of humor" is hardly friendly company. A person without humor is chained to his or her own virtues and outstanding qualities, be they real or imagined, the latter most frequently being the case. The humorless individual is an untouchable, always ready to stand up for his or her value supposedly violated by the carelessness of his or her interlocutors. It is not by chance that this type of individual is called "*pesado*" [literally, "heavy"]. He or she has a certain weight, like a thing, precisely because the individual wants to give his or her value all the weight and certainty of things. This individual neglects, in him- or herself, the presence of the factor that makes him [77] or her human [and] that makes human existence vulnerable and insecure, in spite of the fact that at the same time he or she is founding his or her dignity and covering it with lightness and transparency. Incapable of recognizing and directly confronting one's own self-transcendence, the humorless individual aspires to be filled with value, aspires to universal recognition and respect, but to *necessary* respect and recognition, analogous to the *necessary* recognition we grant to the existence of a present thing. With this, the humorless person negates his or her freedom, the only possible basis for genuine recognition of people by people, and the freedom of others, the only element that could make the recognition valuable. All of us are familiar with that dense, paralyzing atmosphere provoked by the presence of the individual who is "self-satisfied," stuck to his or her "self," enforcer of his or her own rules; all of us have felt the relief of his or her absence.[27]

There is another form of humor that does not consist of a direct showing of freedom, as in the case of black humor. In this [other] form of humor, freedom explodes—so to speak—before our eyes, canceling in one full swing the oppressive tension of the circumstances. Freedom emerges suddenly, like a lightning bolt, over the backdrop of an atrocious and overwhelming adversity: a man with his chest pierced with a dagger: "Only when I laugh." Here, freedom comes forth shining. The humorist's intention alludes directly to it.

But there is [yet] another style of humor that does not directly address freedom but rather alludes to it in an indirect fashion, beating about the bush. The backdrop of negativity, of adversity, of pain, or of human wretchedness is likewise present, and the humorous act consists of reducing the importance of that adversity. It lets us see that adversity is surely considerable and even overwhelming, but its action is not geared toward showing that, even if things are this way, human beings are free, but rather it limits itself to downplaying adversity. It operates on the index of adversity in reality, showing that its magnitude lacks a definitive meaning. It points out that the situation isn't so serious after all, or that it seems more tolerable than what a too-pathetic soul would want to make us believe.

"Thus," Kierkegaard tells us, "when an unfortunate man says, for example, 'It's all over for me; everything is lost,' the humorist could continue by saying: 'Yes. What [78] poor creatures we humans are, in the midst of this many-formed misfortune of life; all of us are condemned to suffering; if only I could see the day when my landlord would have the knocker on my door changed, I would consider myself fortunate.'" The humorist—Kierkegaard adds—does not say this to offend his unfortunate friend, but because "he has understood suffering in such a way that he considers any attempt to document it superfluous, and he expresses this by saying just anything."

That said, "understanding" suffering implies in this context, on the one hand, to take it into account, and on the other to represent it to oneself in a certain way, to put it before oneself; that is to say, to transcend it.

Humor operates here as a palliative for the pathos of adversity, and with this, it shows the humorist's freedom in an indirect fashion. The humorist knows perfectly that human existence is something *essentially* difficult and painful. The humorist's gesture of liberation does not imply despising or mocking. The humorist is not a cynic, nor does this individual attempt to be safe either from suffering or from humor. He or she simply knows that the issue is too serious to make a fuss out of it. The humorist—according to Kierkegaard, who has plumbed into the sense of irony and humor to greater depths than any other—is someone who is in the border zone between the moral and the religious. For the humorist, as for the religious individual, existence is suffering, but in contrast to the case of the religious individual, the humorist does not appeal to a transcendent entity that might contribute to a solution. On the edge of the religious, the humorist turns around and is silent: "He understands the significance of suffering in its relation to existence; (he knows it is essential to it), but doesn't comprehend the significance of suffering (because such a significance only becomes clear in a religious connection); he understands that suffering is a part of existence, but his understanding goes no further." "He touches, in pain, the secret of existence, but immediately, he is once again on himself." This turning back on oneself is accomplished by means of the joke and joking;[28] it is the significance of jokes within humor.

For Kierkegaard, humor has a significance of greater scope than the one we have given it. Although Kierkegaard's doctrine could be of only incidental importance to our purpose of [79] exploring the meaning of irony and of humor, we will present a brief exposition of the function and the sense that Kierkegaard gives to irony and humor within the totality of, and in a certain way, within the development of human existence. Keeping in mind his doctrine can clarify and open up new horizons of meaning for what we have said so far about these two attitudes [irony and humor].

Kierkegaard distinguishes three levels or spheres of existence: the aesthetic, the ethical, and the religious. Irony is the limit between the aesthetic and the ethical; humor is the border between the ethical and the religious. The aesthetic sphere is characterized by a naïveté that looks for happiness in life's immediate goods; it is characteristic of the individual who without thinking much of it devotes him or herself to pleasure, such as Don Juan, or to the attainment of a position in the hierarchy of the values actually current in a given society. This type of existence lacks unity; it is fragmented according to the multiple points of attraction that the world has to offer. The ironist is the individual who has understood this game and looks skeptically at the possibilities of fulfillment offered by the immediate, because this individual is already related to the "infinite ethical demand"; that is to say, with the value's unconditioned demand that demands from the individual a total detachment from the opportunities for pleasure that the world offers him or her. "Irony," says Kierkegaard, "manifests itself when, connecting in a continuous manner the particularities of finite life to the infinite ethical demand, contradiction appears." But one is not moral because one is an ironist. Irony still maintains a relationship with the "particularities of the finite." One is only within ethics when—and to the extent that—one "relates within oneself to the absolute demand"; that is to say, when one has fully assumed responsibility for value in the way that we have pointed out in Socrates' case. The ironist begins to be—or already is completely—a moral person, that is to say, a person who already views existence as a totality. The moral human being, the one who lives within the ethical sphere, relates to existence as a whole, on the one hand; on the other, this person maintains that totality of his or her existence as a unitary whole because he or she refers it all to the absolute datum of value, to the demand of duty. To the moral human being, duty is a total-izing instance that gives unity and freedom to existence.

The person of ethics, the moral person (which is not the [80] same thing as the moralist), however, can come to realize that existence implies, essentially, something inherent to finiteness: suffering. But even if this person understands the situation in all its depth, his or her life becomes tinged with certain skepticism of a superior level: humor. The moral person turns into a humorist when he or she begins to understand suffering as a necessary derivative of finiteness, as something essentially inherent to the human condition. With this, the humorist opens up to a type of superior community when he or she abandons the initial naïveté of the moral human being that pursued selfish ends and attributed a superior value to them, and he or she understands, even, that moral excellence is very far from a radical and universal solution to the enig-mas of existence. "Because humor," says Kierkegaard, "is a hidden suf-fering, it is also an instance of sympathy."[29]

Nevertheless, the humorist is not yet a person who lives in the sphere of the religious. His or her relationship with existence as a whole places this individual in reference to an absolute transcendence; the irrevocable presence of pain and of suffering as unsolvable enigmas point already to a solution at the religious level, but the humorist, even within a deep and living relationship with all these phenomena, never comes to assume them into a religious view; that is to say, as an opening to the transcen-dent and to the infinite. The humorist can expressly elaborate on the pain of the human situation, but he or she revokes it with a "humor-ous" act, with a joke. Being aware of the great charge of problematicity human existence has (an awareness without which he or she could not in any way be a humorist), the humorist verges on the limits of the reli-gious, but, nevertheless, turns his or her back to it.

Kierkegaard comments that "the fact that humor precedes faith, in the Christian religious sense, also shows the enormous game of existence (that is to say, the great number of life possibilities) possible outside of

Christianity, and on the other hand, the detachment required to correctly embrace Christianity."[30]

As we can see, Kierkegaard ascribes to irony and to humor an essential significance in the deeper layers of [81] existence. He doesn't think that these attitudes are simply areas close to the comic, nor does he consider the comic itself a simple "curiosity" of life. To Kierkegaard, these are radical attitudes that show all their sense only when they are understood with the totality of existence as a starting point. Regardless of this "existential" sense of irony and of humor, [these phenomena] interest us only because of their peculiar relationship to freedom; we highlight them in this connection simply to make our vision of the moral sense of *relajo* clearer.

With his or her attitude, the humorist is prevented from falling into sentimentalism and bombast. With this, the humorist outlines in advance a style of existence that we have labeled as Stoic. This individual makes a commitment to not invoke adversity or suffering in order to give him- or herself the luxury of doing nothing. The humorist's attitude implies that human pain or his or her own suffering cannot serve as a valid excuse, that humans continue to be responsible for their lives and for all the things they do, even if they are involved in a difficult situation, [and] in spite of the fact that life drags along with it a formidable volume of difficulties and adversity. With their attitude, humorists point out the fact that we cannot cancel our responsibility, that is to say, our freedom, simply because life is hard; the humorist points out that human beings are called to, always freely, tasks that are a pressing demand, even if life is a "sea of troubles," in the words of Hamlet—who is not a humorist but rather a pathetic man, and like all pathetic people, incapable of an action that is decisive and that imposes order on reality.

RELAJO, HUMOR, AND IRONY

Thus, freedom manifests itself as a positivity both in humor and in irony. It appears as a constant of responsibility, a bit more like an immediate achievement in irony and a bit more like a presupposition in humor. But in both cases, freedom appears as a backdrop of responsibility, like the aura of seriousness and of a commitment. Freedom appears here pregnant with possibilities for action, enveloping existences that are clearly thrust in a direction. It is freedom that is actually realized in the world;

in it, freedom opens up perspectives full of sense in which [82] anybody can participate. Irony and humor are a certain opening up of pathways within the tangle of human pretenses and feelings.

Let us now see what happens to *relajo*: what is its relationship with irony and humor, two attitudes with which, on the surface, it would seem to be related by analogy.

We have seen that *relajo* is an attitude of dissidence. It is a *no* secreted by a consciousness that refuses to support the demand for the realization of a value. At first glance, *relajo* appears, thus, as an attitude whose sense is freedom, since freedom can also be conceived of as pure negation. One can think of freedom as the floating, expectant condition of a consciousness *not* determined by the causal series of physical-natural happening. Freedom can be conceived by negation. This negation which is supposedly constituent of freedom can be extended, no doubt, to the moral world, since the demand of value or of law has no compulsive efficacy over the will. One can refuse to follow the fragile indications of pure value. One can perpetually pass by the unconditional demands of morality. The ethical norm cannot even be conceived of as a natural legality exercised by the spirit on the human will.

If one accepts this negative notion of freedom as valid, if we consider that this nondependence of natural causality and ethical demand (leaving aside the radical differences that evidently separate one from the other) to be full and complete freedom, then there is no doubt that *relajo* is an act of liberation and that in exercising it one attains a certain freedom. This, evidently, is the notion of freedom that *internally* presides over the actuality of *relajo*.

But this notion of freedom is twice as illusory. On the one hand, it interprets a mere negation in positive terms: it gives positive value to something that doesn't have it and whose positivity—if it did have any (as in its being an expression of the freedom of action)—does not come from its negative character. To say it in other words: this interpretation ignores the fact that an act of loyalty to value is just as free as an act of negation of value. I am free when I refuse to follow the indications of value or of duty, but [83] I am equally free when I consent to following them, and I follow them effectively. *Relajo* is an attitude that illegitimately identifies rebelliousness with freedom, without seeing that rebelliousness involves freedom in the same way that nonrebelliousness does. One and the other refer in the same way to value: they are activities in the moral order, and therefore, they are *always already* in the realm of freedom. The interpretation of *relajo* as a liberation toward freedom doesn't realize that its character as a free act does not come from its negation but rather from its spontaneity.

Freedom as pure negation, on the other hand, is not more than a mirage and a deception, since the "freedom from," the negative freedom, is but the negative side of a "freedom to," or the given of responsibility. In the first case, negative freedom is but an aspect of positive freedom that is indeed a genuine liberation, an opening up of the path for effective action in the realization of values. In the second, it is but the negative form of responsibility: I am responsible for my actions; therefore I am *not* absolutely subject to circumstances.

Relajo goes into a blind alley, into the illusion of negative freedom, and it attains only infecundity. It is an action geared toward obstructing action with sense. Thus, to the degree that it is effective, *relajo* is effective for failure. It pursues a mirage of value: freedom as a simple *no*; that is to say, it pursues the value that can exist in not realizing value. It is an action ordered toward disorder, toward tangling and confusing the pathways of action.

Irony cancels the obstacles that block the paths toward genuine value. *Relajo* mixes up paths, values, and situations; it locks us up into a noisy immanence of facticity that obscures value's authenticity and even makes its existence doubtful. With this, *relajo* closes the channels that connect the immanence of the situation and the transcendence of the value, and it promotes an atmosphere of enclosure and lack of communication.

Humor makes freedom obvious as the immovable place where human responsibility is seated. *Relajo* mimes a movement of freedom that is actually a negation of freedom in search of an escape route toward irresponsibility.

The freedom of the ironist originates in a passionate [84] assuming of responsibility for a value, the pseudofreedom of *relajo*, in a radical refusal to assume that responsibility. Irony points toward a world ordered in the sense of authenticity and of the truth of moral life. *Relajo* is a desperate attempt to prevent moral life from manifesting itself as a spirited appeal to an ennobling and a spiritualization of human life.

The action of the ironist is succeeded by a world unencumbered by the obstacles that oppose the sincere search for truth or of some other value, in which the paths of thought and action appear cleared for human endeavors. The action of the humorist is succeeded by a world free of the temptation of pathos that proclaims that everything is useless and that humans are inevitably unfortunate beings incapable of remedying their situation. The action of *relajo* is succeeded by a world in which everything stays the same as before, but in which one more failure has occurred in the endeavor of making values come into reality.

Irony wants truth; humor wants freedom; *relajo* wants irresponsibility. The *no* that *relajo* presents in opposition to the realization of value flows into itself. *Relajo*, literally, wants a freedom for nothing; freedom to choose nothing; it promotes disorder so as not to have to do anything in a prolonged action with sense. *Relajo* has irresponsibility as an end.

If, on the other hand, we conceive freedom as a "possession of oneself within an order," whichever order this may be, as required by the essential reference of freedom to action, then *relajo* appears as a veritable "abdication of oneself in disorder." Indeed, the notion of "order" in human life is but the a priori condition of action. The word "order" implies an idea of finality. One says that an action is "ordered" "toward an end," that a feeling is "ordered" toward an object or toward a person.

The idea of "order" highlights a structure of active meaning. An "order" is a state of the world in which the instrumental relationships between action and its ends are clearly visible. Human beings are all the more free the clearer the notion they have of their own function in a perspective of means and ends, the greater authority humans attain [85] over their own situation, thanks to a precise view of "their" ends within a constellation of effective means. The promotion of disorder is, then, strictly equivalent to the muddling of the channels of action, and that is precisely the result of *relajo*. But the action of *relajo* points toward an even more decisive direction. As negation of value, it attempts to suppress even the general direction of the action, since it prevents the clear expression of the ultimate significance of the means and ends themselves. Not only does it render effective action difficult or impossible, but also, with its negativity, it erases the motivation of the action itself: the value. *Relajo* kills action in its cradle. It negates the only thing that gives sense to action; it prevents the light of value light from illuminating the scaffolding of mediate means and ends that would lead to the action's realization. *Relajo* is a paradoxical inactive call that renders the value's call sterile. It is the sterilizing action par excellence; it is a moral saltpeter in which action with sense—or what is the same thing, responsible action—cannot grow. After *relajo*, things remain exactly the same as before. Because of this, *relajo* cannot be considered a "revolutionary" attitude, as we will see further ahead. Its indisputable effectiveness consists of making another's action ineffective.

Relajo sabotages freedom, while irony and humor—modalities of subjective freedom—clear the paths of action. Nevertheless, the three attitudes [irony, humor, and *relajo*] have something in common. They are, in a sense, responses to a human circumstance in which a value is somehow at stake. Irony annihilates an assumption, and unjustified prestige, and opens up a path for the value. Humor cancels pathos—which is an attitude of desperation toward action. In pathos, the affirmation "There's nothing that can be done" is implicit. Pathos wants to confirm as insurmountable a state of the world. Humor destroys this confirmation and gives back its transitory character to the situation that pathos wanted to make permanent.

But none of these attitudes denies the axiological situation as a whole. Irony preserves the sense of value and the demand to direct one's life according to this value. Humor does not deny that things are the way the pathetic person sees them, but it leaves open the possibility of overcoming them even if it is only by means of an internal attitude. The ironist and the humorist [86] maintain their unity in contradiction. The ironist is also a serious person. The humorist does not lack the pessimistic clairvoyance that pathos would like to raise to the level of the absolute. One and the other preserve and overcome some of the attitude of their opponents. They don't negate the other absolutely, but rather they transcend the other without losing sight of what is valid in [the other's] attitude. Irony and humor are negations that affirm, negations that negate themselves in an ulterior affirmation. *Relajo*, on the other hand, negates as a whole, all of the situation and its very foundation. The unity of *relajo* depends on a totalitarian negation of what is other. "The other,"[31] according to what we have described, is a value that an individual calls on in front of all the other individuals; it is an invitation to a common action.

The *relajo* individual does not "internalize" anything of the situation. This person does not accept the invitation, and he or she leaves all the whole [of the situation] "outside." The ironist and the humorist, in contrast, "assume"; they internalize their opponent in accepting some of the opponent's pretenses. The ironist and the humorist have within themselves some of the very thing that they oppose, whereas the *relajo* individual opposes to the other by externalizing it, by making it other.[32]

Ironists assume within themselves the dialectic tension: "pretense toward the value-transcendence of the value." Humorists assume the tension "adversity-freedom." *Relajo* individuals simply negate the value in their interior, and with this, they free themselves from all internal tension. The unity of *relajo* is not, then, the tense and dynamic unity of two or several contrasted terms, but rather, it is only the abstract and static unity of a negation pure and simple, without ways out, without mobility, without perspectives for the future. The result is that the counterfigure of relajo ends up outside of it. There is a style of relation to value that is a simple and absolute affirmation, just as relajo is a simple and absolute negation. By this, I mean to say that the internal and unitary duality that presides over ironic tension and humorous tension does not appear in the field of relajo, a field presided rather by an external and binary duality. An equally abstract figure—also equally lacking an internal moral tension in the same way that the relajo individual lacks the moral tension found in irony and humor—stands in opposition to the relajo individual. Irony is a synthesis of the Sophist's pretenses and of the philosopher's aspiration to truth; humor is a synthesis of pathos [87] and of responsible freedom. Then, between relajo and its opposite, the "spirit of seriousness," no synthesis whatsoever is possible. The ironist is, in a certain sense, a universal individual, and the same can be said of the humorist. The relajo individual, in contrast, is doomed to singularity, just as is his or her essential counterfigure: the spirit-of-seriousness individual.[33] Relajo and the spirit of seriousness are two opposites that cannot be overcome in any synthesis. The ironist is, as we have seen, a serious person who does not take seriously many things that seem serious but really aren't; [this is] just like the humorist. Seriousness and the ability to make the comic emerge—which is the incidental degradation of some value (even of that of *relajo*) which constitutes the focus of his or her interest—can manifest themselves in unity in one same individual. In contrast, the relajo individual "doesn't take anything seriously." The seriousness that this type of individual lacks is all condensed in another type of individual, who in Mexico is called "*el apretado*."

PHYSIOGNOMY OF THE "APRETADO"

"Apretado"[34] is the name given in Mexico City slang to the individual afflicted with the spirit of seriousness. Originally, the word seems to have a meaning based, especially, on social class differences. It seems that the term was first used to designate an individual who was careful to validate his or her position within a hierarchy of social classes. "Apretado" would thus have been a synonym of "snob."[35] But currently, it denotes in general a type of individual of a certain style, one of whose species is the "snob." This style is none other than the spirit of seriousness, a first outline of which I provided a bit earlier, when we were talking about the individual lacking a "sense of humor."

The spirit of seriousness is that attitude of consciousness which refuses to take notice of the distance between "being" and "value," in any manner in which this could occur. In this sense, it can be an incidental determination of any individual. But in the individual that is called an "apretado" in Mexico, this attitude is a habit. The "apretado" individual considers him or herself valuable, without any considerations or reservations of any type. The external expression of this attitude, its most peripheral manifestation, is this individual's outward appearance. "Apretado" individuals worry about their physical appearance, which is the expression of their internal being. They dress impeccably; they are elegant people, or at least they try at all costs to be so [88]. Their exterior shows the massiveness with no fissures according to which they interpret their own interiority. "Apretado" individuals are a little bit too impeccable; their self-esteem shines forth in their meticulous care for all the details of their external figure. Our colonialist naïveté says that these individuals are "very British," and they themselves have a—often self-proclaimed—weakness for what they call "good English taste."

But this is only external; it is a feature of their personality. "Apretado" individuals are elegant, just as they are any other value that they decide to attribute to themselves in their own interiority. For "apretado" individuals, values are not ever-unattainable guides for self-constitution, but rather actual ingredients of their own personalities. Values are not perpetually evanescent regulatory ideas, but rather properties that "apretado" individuals possess, with the calm certainty with which a rock possesses its hardness. To "apretado" individuals, "being" and "value" are carefully identified with each other at that privileged point in the world which is their own person. "Apretado" individuals carry their value in the same way they carry with them their legs or their liver: as a silent and solid cause of pleasure that they caress in their private moments.

In dubbing such an individual an "apretado," the colloquial language has hit upon the very center of this person's significance. "Apretado" individuals are compact masses of value; they live themselves on the inside like a dense volume of value-filled[36] "being," like a bundle of valuable "properties," conceived according to the model of the properties of a thing. It is not by chance that "apretado" individuals are, essentially, proprietors, although they may not yet possess considerable riches. Perhaps they may not yet be more than an honest official, very intelligent, very effective, and full of qualities. But "apretado" individuals have an infinite advantage over all other individuals: they *are* all these things. No matter what they do, they are intelligent, effective official, full of qualities. If an "apretado" individual says something stupid, if he or she makes a mistake, that doesn't prove anything, since it will be a stupidity said by a very intelligent person; it will be the mistake of a very effective official. When an "apretado" goes for a walk, an official goes for a walk; when an "apretado" eats, an official eats. An intelligent and efficient person sleeps; a person with good taste walks along the street; a person of talent calmly enjoys breakfast . . .

"Apretado" individuals live in calm possession of their "properties": intelligence, brilliance, talent, officialness, (perhaps bank-officialness).[37] Their being is, likewise, naturally a *having*, a *possessing*—these individuals' value-filled being glides magically and [89] imperceptibly toward their value-filled possessing. In a certain sense, "apretado" individuals are also their car, their house, their plots of land, their elegant furniture, their works of art. It couldn't be any other way. Since these individuals have begun to conceive their own being according to the model of things, and since property has started out by being the way in which they relate to themselves, it seems inevitable that property become also their way of referencing the world. "Apretado" individuals are the possessors of their quality-properties as they are of their thing-properties. The general scheme according to which their relationship to other people is founded can be formulated thus: the one who possesses is; the one who does not possess is not.

Very important consequences regarding the position of "apretado" individuals within the Mexican national community are derived from all of this.

In any case, "apretado" individuals seem to be the absolute opposite pole of *relajo* individuals. One could say that the figure of the former is antinomial to that of the latter in all respects. For now, the "apretado" individual seems similar to a fullness of affirmation against the pure negation of the "relajiento" individual. The "apretado" seems to be the positive pole of a unitary correlation, at the other extreme of which would be the negativity of *relajo*. If, as we have shown, *relajo* implies a nonfreedom, a false, negative freedom, the "apretado" individual could seem to be a bringer of freedom. This individual would be genuinely free.

But this is false: such a manner of reasoning is not more than an abstraction. Within reality, the spirit of seriousness ends up being just as negative and just as lacking in freedom as *relajo*. This will become evident as soon as we examine the way in which "apretado" individuals refer to others.

No doubt, "apretado" individuals begin by conceiving themselves as an impenetrable block of *value-filled being*, and this attitude motivates all their way of relating to the world; a value-filled being is a good, and a good is something that one possesses. But when this good is oneself, possession necessarily implies a relationship with others. Indeed, in the pure relationship with oneself, there is no way to grasp oneself immediately as value-filled. I very well can "consider" [literally, "have"][38] myself intelligent, but I cannot see my intelligence as I see this table in front of me. In order to do this, I would have to adopt someone else's point of view in relation to myself [90], like . . . I do when I see my image in a mirror. "Apretado" individuals need a mirror that will reflect their inner excellence. Since, for the "apretado" individual, values are not that unattainable transcendence that outlines the pathways of their behavior but rather are real ingredients of their being, and since that value-filled being cannot be contemplated in a reflection that only places it facing itself as a neutral presence, "apretado" individuals are condemned to make themselves present before others in order to seek recognition by them.

That being said, this recognition that "apretado" individuals seek is recognition of "their" value as being-value; they need witnesses, without which their supposed value-filled being would disappear into silence and into unreality. An "apretado" individual cannot be an "apretado" in the desert. These individuals need for their value to appear before other people. They need to be able to read their value in the gaze of others. An "apretado" individual can only see his or her character of official in the submissive respect of subordinates, even if this only serves as a way to later—when he or she is left alone—hold on to the delicious certainty that he or she is important. "Apretado" people need the admiring gazes of others in order for the sweet certainty of their elegance to rush through their veins. All the actions of "apretado" people are geared toward this perpetual reading of the self in the other-mirror. These individuals need those testimonies to be able to sustain themselves in their beatific self-esteem. Without noticing it, given their continual orientation toward themselves, "apretado" individuals are condemned to others' gaze, which to them is indispensable for recovering the stability of their value-filled being. "Apretado" individuals—who start out being a fullness and a self-affirmation—begin to move toward the periphery of their being; they have a need for other people, but not in order to communicate with them. They have a need for other people, not in order to constitute a "we" with them, but rather to negate them while self-affirming themselves: they only need others as spectators of their own excellence. The "apretado" individual begins by affirming him- or herself as essential, but in order to be essential, it is the other who is essential. The other is essential, so he or she can be negated and, in this way, for the "apretado" to recover his or her original essentiality. "Apretado" individuals need the other in order to not be the other; they need others precisely to be able to distinguish themselves from them. The "apretado" individual is one who distinguishes him or herself from others. This is a "distinguished person." But this person needs to be distinguished by others. Nobody can be distinguished by him- or herself. Being distinguished cannot be anybody's intrinsic determination. To this negation, which the others must [91] exert on this individual by "distinguishing" him or her, there corresponds a negation that the "apretado" individual performs on the others: he or she excludes them. "Apretado" individuals are "distinguished" by others; but to themselves, they are "exclusive." "Exclusivity" is the supreme category in the world of the "apretado." "Apretado" individuals eat at exclusive restaurants; they attend exclusive schools; they belong to exclusive circles. In this way, a type of competition of exclusivities is established: the greater the exclusivity, the greater the value, until one reaches—by elimination—a supreme degree of exclusivity that constitutes the paradise of "apretado" individuals. Their supreme aspiration is to belong to the most exclusive of exclusivities. "Apretado" individuals simply exclude others and distinguish themselves from them. What is left when we exclude "apretado" individuals is an empty and universal concept, just as the very exclusion of the "apretado" individuals is. What remains—purely and simply—is "people" [gente]. This structure of exclusions and distinctions is also reflected in the language of our community and has made it possible for the word "people" [gente] to mean a positive quality. This concept,

which designates only the human being in an empty and faceless gener-
ality, has been transformed in Mexico—thanks to the exclusive activity
of "apretado" individuals—into a compliment. In Mexico, one is saying something positive about someone when one says that he or she is
"people" [gente].[39] So and so is "people" or so and so is "very people"
means that so and so does not consider him- or herself exceptional; he or
she does not exclude other people; this is a generous person with a good-
ness capable of communicating with and of understanding the other,
and so on. It means, all things considered, that Mr. So-and-so is not an
"apretado." This also shows us, on the other hand, the degree to which
the influence of the "apretado" has penetrated into Mexico.

But distinction and exclusivity—negative categories—essentially
require that which is excluded and that from which one distinguishes
oneself. The one who is exclusive and distinguished has to *appear* as
exclusive and distinguished, since if one doesn't appear thus, if one does
not "show oneself" in the light of the world of those who participate
in the game, one would only be able to adhere to positive, substantial,
real determinations in order to be. To exclusiveness and distinction considered as constitutive categories, one must also add ostentation [and]
appearances in order to be able to finish the game of reflections that the
"apretado" individual establishes in his or her world: a world of negations founded on a false affirmation: the greater the appearance, the
greater the distinction and the exclusivity; but at the point of supreme
exclusiveness [92], the supposedly embodied value has disappeared.
The most exclusive person of exclusive people can be—and often is—an
insignificant man or woman who doesn't even bother to consider him-
or herself excellent, one who maintains him or herself in a perpetual
nonreflexive ecstasy in the world of appearances.

The belt of negations that constitutes the world of appearances gets
tighter each day and ends up excluding even the value-filled being of the
naïve "apretado" whose supposed value-filled substance ends up totally
out of play when it comes to the hierarchical founding of the world of
the "best" [individuals]. The only thing that remains standing is the
form of the "apretado's" relationship with the world: property—and at
the extreme opposite—the appearance of property.

All this game of negations is based only on property. The aspir-
ing "apretado" bows reverently before those who possess more than
he or she does and despises the mass of those who do not possess. The
one who possesses is, and the one who does not possess is not. Within

this horizon, the best thing that can be done in any case is to maintain appearances. The world is like that, and there is nothing more to find out. In this way, "apretado" individuals are slaves of others: slaves of the dispossessed, whom they fear but whom they need in order to be "apretado" and distinguished; slaves of the possessors, whom they fear and they flatter; slaves of appearances to which they subjugate their entire lives; slaves of their apparent virtues and of their maxims, which they consider threatened by negation since "apretado" individuals are immersed in a world of negations. They are continually obligated to stand up for these virtues and maxims, since casting doubt on them is equivalent to casting doubt on themselves. They are slaves of property, doomed to pursue it or to simulate it in order to be valuable, or—to say the same thing—in order to be. "Apretado" individuals are the living denial of freedom. They also do have an idea of freedom, but it is a negative idea, a small idea. Their idea of freedom is limited to the belief that the State has no right to violate private property.

The very same movement through which "apretado" individuals attempt to embody value condemns them to transform this fullness of value into mere appearances. The very same movement with which "apretado" individuals attempt to be a block of affirmation entangles them in a dialectical game in which negation installs itself as a constitutive force of their being. The very same act with which the "apretado" individuals establish themselves in the world as value-filled beings implies [93] a negation of the freedom of others, who are then condemned to be nonvalue filled, and also a negation of their own selves, since if the "apretado" individual's value is an attribute of his or her being, the foundation of this value is not a free and contingent choice but rather a necessary attribute, like extent is a necessary attribute of things. Freedom then ends up "outside," conceived of negatively as independence, as nonobstruction by others of the field of the "apretado" individual's activities, and above all as nonintervention by the State in the "apretado's" property [issues]. In this sense, the "apretado" individual loves freedom, but when he or she hears this very same word on the lips of the nonpossessors, his or her capacity for love becomes irresistibly attracted to another magic word: "order." Deep down, "apretado" individuals love order more than freedom. Order is that stable situation of society that allows these individuals to play the exclusivity game and to give themselves the pleasure of embodying value. The objective expression of that order is Law. Law allows "apretado" individuals to comfortably be all of what they are: an efficient official, a prosperous proprietor, an exemplary human being.

Relajo individuals, in contrast, detest order, and they destroy it whenever they can. Nevertheless, both relajo individuals and "apretado" individuals conceive of freedom as independence and as negation, which does not prevent these two—as moral styles—from being on opposite poles. "Apretado" individuals not only "have" a negative notion of freedom, but they also embody—with their attitude—an actual negation of the freedom of *people*, of those people from whom they simply demand the recognition of their value and respect for their person. "Apretado" individuals demand not only the recognition of value by positioning themselves next to the others in the attitude of respect, but they also demand recognition of themselves as value-filled beings before others. The other must bow respectfully before the "apretado" individual, without any hope of participating with this individual in the realization of value, since the apretado individual is the value. When others refuse to be submissive, "apretado" individuals refer to them as "alzado" or "levantado,"[40] that is to say, individuals who refuse to bow down. "Apretado" individuals essentially want others to submit to them; they want them to bend. From this, we derive the fullness of meaning and the popular resonance of the expression "I break but I don't bend," as a response to an attitude of rebelliousness that "apretado" individuals provoke with their monopolizing pretense of being value in its fullness. This monopoly and the personal preeminence [94] to which "apretado" individuals aspire dissolve all the possibilities for the formation of a community that is genuine in its contours. The individual who considers him- or herself value-filled or fully significant radiates sterility and distance. If such an individual is an intellectual, his or her vulnerable points become veritable taboos. The slightest dissent from his or her opinions is considered by this person as serious as an insult, because his or her character as a "source" of value suffers a crisis. To dissent is to suppose that something worthy of attention exists (even if it is pure truth) apart from this person, and, thus, dissenting is to rob the "apretado" of his or her own substance because it diverts the attention of others [away from him or her]—and "apretado" individuals need such attention in order to be what they are. Dialogue is impossible with an "apretado" individual. Genuine dialogue presupposes the transcendence and the evanescence of value; but when value is there—completely made out of flesh and English cashmere—the only thing left to do is listen attentively and

assent respectfully, or dissent—but not a lot and only with the greatest
possible prudence. If the "apretado" individual is a Catholic, he or she
possesses Catholicism. This person is definitely, infinitely, and irrevocably Catholic, just as a stone is definitely, infinitely, and irrevocably
a stone. It doesn't matter, for example, that in their professions "apretado" individuals allow themselves to be rogues. Those are things of
no importance. [These] "apretado" individuals absorbed Catholicism
through their mothers' milk. They have Catholic blood, Catholic bones,
Catholic entrails—although this does not prevent them from despising
priests a bit and from speaking about the fanaticism of pilgrimages to
the Shrine of the Virgin of Guadalupe. "Apretado" individuals possess
an infinite and perfect source of justification that will allow them—if
not always to "be," at least to always "be in good."[41] The "apretado"
individual's exceptional person possesses an overwhelmingly comfort-
ing protection because it also protects his or her property. The gates
of hell—both of the religious and of the social one—will not prevail
against him or her. There are twenty centuries (twenty centuries!) of
tradition giving this individual a pat on the back and telling him or
her that everything is going well. Against twenty centuries of tradition,
Communism is a storm in a teacup. "We Catholics have been through
a lot worse." Catholic tradition is an extremely comfortable seat, and
Francisco Franco has proven in Spain that even bayonets can end up not
being entirely uncomfortable.

Both the freedom of the "apretado" individual and that of the "relajiento" are negative freedoms. That is why, in both attitudes there is a
negation of community. One and the other dissolve the community—
which can only be founded upon a value that is transcendental [95] to
its members.

Indeed the foundation of a community, coexistence, can be thought
of as the continuous self-constitution of a group in reference to a value.
Value as a model or guide for the constitution of the group turns out to
be, for the group, just as unattainable as the guide-value is for the individual. "Apretado" individuals negate the transcendence of value appro-
priating it for them and thus turning themselves into the *foundation* of
the community. But, as we have seen, "apretado" individuals come to be
involved in a dialectic in which this attitude reveals itself to be exactly
the opposite: the "apretado" turns out to be the foundation of the dissolution of the community by means of the double negation of distinction

and exclusion. For their part, *relajo* individuals prevent the integration of the community by preventing the manifestation of the value.

"Relajientos" and "apretados" constitute two poles of dissolution of that difficult task on which we have all embarked: the constitution of a Mexican community, of a genuine community, and not of a society divided into proprietors and the dispossessed.

Notes

Chapter One

1. Fuentes was intimately aware of Portilla and Portilla's associates. In an interview with *La Jornada* in 1993, he claims to have been a "really good friend of Portilla's." When asked about Portilla and his associates, the members of el Grupo Hiperión, he says: "Se trataba de gente de inteligencia excepcional. Yo fui muy amigo de Jorge Portilla. Lo sigo siendo de Leopoldo Zea, de Luis Villoro. Fue mucha la gente que participó en ese movimiento. Fue un momento sumamente serio, de gran reflexión, de imaginación también, que abrazó a muchas generaciones, que incluía a españoles como De Novilla, a gente de generaciones anteriores, como Alfonso Reyes, que publicó La x en la frente, en la colección México y lo Mexicano; en fin, creo que fue un monento de reflexión, un paso hacia adelante, un dejar ciertas cosas atrás. A mí me parece importantísimo que Reyes haya publicado La x en la frente y recordado a todos a través de A vuelta de correo que el nacionalismo estrecho es algo que nos reduce, que nos empobrece, que nos empequeñece y que no tenemos porqué cargar complejos para hacer una literatura que, como dijo el propio Reyes, será buena por ser literatura y no por ser mexicana" (Solares 1993).
2. "Confiaba en la voluntad de los hombres si no para vencer si para no dejarse vencer."
3. The phrase "borracho, parrandero y jugador" is a line from a popular Mexican song, "El Corrido de Juan Charrasquiado," written by

Victor Cordero. Juan Charrasquiado is gunned down by a cowardly bunch, and the song tells his tale. It remembers a man loved by women, a gambler (*jugador*), a drinker (*borracho*), and a wanderer (*parrandero*) whose life, as the song itself testifies, was both tragic and heroic.

4. According to Michael, however, Portilla's failure was not as offensive as that of Leopoldo Zea, an original member of el Grupo Hiperión and the leading Latin American philosopher at the time of his death in 2004, who leaves the project of a "Mexican philosophy" behind to deal with the problem of a "Latin American" philosophy, "an even bigger stupidity, if simply for quantitative reasons" (Michael 1996, 10).

5. Portilla 1984 will be the primary text for the remainder of this investigation. It will be cited frequently throughout. Hence, I will cite it by placing the page number within square brackets [pg], to distinguish it from the rest of the secondary literature. The page numbers, in brackets, refer to the pagination of the Spanish text, which is translated in the appendix of this work.

6. Not only is there a lack of an English equivalent, but Portilla's project depends on the uniqueness of the word. So I leave it in its original. While I am not trying to consciously play with the rules of translation, my approach is similar to that of John McCumber, who "translates" Martin Heidegger's "Gestell" (in quotes) as *Gestell* (sans quotes). See (McCumber 1999).

7. José Gaos is the first translator of *Sein und Zeit*. His influence on Mexican thought is immensurable.

8. This work is a collection of lectures delivered in 1945, which has also been published as *Existentialism Is a Humanism*. It seems to have been available in Spanish as early as 1946, via a translation of Manuel Cardenal.

Chapter Two

1. For a first-person account of this group, its formation and dissolution, see Guerra 1984.

2. The intellectuals who fled Spain did not consider themselves "exiles" or "refugees"; rather they thought of themselves as "transplanted" into a different patch of their Hispanic soil, but nevertheless into a

circumstance that they would have to reckon with. For more on the *transterrados* who took up residence in Mexico, see Oliver 1993.

3. Domínguez Michael writes: "Few episodes of our intellectual past have been forgotten as quickly as [Hyperion]" (Michael 1997, 8).

4. Another way to explain the adoption of "Hiperión" as the group's public image is provided by Hurtado: "If Hiperión was, according to the group myth, son of the heavens and the earth, they [the members of the philosophical group] aimed to realize a synthesis of the universal and the particular" (Hurtado 2006, xiii).

5. "*Lo* mexicano" cannot be consistently translated as "*the* Mexican," as one would assume, since the intention by these thinkers is to speak of a particular *manner* or *mode* of *being Mexican* which "the Mexican" leaves out; "the Mexican" will be reserved for "*el* mexicano," which actually refers to concrete Mexican individuals. I mentioned above that the theme of Hyperion's project was grounded on a philosophical understanding of "lo mexicano." Literally translated, "lo mexicano" means "that which is Mexican," or, even, *Mexicanness*. Thus, Portilla, Zea, and Uranga ask: *What is Mexicanness?* This is a question which guides their studies into history, values, and ontology. But can we even ask such a question *philosophically* without seeming relativistic or unnecessarily provincial? Indeed, a respected chronicler of Mexican philosophy, Abelardo Villegas, asks rhetorically: "Is a philosophy of *lo mexicano* possible?" (Villegas 1979). In other words, can philosophy genuinely engage the theme of *lo mexicano*—or "that which is Mexican"—at all? It is a rhetorical question because for Villegas philosophy must treat of universal concerns so that when philosophers ask about a particular *sort of living*, such as Mexican, they are not asking a genuinely philosophical question. So, no, a philosophy of *lo mexicano* is not possible—nor its attempt advisable, according to Villegas. But it was with the "philosophical question" of *lo mexicano* that Hyperion was concerned. So were they, then, *not* doing philosophy? As early as 1952, Emilio Uranga considered this objection as grounded on the stubbornness of the colonial influence. In section 9 of *Being and Time*, Uranga read the following: "That Being which is an *issue* for this entity in its very Being, is in each case mine. Thus Dasein is never to be taken ontologically as an instance or a special case of some genus of entities as things that are present-at-hand . . . Because Dasein has *in each case mineness* [*Jemeinigkeit*], one must always use the *personal* pronoun

when one addresses it: 'I am,' 'you are.'" Uranga interpreted this as a way around the European bias. The *being* to be interrogated *could only be* Mexican! That is, if the question is the question of existence or the ontological question of being, the being of the Mexican (a Dasein which is "mine") must be that which is interrogated *because* of its proximity to the questioning. This meant that *lo mexicano* served as a stand-in for humanness. In fact, *lo mexicano* was a metaphor in the language of the Mexican experience for all human experience. It had to be; *lo mexicano*, or "that which is Mexican," was the most proximal being. Uranga writes in *Análisis del ser del mexicano* that to begin the phenomenological interrogation with "man in general" presupposed an intuition which was unattainable in principle, one constituted in part by a European bias toward *its own* "substantial" conception of man (see Uranga 1952; also Sánchez 2008). Ultimately, the focus on *lo mexicano* is meant as a way to access the realm of the universal through the particular, but as "belonging" to Mexicans, it is the only way. Mexican reality, properly understood, ought to reveal structures of human existence which are not just events of a Mexican experience, but which are events of experience in general. What is more important, however, is that these universal aspirations mean that Mexican reality must give up its secrets in the process of its testimony—secrets which should give way to praxis and liberation.

6. As Hurtado tells us, this group was not merely a group of intellectuals with similar interests, but "an investigative team" intent on "bringing about profound transformations" in Mexico and in Mexicans (Hurtado 2006, xi).

7. English translations of Zea's work abound. The secondary work is also vast. For a well-written analysis of his thought see Sáenz 1999. In *The Making of the Mexican Mind*, Romanell attends a great deal to Zea and his philosophical contributions. Hiperion, on the other hand, he says, is in its youth as a movement (this was 1952), so he skips it (See Romanell 1952, 184).

8. An example of this view is J. L. Mackie's *Ethics: Inventing Right and Wrong*. He begins chapter 15 with the sentence, "There are no objective values," and he proceeds to show how all values are subjective. (Mackie 1991).

9. We can say that "relajo" is a "metaphor" for the activity Portilla describes, which makes proper translation even harder. As Derrida

reminds us, "Metaphor [is] a provisional loss of meaning" (Derrida 1982, 270).

10. *Choteo,* like *relajo,* is impossible to properly translate. I am doing it here, since my aim is not to offer a sustained analysis. "Raillery" comes close in that it preserves the essential characteristics of *choteo* without *adding* new significations. I will alternate between the English and the Spanish.

11. For a short yet informative article on Cantinflas' life and work, see the *Encyclopedia of Contemporary Latin American and Caribbean Cultures* (Balderston et.al. 2000, 274ff).

Chapter Three

1. As Merleau-Ponty pointed out, "For Sartre, there are no causes which can truly act upon consciousness. Consciousness is total, absolute freedom" (Merleau-Ponty 1998, 501).

2. As Reyes puts it: "In our own time [*relajo*] is something kids do, a matter of college pranks. These days, chaos [*desmadre*] has its time, its place . . . its music" (Reyes 2003).

Chapter Four

1. What I am calling the "particular-universal structure" of Mexican philosophy can be seen most clearly in Portilla's predecessor, the philosopher Samuel Ramos. Ramos was the first, in his 1934 *Profile of Man and Culture in Mexico,* to subject Mexican culture and the Mexican character to philosophical scrutiny. It is an understatement to say that Ramos set the agenda for what was to come, first with Zea and then with Paz, Emilio Uranga, and Portilla. In Ramos, the particular character complexes of Mexicans are raised to the level of universality, where they are inserted into a vision of humanity and set as examples of what is lacking and what is required for human, and not just Mexican, overcoming. Observing that "Mexicans up to now have not cared about getting to the bottom of culture . . . [but] instead . . . have been dazzled by its brilliant outward effects" (Ramos 1982, 95; Gracia and Millán-Zaibert 2004, 285), Ramos adds, "We must have the courage to be ourselves and the humility

to accept the life that fate bestowed upon us without being ashamed of its poverty" (Ramos 1982, 91; Gracia and Millán-Zaibert 2004, 282). This last statement is a statement carrying universal weight, but is one picked out of the rubble of his particular deconstructions. "By Mexican culture," he concludes, "we mean universal culture made over into *our own*" (Ramos 1982, 95; Gracia and Millán-Zaibert 2004, 285).

2. By history, I mean the history of philosophy, which resists recognizing its other. As Zea puts it: "The history of philosophy [. . .] is also the history of Western culture . . . However, that history never offered the possibility that someone might ask whether or not he or she had a right to Logos [Verbo, Logos o Palabra], even if that same inquisitiveness already signals the use of this right" (Zea 1952, 10).

3. According to Zirión Quijano's *Historia de la fenomenología en México*, the history of phenomenology in Mexico *is* "the history of *Husserlian* phenomenology in Mexico" (Zirión 2004, 22).

4. Amy Oliver, who has been at the forefront in the effort to introduce Mexican philosophy into the US academy, argues against the view that these "other" philosophies are somehow lacking in seriousness. "If serious philosophy is not a skill or a method," she writes, "but an attempt to embody vital truths that make life intelligible and provide a way to orient everyday living, then serious philosophy is done in Mexico" (Oliver 1993, 218).

5. Husserl explains this method in his *Encyclopedia Article*: "This *eidos* must manifest itself throughout all the potential forms of mental being in particular cases, must be present in all the synthetic combinations and self-enclosed wholes, if it is to be at all 'thinkable,' that is, intuitively phantasized or objectified" (Husserl 1971, 80).

6. The claim here is that Portilla's philosophical tendencies are in line with those of the European phenomenologists who dictated the manner in which phenomenology would be practiced worldwide. It is true that Portilla belongs to a rich history of philosophy in Mexico, one which finds its most significant moments with the antipositivists of the early part of the twentieth century. These early thinkers would dictate an "authentic" direction for Mexican philosophy, one that moved away from positivism's "depreciation of traditional Mexican culture and institutions in favor of an attempt to copy, at least symbolically, the organizations and ideologies of more 'advanced' Western nations" (Weinstein 1976, 1). The authentic direction mapped

out in particular by Antonio Caso and José Vasconcelos was thus one aimed toward the rediscovery of the Mexican's role in the cosmos (see Hurtado 2010). While Portilla's project is ultimately one aimed toward a similar goal, the cultural crisis which is the subject of his essay is one never before subjected to philosophical scrutiny. For this reason he considers the philosophical methodologies of his predecessors inadequate, or, at least, not up to the task. As he says in the first pages of the essay, no one, or *no philosophers*, would consider what he does here "serious philosophy." Hence, he undertakes his deconstruction as if from a presuppositionless starting point.

Chapter Five

1. Of course, "colonialism" is not a *place* to which one can *go back*. It is a persistent condition of subjugation and dependence which imposes itself in various forms, not all of them material or economic. In Mexico, material and economic colonialism is traced back to the devastating arrival of the Spanish in the sixteenth century. After the wars of independence in the nineteenth century, colonialism persists as a form of power and hegemony which infiltrates all aspects of Mexican life. This infiltration is what interests me, since values which regulate obedience, propriety, and civil conduct, for instance, represent the colonialism one can *go back* to.
2. These philosophers did not problematize their notion of "Mexicans," which means that Mexicans were assumed to be largely homogenous. José Gaos pointed out this difficulty in his critiques of the project (Gaos 1954).

Chapter Six

1. By "axiological imperialism," I mean the manner in which value schemes can be presented as absolute by those in positions of power. Axiological imperialism follows, and is sometimes motivating, the political and cultural conquest or oppression of peoples throughout the world.
2. "Historical reason" is opposed to "instrumental reason." Historical reason privileges the value of the past for the sake of self-knowledge

and internal/external liberation. If Portilla were to criticize instrumental reason on the basis of historical reason, *relajo* would be
seen as a move against the seduction of the technological life-world
which instrumental reason has created. It would seem, instead, as a
nostalgic withdrawal to a space lacking in commitments and imper-
vious to the demands of *what matters to us now* (our "modern"
values).

3. Portilla himself is indecisive on this issue. On page 20 he calls *relajo*
"reflexive," on page 22 he says that "it is not an introspection," and
on 39 he says that *relajo* is not "spontaneous." We would have to
conclude from this that *relajo,* as a disruptive act, involves a reflection which does not involve *thinking* about the disruption itself (as
one would do in introspection) but only about disrupting. *Relajientos* are not very effective consequentialists, it seems—another reason
why they are an offense to instrumental reason.

4. One could, possibly, take Portilla's characterization of *relajo* in an
entirely different direction and argue that to bring about the "state"
of *relajo* is akin to brining about that state of nothingness and
indecision which Sextus Empiricus spoke about in *Outlines of Pyr-
rhonism*. There, Sextus Empiricus tells us: "Skepticism . . . places in
antithesis, in any manner whatever, appearances and judgments, and
thus—because of the equality of objects and arguments opposed—
to come first of all to a suspension of judgment and then to mental
tranquility" (Empiricus 1964, 32). However, Pyrrhonian skepticism
is completely rational. It has an end: tranquility. *Relajo* does not
have this end in mind. Tranquility of some sort might be achieved,
but only accidentally, and surprisingly.

Translation

1. The first edition of this work was published by Ediciones ERA in
1966. The following text is a translation based on the 1984 Biblioteca Joven edition, *Fenomenología del relajo y otros ensayos*.
Mexíco D.F.: Fondo de Cultura Economica. Numbers in square-
brackets [page numbers] refer to the 1984 edition. I thank the Fondo
de Cultura Economica for permission to publish the translation of
Portilla's essay in its entirety.—Translator's note.

2. In the original text, the expression is "la situación del hombre," "the

situation of man." Keeping in mind that Portilla wrote at a time when the terms "hombre" (man) and "hombres" (men) could also denote human beings and humanity in general and were not limited to the designation of male humans, gender-inclusive language has been employed in the present translation. English terms such as "human being," "human," "humankind," "individual," "person," and "people" have been used in place of the Spanish equivalents for "man" and "men" when these do not necessarily denote males—Translator's note.

3. In the original, "el recogimiento del trabajo." The noun *recogimiento* has strong religious connotations and usually refers to the act of withdrawing or isolating oneself from social contact (sometimes to or within a monastery or convent) to concentrate one's thoughts on inner spiritual activities such as meditation.—Translator's note.

4. In the original, "el prójimo" (used and translated as "one's neighbor" in religious contexts).—Translator's note.

5. In the original "una desolidarización," literally an act or action of dissolidarity.—Translator's note.

6. By an action that Husserl calls "phenomenological reduction." Author's footnotes will be numbered.

7. In the original, "el relajamiento de una situación seria." The *–miento* suffix attached to a verb root transforms the verb into an abstract noun and roughly corresponds to the English suffix "(en)ing," as in the word "awakening" (the act of waking). The word "relajamiento," which exists in Spanish and normally means "a relaxing," is being used here by Portilla in a new sense as part of a creative play on words which would translate as "a *relajo*-ing," or transformation of a situation into *relajo*.—Translator's note.

8. In the language of E. Husserl, the "noema" of *relajo* is a value, even if the value is merely a noematic nucleus; the full noema is the theme: "negated value," "value put in parenthesis," "neutralized value," "value to be degraded in the name of another value," etc. The noematic nucleus (the value pure and simple) remains always invariable with its essential constituent of appealing to my freedom, but the aura of negation that unites with the nucleus to constitute the full noema points back retrospectively to the noesis: "negation of the value," "comparative degrading of the value," etc. as a mere noetic correlate and not as a *psychological act*. The displacement of attention and the self-positioning in lack of solidarity are, then,

essential characteristics that can be read in the intentional horizon of *relajo* as such and not as "real," individual, localizable, and datable psychological movements of the individual that provokes *relajo*. This is to say, the "intimate" nature of *relajo* alludes rather to an activity (noesis) rather than to a psychological "interiority." On the other hand, a psychological interiority lends itself to introspective reflection, to the degree that the operation that allows us to grasp the described phenomena is a phenomenological reflection.

9. "*Echar relajo*" is an idiomatic expression that means "to create *relajo*." *Echar* is a verb with multiple meanings, used in a wide variety of idiomatic expressions in Spanish. Some of the meanings of *echar* include, "to throw" (echar la pelota: "to throw the ball") to expel, to fire, or to let out (echar de la escuela: "to expel from school"), to put or pour in (echar sal: "to put salt in"), to emit or to give off (echar chispas: "to give off sparks"), and to tell (echar mentiras: "to tell lies"). Portilla's play on words hinges on the idiomatic expression "echar relajo" and the most basic meaning of the verb *echar*, "to throw."—Translator's note.

10. The positional consciousness of a "seriousness to be suspended" with respect to a value is not a positional consciousness of "my decision" to suspend seriousness, no matter how much a nonpositional consciousness of my activity may be inherent to that prereflexive positional consciousness. In relajo, the individual is in the world, dislocating a situation articulated by the realization of a value, and not deliberating with him- or herself or contemplating his or her future behavior or emotional moods.

    It is not hidden to me that these assertions bring up the problem of the possibility of a prereflexive consciousness and that of an involuntary action that, not because of this, is unconscious or lacking in purpose. Such an issue, no matter how important it may be in and of itself, cannot be dealt with in detail within the limits of this essay without excessively diverting it from its main purpose.

11. Mario Moreno, known as "Cantinflas" (1911–1993) was a widely famous Mexican comic film actor whose films combined comedy with social commentary. He is best known for slapstick humor highly dependent on gestures and body movements and for his use of a discourse full of nonsense to achieve comic effects.—Translator's note.

12. The term "fiesta" ("party") has been left in the original Spanish in most instances in the translation, in part because of the uniquely Mexican cultural overtones the term has, which the English term "party" does not quite capture.—Translator's note.

13. In the original, "un relajiento." The word *"relajiento"* literally means "full of *relajo,*" since the –iento (feminine form –ienta) suffix in Spanish primarily means "full of" and corresponds roughly to the English suffix –y attached to nouns to transform them into adjectives meaning "full of (a particular thing)," as in the words "greasy" (full of grease) or "hungry" (full of hunger). However, unlike in English, the Spanish suffix –iento meaning "full of" generally carries a pejorative nuance and is used as an adjective maker attached to nouns that denote things with at least some negative semantic characteristics or connotations. For example, the –iento suffix can be found attached to nouns such as *mugre* (grime, dirt), *grasa* (grease), *polvo* (dust), *pulgas* (fleas), *sangre* (blood), and *hambre* (hunger) to produce the adjectives *mugriento* (grimy or dirty), *grasiento* (greasy), *polvoriento* (dusty), *pulguiento* (flea-ridden or full of fleas), *sangriento* (bloody), and *hambiento* (hungry), respectively. The attachment of the suffix -iento on the noun *relajo* produces the adjective *relajiento*, a word with a decidedly pejorative ring. Since many adjectives in Spanish can be used as nouns by preceding them with an article, the expression "un relajiento" means "one who is full of *relajo.*"—Translator's note.

14. The concept of the "German joke" or "chiste alemán" denotes a type of joke that makes fun of cultural or linguistic stereotypes associated with a particular nationality or the sounds of a particular foreign language. A similar—although not entirely analogous—concept for English speakers might be so-called "Polish jokes."—Translator's note.

15. The original text says "vivible" (livable) instead of "visible" (visible). This is a quite obvious typographical error in the original edition, since "vivible" does not make sense in the context of the sentence while "visible" does.—Translator's note.

16. *Philosophie du Rire et des Pleurs* (Presses Universitaires de France, Paris, 1949).

17. It isn't clear that the comic provokes laughter. William James asserts that the comic is created by laughter. At the bottom of such an

opposition of opinions lies the philosophical problem of the opposition between realism and idealism. The problem of the primacy of the object or of the subject in the theory of knowledge extends to all fields of reality and reveals its difficulty very conspicuously in this little issue of laughter, in which one can clearly see the difficulty of reducing the origins of the phenomenon [laughter] to either of the two terms at stake.

18. In the original, "a mandibula batiente" (literally, "with beating jaw").—Translator's note.

19. In the original, "la clave del 'es' a la clave del 'tal vez'" (literally the key of the "is" to the key of the "perhaps").—Translator's note.

20. Freedom, as a given of human action as a priori condition of attribution can be negated by a theory that explains human beings using nature or another nonhuman or nonpersonal entity as a starting point. But theories, no matter how coherent or ingenious they are, cannot erase the conditions of possibility from human behavior. Theories are always secondary with respect to those conditions, and they themselves presuppose them as conditions of their own possibility, since it is always possible for human beings to negate or to affirm anything by means of any theory. What can be achieved with some of these [theories] is that some individuals decide to adopt any behavior without assuming the responsibility that the behavior implies, [rather] transferring their responsibility to history, to destiny, to their blood, to their boss, to passion, or to any other thing. The results can be unfortunate. By following this path, a type of degraded or "dehumanized" human being can emerge, although this in no way means a nonhuman being.

21. It is evident that what these days is called "economic freedom" is nothing other than a particular form of political freedom. To the degree that the instrument of domination that inhibits the evolution of the person until his or her fulfillment is the system of production and not simply the polity or the exclusion of one [social] caste by another, the reform of the system of production becomes the means of a *liberation that is economic in its content but political in its form.* Undoubtably, a person abandoned on the periphery of the community in an individualistic society lacks the necesssary means for full development and therefore is and "feels" "less free" than one who has access to such means, since this individual has a limited field of choice. *Political freedom means, then, on the one hand, a greater number of possibilities for self-realization and, on*

the other, easy access to the means necessary to it. In the case of the marginal individual, possibilities and the means of attaining them are considerably limited, but this does not strip this individual of the subjective freedom that allows him or her to be a revolutionary; *to be a revolutionary* is not an economic determination but rather a political one, although it may be conditioned by economics.

22. In the original, "relajaciones" ("relaxations"). The word "relajaciones" is a synonym of "relajamientos" in its usual sense to mean "relaxings." However, considering the context of the passage and Portilla's previous play on words with the noun "relajamiento" to mean the "transformation of a situation into *relajo*," it is unlikely that this is another pun to mean "transformations into *relajo*." The context points more convincingly to the possibility of a typographical error for "relaciones" (relationships). Indeed, in the section that follows the passage, Portilla deals with the relationships of irony, humor, seriousness, and the spirit of seriousness to freedom.— Translator's note.

23. In the original, Portilla uses the verb "estar," one of two main verbs in Spanish meaning "to be." "Estar" usually denotes being in a location or in a state or condition. It is not used to denote being as existence. By using this verb, rather than "existir," "to exist," Portilla may be emphasizing the "location" or "place" of irony within human beings or history rather than the existence of irony.—Translator's note.

24. The expression "poner banderillas *al quiebro*" refers to a maneuver in bullfighting in which the bullfighter—when applying the *banderillas* (sharp-pointed metal rods decorated with crinkled crepe paper) to the bull's neck—runs up to the bull and then shifts his body sideways at the waist, dodging the charging animal.—Translator's note.

25. "Menudo": a typical Mexican soup made with beef stomach and tripe.

26. Comadre: technically, the godmother of one's child.

27. This is a possible typographical error. The original says "resentido el alivio" ("felt pain in, resented the relief ") rather than "sentido el alivio," "felt the relief." The idea of feeling relief with the absence of the self-satisfied individual makes more logical sense given the context of the passage.—Translator's note.

28. In the original, "el chiste y la broma"; both "chiste" and "broma" correspond to the English noun "joke." However, there is a nuance of difference between the two terms. A *chiste* usually denotes the

kind of joke that one tells. It follows some type of formula and has a punch line. A *broma* can be a practical joke that one plays on someone, or it can be an act of joking. The translation attempts to capture the nuances of the original by distinguishing between the joke (which is told to someone) and joking (which can include practical jokes played on someone).—Translator's note.

29. These references and the previous ones regarding Kierkegaard can be found in the edition of *Concluding Unscientific Postscript*, Princeton University Press, 441ff.

30. Ibid, 259.

31. In the original, "lo otro," with the neuter pronoun "lo" instead of the definite article "el." Portilla here is not referring to the concept of "the other" as a person who is other. "Lo otro," in this context, denotes "that which is other," as opposed to "el otro" "the person who is the other."

32. The expression in the original is "ajeno," meaning "belonging to another," "alien," or "foreign" (not belonging inside something).—Translator's note.

33. In the original "el hombre del espíritu de seriedad," literally "the man of the spirit of seriousness."—Translator's note.

34. "El apretado," literally, "the tight one."

35. Portilla uses the English term "snob" in the original text. The English term exists in Spanish as a loan word.—Translator's note.

36. The Spanish term here is "valioso," usually translated as "valuable." Although the term can and does mean the same thing as the English "valuable," it has been rendered as "value-filled" in this translation because this expression captures the nuance of the Spanish "-oso (feminine –osa)" suffix, a suffix that corresponds roughly to the English –ous and means "full of" something. The English word "valuable," in contrast, has the –able suffix, which means "able to be ____-ed," as in "lovable" (able to be loved). Thus, "valuable" conveys the idea of "able to be valued, or worthy of being valued," whereas the Spanish "valioso" conveys the idea of being filled with value. Portilla seems very aware of this linguistic nuance, since he asserts that "apretado" individuals consider themselves "filled" with value.—Translator's note.

37. Here, Portilla plays once again with suffixes and exhibits his sense of humor. He creates new abstract nouns by adding the –(e)dad suffix,

which is roughly equivalent in this context to the English suffix "–ness." The original text says "funcionariedad" (literally official-ness, the property of being a *funcionario*, or bureaucratic official) and bancariedad (literally "of a bank-ness," derived from the adjective "bancario," meaning "of or pertaining to banks." One of his sample "apretado" individuals, then, seems to be a "funcionario bancario (bank official), who is filled with "bank-official-ness."—Translator's note.

38. Here, Portilla plays with the form and meaning of an idiomatic expression in Spanish that hinges on the verb "tener" (to "have" or to "possess"). The expression "tener por" or "tenerse por" followed usually by an adjective, means "to consider someone" or "to consider oneself," respectively, as having a certain quality. Literally, one "has oneself (as) _____"; "tenerse por inteligente" is literally "to have oneself as intelligent."—Translator's note.

39. The feminine collective noun "gente," meaning "people" (as in a group of more than one person), is plural in meaning but grammatically singular in form. However, "gente" can be used adjectivally, especially in certain idiomatic expressions, to describe a singular person. A single person can be described as being *buena gente* (nice, friendly), *mala gente* (mean, unfriendly), "gente de bien" (doing good or having goodwill), or "gente bien" (upper class, wealthy). When Portilla says that a particular individual is "people," or "very people," he is using "gente" as an adjective to describe the individual, not as a predicate noun equivalent to "person." He is not affirming the individual's personhood or asserting that the individual is "a person."—Translator's note.

40. "Alzado" or "levantado," literally "raised"; the closest English equivalent might be "uppity" when applied to servants.—Translator's note.

41. In the original, "ser [el bien]," "to be [the good]" and "estar en el bien," "to be in the good." Portilla here plays with the grammatical distinction between the two verbs meaning "to be" in Spanish, *ser* and *estar*. "Ser" is usually used to denote being associated with characteristics seen as part of the "essence" of a person or thing. It also denotes existential being and is always used with predicate nouns, when "to be" means "to equal"; hence "ser el bien" would mean "to be or to equal the good." In contrast, "estar" is primarily used

to denote being in a particular state or condition—which may be temporary or permanent—or in a particular location. Thus, "estar en el bien" might convey the notion of "to be within the location of the good" or "to be in the state of the good."—Translator's note.

Bibliography

Aurelius, Marcus. *The Meditations*. Translated by G. M. A. Grube. Indianapolis: Hackett, 1983.

Badiou, Alain. *Ethics: An Essay on the Understanding of Evil*. Translated by Peter Hallward. London: Verso, 2001.

Barthes, Ronald. "Historical Discourse." In *Structuralism: A Reader*, edited by Michael Lane. London: Jonathan Cape, 1970. 145–164.

Bartra, Roger. *La jaula de la melancholia: Identidad y metamorfosis del Mexicano*. Mexico: Editorial Grijalbo, 1987.

Bakhtin, Mikhail. *Rebelais and His World*. Translated by Helen Iswolsky. Bloomington: Indiana University Press, 1984.

Berlin, Isaiah. *The Proper Study of Mankind: An Anthology of Essays*. Edited by Henry Hardy and Roger Housheer. New York: Farrar, Straus, and Giroux, 2000.

Camarena, Juan Manuel Silva. (2004). "*Reseña de 'Historia de la fenomenología en México' De Antonio Zirión*." *La Lámpara de Diógenes* 5, nos. 8 and 9 (2004): 157–163.

Carpenter, Victoria, ed. *(Re)collecting the Past: History and Collective Memory in Latin American Narrative*. Bern: Peter Lang, 2010.

Castro, Rafaela. *Chicano Folklore: Folktales, Traditions, Ritual, and Religious Practices of Mexican-Americans*. Oxford: Oxford University Press, 2000.

Deleuze, Gilles. *Empiricism and Subjectivity: An Essay on Hume's Theory of Human Nature*. Translated by Constantin V. Boundas. New York: Columbia University Press, 1991.

217

Derrida, Jacques. *Margins of Philosophy*. Translated by Alan Bass. Chicago: University of Chicago Press, 1982.

Empiricus, Sextus. *Scepticism, Man, and God: Selections from the Major Writings of Sextus Empiricus*. Edited by Philip P. Hallie. Translated by Sanford G. Etheridge. Connecticut: Wesleyan University Press, 1964.

Faber, Sebastián. *Exile and Cultural Hegemony: Spanish Intellectuals in Mexico, 1939–1975*. Nashville: Vanderbilt University Press, 2000.

Farr, Marcia. *Rancheros in Chicagoacan: Language and Identity in a Translational Community*. Austin: University of Texas, 2006.

Freire, Paulo. *Pedagogy of the Oppressed*. Translated by Mayra Bergman Ramos. New York: Continuum, 2006.

Friedman, Milton. *Capitalism and Freedom*. Chicago: University of Chicago Press, 1962.

Gracia, Jorge J. E., and Elizabeth Millán-Zaibert, eds. *Latin American Philosophy for the Twenty-first Century: The Human Condition, Values, and the Search for Identity*. Amherst, NY: Prometheus Books, 2004.

Gaos, José. *Filosofía mexicana de nuestros días*. México: Imprenta Universitaria, 1954.

Giddens, Anthony. *Conversations with Anthony Giddens: Making Sense of Modernity*. Stanford: Stanford University Press, 1998.

Guerra, Ricardo. "Una historia del Hiperión." *Los Universitarios* 18 (1984): 1–10.

Heidegger, Martin. *Being and Time*. Translated by John Macquarrie and Edward Robinson. San Francisco: Harper & Row, 1962.

———. *Supplements: From the Earliest Essays to Being and Time and Beyond*. Edited by John Van Buren. Albany: State University of New York Press, 2002.

Husserl, Edmund. (1964). *The Idea of Phenomenology*. Translated by William Alston. The Hague: Martinus Nijhoff, 1964.

———. "Phenomenology': Edmund Husserl's Article for the Encyclopedia Britannica (1927)." Edited and Translated by Richard E. Palmer." *Journal of the British Society for Phenomenology* 2, no. 2 (1971): 77–90, 83.

———. *Ideas Pertaining to a Pure Phenomenology and to a Phenomenological Philosophy*, First Book. Translated by F. Kersten. Dordrecht: Kluwer, 1998.

Hurtado, Guillermo. (2010). "The Anti-Positivist Movement in Mexico." In *A Companion to Latin American Thought*, edited by

Susana Nuccetelli, Ofelia Schutte, and Otávio Bueno. Malden, MA: Wiley-Blackwell.

Hurtado, Guillermo, ed. *El Hiperión*. México: UNAM, 2006.

Kierkegaard, Søren. *The Sickness unto Death*. Translated by Alastair Hannay. New York: Penguin Classics, 1989.

Krauze, Rosa. (1966). "Sobre la Fenomenoloogía del relajo." *Revista de la Universidad de México* 20, no. 8 (1966): 1–11.

Lacoue-Labarthe, Philippe, and Jean-Luc Nancy. (1988). *The Literary Absolute: The theory of Literature in German Romanticism*. Translated by Philip Barnard and Cheryl Lester. Albany: State University of New York Press.

Lauria, Anthony. "'Respeto,' 'Relajo' and Inter-personal Relations in Puerto Rico." *Anthropological Quarterly* 37, no. 2 (1964): 53–67.

Levinson, Bradley A. U. *We Are All Equal: Student Culture and Identity at a Mexican Secondary School*. Durham: Duke University Press, 2001.

Lomnitz, Claudio. *Exits from the Labyrinths: Culture and Ideology in the Mexican National Space*. Berkeley: University of California Press, 1992.

Lyotard, Jean-Francois. (1987). "The Postmodern Condition." In *Philosophy: End or Transformation*, edited by Kenneth Baynes, et. al. Cambridge: MIT Press, 1987.

Mañach, Jorge. *La Indigación del choteo*. Linkgua ediciones S.L., 2009.

Marx, Karl. *Selected Writings*. Edited by David McLellan. Oxford: Oxford University Press, 1977.

———. *Capital: An Abridged Edition*. Edited by David McLellan. Oxford. Oxford University Press, 1999.

McCumber, John. *Metaphysics and Oppression: Heidegger's Challenge to Western Metaphysics*. Bloomington: Indiana University Press, 1999.

Merleau-Ponty, Maurice. *Sense and Nonsense*. Translated by Hubert Dreyfus and Patricia Allen Dreyfus. Evanston: Northwestern University Press, 1964.

———. "The Philosophy of Existence." In *The Debate between Sartre and Merleau-Ponty*, edited by Jon Stewart. Evanston: Northwestern University Press, 1998.

Michael, Christopher Domínguez. "¿El existencialismo fue un relajo?" *Tinta Seca* 25 (1996): 7–10.

Murfin, Ross and Supryia M. Ray. *The Bedford Glossary of Critical Literary Terms*. Boston: Bedford Books, 1997.

Nietzsche, Friedrich. *Unfashionable Observations*. Translated by Richard T. Grey. Stanford: Stanford University Press, 1995.

———. *The Gay Science*. Edited by Bernard Williams. Cambridge: Cambridge University Press, 2003.

Oliver, Amy. "Values in Modern Mexican Thought." *The Journal of Value Inquiry* 27 (1993): 215–230.

Ortega y Gasset, José. *Man and People*. Translated by Willard R. Trask, New York: Norton, 1962.

———. *Meditations on Quixote*. Translated by Evelyn Rugg and Diego Marin. Champlain: University of Illinois Press, 2000.

———. *What Is Knowledge?* Translated by Jorge García-Gómez. Albany: State University of New York Press, 2002.

Paz, Octavio. *The Labyrinth of Solitude*. Translated by Lysander Kemp. New York: Grove Press, 1985.

Portilla, Jorge. *Fenomenología del relajo*. México, D.F.: Fondo de Cultura Económica, 1984.

Pilcher, Jeffery M. *Cantinflas and the Caos of Mexican Modernity*. Wilmington DE: Scholarly Sources, 2001.

Quijano, Aníbal. "Modernity, Identity, and Utopia in Latin America." *boundary 2* 20, no. 3 (1993): 140–155.

———. "Coloniality and Modernity/Rationality," *Cultural Studies* 21, nos. 2–3 (2007): 168–178.

Romanell, Patrick. *The Making of the Mexican Mind: A Study in Recent Mexican Thought*. Lincoln: University of Nebraska Press, 1952.

Ramos, Samuel. *Perfil del hombre y cultura en México*. México D.F.: Espasa-Calpe Mexicana, S.A., 1982.

———. *Profile of Culture and Man in Mexico*. Translated by Peter Earle. Austin: University of Texas Press, 1962.

Reyes, Juan Jóse. "Jorge Portilla, por los caminos de la libertad." *Crónica de Hoy*. http://www.cronica.com.mx/nota.php?id_nota=99164, 2003.

Sáenz, Mario. *The Identity of Liberation in Latin American Thought: Latin American Historicism and the Phenomenology of Leopoldo Zea*. Lanham: Lexington Books, 1999.

Salmerón, Fernando. "Una imagen del mexicano." *Revista de Filosofía y Letras* 21, nos. 41–42 (Enero–Junio, 1951): 175–188.

Sánchez, Carlos Alberto. "Jorge Portilla's Phenomenology: *Relajo*, *Gelassenheit*, and Liberation," *APA Newsletter on Hispanic/Latino Issues in Philosophy* 6, no. 2 (2007): 1–7.

———. "Heidegger in Mexico: Emilio Uranga's Ontological

Hermeneutics." *Continental Philosophy Review* 41 (2008): 441–461.

Sartre, Jean-Paul. *Existentialism*. Translated by Bernard Frechtman. New York: Philosophical Library, 1947.

———. *Being and Nothingness*. Translated by Hazel Barnes. New York: The Philosophical Library, 1956.

———. *Search for a Method*. Translated by Hazel Barnes. New York: Vintage Books, 1968.

———. *The Family Idiot: Gustave Flaubert*. Translated by Carol Cosman. Chicago: University of Chicago Press, 1989.

Scheler, Max. *Formalism in Ethics and Non-Formal Ethics of Values*. Translated by Manfred S. Frings and Roger L. Funk. Evanston: Northwestern University Press, 1973.

Sobrevilla, David. "Phenomenology and Existentialism in Latin America." *Philosophical Forum* 20 (1989): 85–113.

Stabb, Martin S. *In Quest of Identity: Patterns in the Spanish American Essay of Ideas, 1890–1930*. Chapel Hill: University of North Carolina Press, 1967.

Solares, Martin. "Entrevista con Carlos Fuentes." *La Jornada*. Semanal 222. México (12 de septiembre de 1993).

Taylor, Charles. *Sources of the Self: The Making of the Modern Identity*. Cambridge: Harvard University Press, 1989.

Taylor, Diana. *The Archive and the Repertoire: Performing Cultural Memory in the Americas*. Durham: Duke University Press, 2003.

Thomson, Iain. "Can I Die? Derrida on Heidegger on Death." *Philosophy Today* 43, no. 1 (1999): 29–42.

Villegas, Abelardo. *La filosofía de lo mexicano*. México: UNAM, 1979.

Weinstein, Michael A. *The Polarity of Mexican Thought: Instrumetalism and Finalism*. University Park: Pennsylvania State University Press, 1976.

Zea, Leopoldo. *La Filosofía Como Compromiso y Otros Ensayos*. México, DF: Fondo de Cultura Económica, 1952.

———. *La filosofía americana como filosofía sin más*. México: Siglo XXI Editores, S.A. de C.V., 1969.

———. *The Role of the Americas in History*. Translated by Sonja Karsen. New York: Rowman & Littlefield, 1992.

Zirión Quijano, Antonio. "Phenomenology in Mexico: A Historical Profile," *Continental Philosophy Review* 33 (2000): 75–92.

———. *Historia de la Fenomenología en México*. Morelia: Jitanjáfora, 2004.

Index

92–94, 104, 106, 111, 112, 113; and liberation, 100; and modernity, 100–102; in Ortega y Gasset, 90–92; and *relajo*, 98–100, 114, 117

suspension, 8; ; and the future, 116; and judgments, 208n4; and phenomenology, 12; and post-modernity, 102; and *relajo*, 18, 20, 32, 35, 44, 57, 58, 61, 72, 73, 78, 79, 86, 87, 107, 108, 110, 117, 118, 129, 133, 176; and *relajientos*, 16, 117; of seriousness, 6, 7, 12, 30, 33, 37, 38, 43, 44, 51, 63, 76, 81, 83, 111, 120, 128, 134, 135, 137, 142, 176

solitude, 4, 79, 92, 132, 133

suspicion, 37, 126

Taylor, Charles, 81, 87, 99

Taylor, Diana, 50, 113

technology, 118, 119, 170

temporality, 95, 113, 149, 150

terrorism, 37

transcendence, 53, 55, 59, 60, 85, 91, 92, 94, 95, 96, 97, 136, 142, 166, 167, 168, 174, 177, 178, 179, 180, 181, 184, 187, 190, 193, 197, 198

trasnscendental subjectivity, 70, 79, 89, 94, 97, 98, 144

truth, 10, 12, 15, 18, 40, 42, 57, 58, 59, 60, 61, 80, 81, 105, 106, 107, 111, 121, 127, 134, 145, 167, 173,

174, 175, 176, 187, 188, 190, 197, 206n4

Uranga, Emilio, 25–26, 203n5, 205n1

values, 6, 7, 10, 19, 25, 27, 28, 31, 32, 37, 40–43, 54, 63, 67, 70, 82, 86, 92, 93, 94, 99, 103, 107, 111, 112, 114, 115, 116, 117, 118, 119, 120, 121, 134–140, 141, 145, 146, 149, 157, 164, 166, 167, 177, 178, 183, 187, 203n5, 204n8, 207n1, 208n2; and *apretados*, 17, 61, 62, 191, 193; and freedom, 54, 55, 77; and laughter, 47, 48, 49, 153, 154, 156; and *relajo*, 8, 16, 20, 30, 31, 36, 37, 44, 48, 50, 51, 62, 71, 76, 79, 103, 106, 107, 108, 111, 112, 119, 120, 134, 142, 147, 187, 188

Vasconcelos, José, 1, 66, 207n6

Villegas, Abelardo, 203n5

Villoro, Luis, 6, 9, 25, 26, 201

virtue, 38, 39, 62, 90, 95, 105, 106, 173, 175, 181, 196

Zea, Leopoldo, 1, 23, 25, 66, 83, 84, 87–89, 201n1, 202n4, 203n5, 204n7, 205n1, 206n2

Zirión Quijano, Antonio, 2, 3, 11, 20, 23, 68, 72, 109, 110, 206n3

Zócalo (Mexico City), 4